ATHEIST
UNIVERSE

ATHEIST UNIVERSE

The Thinking Person's Answer to Christian Fundamentalism

DAVID MILLS

Ulysses Press

To all freethinkers, past and present, whose independence of mind isolates them from the sympathy and understanding of their community, but whose courageous and unwavering devotion to the scientific method has liberated their community from the Dark Ages

▲▼▲

Published in the U.S. by
ULYSSES PRESS
P.O. Box 3440
Berkeley, CA 94703
www.ulyssespress.com

ISBN13: 978-1-56975-567-9
Library of Congress Control Number 2006903812

Editor: Lily Chou
Cover design: what!design @ whatweb.com
Cover photographs: ©iStockphoto.com/Stasys Eidiejus
    ©iStockphoto.com/Camilo Jimenez
Typesetting: Matt Orendorff, Lisa Kester
Indexer: Sayre Van Young

Printed in the United States by Bang Printing

20 19 18 17 16 15 14 13 12 11 10 9 8

Distributed by Publishers Group West

Contents

Foreword:
Paper Cut Stigmata
by Dorion Sagan

When I got a paper cut, slicing my thumb while reading the uncorrected proofs of this edition of *Atheist Universe*, I thought it might be a sign—not as dramatic, perhaps, as being struck by a lightning bolt in a sensitive part of the anatomy during an extremely arduous act of premarital lovemaking, but a sign nevertheless.

Creationists are funny. They want to be taken seriously as scientific and have their or their comrades' writings taught as science to our children in schools. But their attitude is unscientific. Rather than engaging in open-minded investigation to figure out how things are done, at the first glimmer of mystery they throw up their hands and say it is beyond science. This is like not knowing how a magic trick is done and thinking no one else can know, either. We can give up trying to understand because God—who in their view is like a 2000-year-old petty Middle Eastern tyrant, quick to anger and condemn to the eternal prison of Hell those who don't obey Him—must have done it. As soon as they (to *sound* scientific) ascribe the phenomenon to irreducible complexity, Intelligent Design, the Flying Spaghetti Monster,[1] or something else, they have abandoned the search. Needless to say, suggesting

something is beyond science evinces neither the spirit of entre-
preneurial inquiry and American ingenuity nor is it, in any way,
shape or form, science. Science does not stop at some artificial
limit of inquiry. It continues on. It, to borrow an apposite religious term, perseveres. Creation "science" and Intelligent Design
theory do not persevere. They throw in the towel.

Science, in the words of quantum physicist David Bohm, is
about finding the truth *whether we like it or not.* Apparently
some fundamentalists are not comfortable with the truth—
so much so that they have gone undercover, pretending to be
scientists, except that (as David Mills shows here) they invent
facts and contradict themselves to arrive at their preconceived
conclusions.

One can hardly underestimate the power of religious fundamentalism. Nor is it limited to Christian fundamentalism. As
shown by the recent Islamic example of suicidal terrorists
attempting to reap their reward of 72 dark-eyed menstruation-,
urination- and defecation-free *houris,* each more beautiful than
any combination of earthly sexpots, the unlikelihood of a belief
does not lessen its power. Not if it appeals to what we wish or
fear to be true. A God who *commands* that you love Him (does
this sound like true love?) and threatens you with eternal torture
in Hell (no matter what good works you might have done) if you
don't believe in Him may be an extremely effective transgenera-
tional ideological scare tactic. But that doesn't make it true. As
Mills shows in this remarkably clear text—which *should* be taught
in schools—the founders of the United States were not fundamentalists. Indeed, the phrase "under God" in the Pledge of Allegiance
and the words "In God We Trust" on U.S. currency were only
added during the fear-laden Cold War 1950s.

Fundamentalism—whether Christian, Islamic or some other
distinct vintage—is an atavistic human thought structure. It is,
however, quite natural. When threatened, we revert to old pat-
terns that aid group survival—never mind the epistemological
taint nor the abdication of an honest search for truth. The truth

may set you free but societies require obedience, hierarchy and cohesion—ergo the paradox that the wheels of survival, especially during times of duress, are greased more readily by easy lies than hard truths. In terms of the scientific quest for human origins and those of life, the religious answer that God did it resembles the conclusion of a corrupt police official who frames a suspect without looking at old, let alone new, clues. When you look at creationism or Intelligent Design theory in this way—as pretend science involved in a dishonest investigation—you see it revealed in all the ultraviolet glare of its own petty offices. As David Mills shows, it's not a pretty picture.

All of which is a shame, because there is no greater tonic for true spirituality than science itself. The word "religion" comes from Latin *religare* for re-linking. Ironically, such re-linking occurs most effortlessly and profoundly when backed up by the realities of science rather than the fantasies of religion. For example, when Nicolaus Copernicus showed that Earth was not at the center of the solar system, he provided part of the process that gave us cosmic passports and citizenship to the galaxy—passports which have already been stamped with men on the Moon, and machines on Venus, Mars and photographing Earth from space. Friedrich Wöhler, the chemist who found that substances in urine were related to substances outside the body, deflated the notion that life was made of some special and magical stuff. But his revelation of life's ordinary nature helped set the stage for understanding the role of DNA, for describing life as a complex chemical phenomenon. Our connection to the universe may be grounds for religious divorce but it is also a platform for spiritual renewal. We can confront reality *and* appreciate it; we can have our cake and eat it too.

So, too, the discoveries by astrophysicists of hydrogen, carbon and other chemical elements in and around the stars shows that the ingredients of life exist throughout the universe and may be present in extraterrestrials who have lessons to teach us far beyond anything we have yet learned. Each scientific realization is, in other words, the occasion for reflection on our connectedness as well as our commonness.

Montana scientist Eric D. Schneider and I argue that not only is the *stuff* of our bodies common, but even the *process* of life as a complex energy-based system is shared. "I am as pure as driven slush," quipped Alabama socialite Tallulah Bankhead. So are we: technological humans, and all life forms, are part of a class of three-dimensional complex systems that naturally cycle matter in areas of energetic flux. Such naturally complex systems include convection cells, cycling storm systems (e.g., hurricanes), and autocatalytic chemical reactions such as chemical clocks.[2] All these systems, including life, not only obey the second law of thermodynamics, but disperse energy more effectively—more quickly, more sustainably or both—than would be the case without them. That is their natural function. Complex systems arise in nature "to" disperse energy or produce entropy. Thus, we argue that life's physical purpose as a process—to disperse energy but to do so more effectively than would be the case without it—has been found. Far from violating the second law (as creationists wrongly claim), life is one of its most effective manifestations.

Life's measurable function has been detected by weather satellites. This natural function is to reduce the long wave radiation gradient between Earth and sun, thereby dispersing energy in accord with the second law. Moreover, life is not random but displays direction over evolutionary time: There has been, since life's inception, an increase in the kinds of life and number of species, an increase in the amount of energy stored by life and deployed in its operations, an increase in life's areal extent, an increase in the efficiency with which energy is used, an increase in cell types, an increase in overall intelligence and sensitivity, and an increase in the number of chemical elements involved, either structurally or peripherally, with metabolizing, living beings. These evolutionary increases, while dependent upon gene-based reproduction and natural selection, reflect the growth of the massive second law–based baby blue biosphere, so striking when we look at it from space. Evolution (and here the religionists are right in their critique of neo-Darwinism) is not random but has a direction. However, this direction is not that of a willful deity; rather, it is the natural direction of spreading, naturally complex, entropy-fomenting systems. And again our cosmic humiliation or debasement is the occasion for a moment of cognitive uplift or expansion. We are part of a cosmic system of energy degradation.

Science's Copernican centrifugations do not seem to rule out religion but they do seem to call for the sort of *im*personal God discussed by Einstein and Spinoza—a "God" "who" includes all of nature and no doubt much else besides our cosmically puny and all-too-human minds. As geneticist J. B. S. Haldane famously remarked, "The universe is not only queerer than we suppose, it is queerer than we can suppose." Science, religion and philosophy come together in recommending a humility proportional to our ignorance. "Only two things are infinite," said Einstein, "the universe and human stupidity."

Spinoza's God was an entity partially contiguous with nature, a deity that did not interfere in time and therefore did not perform miracles or tamper with creation via divine intervention. His was an impersonal God as eternal as the laws of nature. Such a God, which has lost all traces of the taste for punishment and anger management problems of the Great Steroidally Poisoned Despot in the Sky, accords with science, with nature and with the intellectual legroom to accommodate our ignorance. Spinoza's is a possible God. Spinoza, though a great advocate of freedom of the press and freedom to worship (his *Theologico-Political Treatise* is said to have influenced the United States' founding fathers), did not believe in free will. He thought it was an illusion, the result of our parochial ignorance of the higher state of affairs—one described by the eternal laws of nature, one outside of time, one not open to divine intervention. Spinoza argued for the deterministic world Einstein defended in his letter to Max Born when he wrote, "He [God] does not play dice." Freedom for Spinoza was equivalent more to the growth of knowledge than the real exercise of free choice. As Mills points out, the men who started this country were deists, not fundamentalists: their god, insofar as they had one, was on the side of science and nature, and not a supernatural force operating beyond nature with jealousy jags, temper tantrums and afterlife ultimatums. The argument for atheism is the same as the argument for monotheism except there's one fewer god. This brings to mind Alexander Hamilton's reputed response to Ben Franklin's apparently absurd suggestion that each session of the Constitutional Convention be opened with a prayer: "No, we don't need any foreign aid."

Postscript

Miraculously my paper cut is almost healed, a natural process that reminds me of a joke. A muttering man of religious bent, late for an assignation, says aloud: "Jesus, if you'll only find me a parking space I swear to God that I'll give up the women and the Irish whiskey for the rest of my life." Sure enough, a parking space appears, and he turns in. "Never mind, I found one myself."

To conclude, I am delighted to have been asked by Mr. Mills to write the Foreword to his fine book. With impeccable logic, intellectual bravery and professional clarity Mills points the way past religious prejudice to a far more believable—and ultimately enchanting—view of ourselves and the world.

Preface

Five years have now passed since I completed the original manuscript of *Atheist Universe*. To my surprise, book sales have been robust since publication in April 2004. Of the 400 titles on "atheism" catalogued and sold by Amazon.com, *Atheist Universe* soon became their best-selling volume, even when popular Christian classics refuting atheism were included in the sales rankings. For over two years thereafter, *Atheist Universe* maintained its distinction as Amazon's best-selling atheist title, finally being superseded in late 2006 by sales of *The God Delusion* by Richard Dawkins, who quotes this book extensively in his own recent writings. Of the 3 million books in print in the English-speaking world, sales of *Atheist Universe* continue in 2009 to rank among the top one-tenth of one percent. Literally, only one book in a thousand (on any subject) sells more copies than *Atheist Universe* on Amazon.com. This book's commercial success thoroughly blindsided me.

Prior to publication, I scoffed at—and publicly corrected—anyone who over-optimistically suggested that this book might sell more than a handful of copies to a few special-interest groups. I had written this book not for money, but because of my life-long interest in the subject and ongoing debate. I had so little confidence in the commercial viability of *Atheist Universe* that I thought it futile even to shop the manuscript to a Madison

Avenue publisher. Instead, I initially sent the book electronically to Xlibris, which, although partially owned and controlled by Random House, usually publishes titles on obscure subjects, with limited press runs.

I was therefore both delighted and honored when, in 2006, Ulysses Press stepped in to significantly broaden the availability of *Atheist Universe*, expanding its presence from the online-only market to brick-and-mortar bookstores as well. Nick Denton-Brown, Acquisitions Editor at Ulysses Press, discovered my needle in the Amazon haystack and is to be praised—or reprimanded, depending on your point of view—for making possible the Ulysses Press edition of the book you now hold.

My lack of foresight on the book's marketability was not due to a lack of personal confidence in the substance or coherence of the book's arguments. Rather, I recognized the indisputable fact that atheism is embraced by only a modest minority of the population. Public opinion surveys consistently show that nineteen of twenty Americans profess a belief in God. It would be unrealistic, I thought, to expect a book promoting atheism to sell briskly. So, while I didn't irrationally overestimate the book's market, I did significantly underestimate the book's potential.

I am proud to say that *Atheist Universe* became one of the flagship titles later dubbed the "New Atheism." Many subsequent works were published by others soon afterward, and a critical mass was reached in which the general public, not just free-thought groups, became aware that Christian Fundamentalism was being challenged in a visible and forthright way as never before. *Atheist Universe* thus rode two separate sales waves. When originally published in 2004, this book had little competition in the marketplace. There were other anticlerical books of course, but most had been written in past decades—if not past centuries. Up-to-date atheist books were scant and, to my astonishment, positively in demand. When antireligion books by Richard Dawkins, Sam Harris, Daniel Dennett and Christopher Hitchens later became *New York Times* bestsellers, *Atheist Universe* also benefited from the publicity stir, experiencing its second wave of popular sales—a wave in which, perhaps, it had played a tiny role in setting into motion two years beforehand. Sales of free-thought books therefore expanded from atheist activists preparing for debate to a newly-curious general readership.

Whether a book sells well or poorly is, of course, no necessary indication of its merits. Many superb books sell very few copies, especially when they are geared to academic or scholarly audiences; and some runaway bestsellers are often popular only because they capitalize on momentary media frenzy over a particularly lurid crime or a hot new celebrity scandal. If we are to judge a book's credibility by sales numbers, then books endorsing religion are clear winners over books on atheism. There's no doubt about that. Religious leaders often point out that the bestselling book of all time is none other than the Holy Bible itself. Bertrand Russell once observed that "The fact that an opinion has been widely held is no evidence that it is not utterly absurd; indeed, in view of the silliness of the majority of mankind, a widespread belief is more likely to be foolish than sensible."

Having duly noted and accepted Russell's wise admonition on the folly of popular opinion, I nonetheless wish to express gratitude to all who welcomed the original publication of *Atheist Universe* and who helped its sales through positive reviews, word of mouth, and links on popular free-thought websites. I hope that this updated and expanded edition successfully addresses some important issues that were omitted in the earlier printings of the book or that have newly arisen since original publication.

Introduction:
Is This Book an Outrage?

Winston Churchill once observed that "Everyone is in favor of free speech. Hardly a day passes without its virtues being extolled. But some people's idea of free speech is that they are free to say what they like, but if anyone else says anything back, that is an outrage."

Most people will consider this book to be an outrage. This book strikes directly at what is, for many people, their most private and deeply held convictions: their beliefs about God, the Bible, and life-after-death. The old adage warns us that "If we want to keep our friends, we should never discuss politics or religion." We take offense. We resent those who tell us that our shoes need polishing or that our clothes are wrinkled, much less that our most sacred beliefs are, in the end, a complete fiction. Whether our critics are right or wrong, we simply don't want to hear about it. We craft rationalizations for clinging to our current set of beliefs. We don't want to stray beyond our familiar zone of comfort.

Privately, most people do entertain doubts about whether science and Scripture truly agree with each other. Religious leaders *claim* that the Bible and science harmonize completely. Scientists, not wanting to rock the boat and upset their audience, rarely make a deliberate, concentrated effort to point out disparities between their laboratory findings and the "truth" as revealed in the Word of God. The result is that religious belief is inculcated into children long before they are capable of independently scrutinizing their parents' mystical assertions. The children become believers for life. When, as adults, something appears to contradict the religious beliefs we adopted as toddlers, we feel a "cognitive dissonance" and fear that something immoral is impinging itself upon us unwanted. In the final analysis, much religious belief is sustained by tarring the nonbeliever as a person without a conscience, having no valid standard for a workable system of ethics.

To millions of churchgoers, the terms "ethical conduct" and "Christian conduct" are synonymous and interchangeable. A "Christian act" is by definition an "ethical act." And an "immoral deed" is necessarily "un-Christian." The logical problem posed by these definitions, however, is that non-Christians—be they Jews, Muslims, Hindus, Buddhists or atheists—must necessarily be perceived as unethical—or at least less ethical—when compared to "true" Christians, simply because they hold differing religious beliefs. For if *your* beliefs are absolutely, positively true and "ordained of God," then anyone who disagrees with you is absolutely, positively wrong and is a damnable tool of Satan. Such "thinking" leads to religious bigotry and prejudice—and to Holy War. So, perhaps, we should think twice before introducing our children to such a biased and discriminatory "ethical" system—a system that admittedly promises heavenly rewards for faith and proper religious beliefs, rather than for real-world ethical treatment of others.

For example, a man could theoretically kill hundreds of innocent people, rob fifty banks, poison the drinking water of an entire region, or even start a world war. But if this man, during his last few seconds of life, sincerely repents of his sins and "accepts Jesus into his heart," he will be taken to Heaven and rewarded eternally. By contrast, a woman can sacrificially devote her entire life to charitable work and to generously helping disadvantaged children throughout the world. But if she neglects to recognize the existence of a supernatural Power, then she will be barbecued forever in the pits of Hell, according to Christian doctrine.

Christianity, therefore, defines ethics primarily in terms of an individual's religious *beliefs*—which affect no one else—rather than in terms of unselfish *conduct* toward others. Martin Luther King, Jr., taught us to judge individuals, not by the color of their skin, but by the content of their character. Many Christian Fundamentalists, however, judge individuals, not by the content of their character, but by the color of their religious beliefs. If your opinions on religion disagree with those of the Fundamentalists, they will for that reason declare your character to be bankrupt. Moreover, Fundamentalists sincerely believe that, because of your "bankrupt, un-Christian character," you are more likely (than the Fundamentalists) to commit immoral deeds. In other words, "true" Christians are necessarily more ethical than non-Christians. Such religious bigotry is no less offensive than claiming that a man born African American or Chinese is for that reason more likely to commit immoralities. So, while masquerading as a fountain of ethical virtue and love, Christian Fundamentalism instead teaches an unhealthy (and unethical) religious prejudice and hostility toward individuals of diverse opinion and background.

Politically active TV evangelists, like Pat Robertson and James Dobson, define "ethical conduct" to mean that you support and campaign for the most ultra-conservative right-wing extremist on the ballot. To be "moral," you must also oppose gay rights, oppose gun control, oppose stem-cell research, oppose the 2009 economic stimulus package, oppose physician-assisted suicide, be violently anti-abortion, loathe the United Nations, despise Barack Obama, Bill Clinton, Hillary Clinton, Nancy Pelosi and Harry Reid, and believe that men should rule over women within the family. If you deviate from these hallowed beliefs, then you will burn eternally in the fires of Hell. Personally, it is difficult for me to fathom how we derive any true lessons on ethics from these politically inspired sermons. The only message that children are likely to absorb is one of intolerance and hatred of people with opposing viewpoints.

Bill Bennett, conservative author of *The Book of Virtues* and *The Children's Book of Virtues*, invariably scowls with contempt and disgust whenever someone takes issue with his political or religious views. Perhaps Bennett's face was permanently frozen into a sour grimace by all his years of virtuous chain smoking and by his virtuous high-stakes gambling losses in Las Vegas.

Talk-radio icon Rush Limbaugh, while demanding long prison sentences for all drug traffickers, was himself purchasing and ingesting each day enough illegal narcotics to euthanize a dozen African hippos.

Old-fashioned family-values conservative Bill O'Reilly cruelly lambasted any moderate whose sexual ethics differed from those of traditional Christianity. Yet, unknown to O'Reilly (and his wife), his female TV producer kept audio recordings of the moralizing celebrity making lewd and unwanted sexual advances toward her, demanding phone sex, fantasizing about threesomes and vibrators and, finally, masturbating over the phone into her startled ear.

In late 2003, right-wing commentator Ann Coulter published a book titled *Treason*, which openly accuses all liberal thinkers of being criminals, since treason (of which all liberals are supposedly guilty) is a high crime. Coulter's venomous, hate-filled books are quite typical, though, of how the Christian right views ethics. If you agree with them on politics and religion, then you're a patriotic American bound for Heaven. If you disagree with them on politics or religion, then you're an unpatriotic criminal destined for Hell.

I myself have been publicly labeled a "spokesman for Satan," a "disgrace to human dignity," a "moron," a "shrimp head" and, my favorite, a "pitiful middle-aged man, embarrassed by his lifelong unemployment, and frozen, emotionally and intellectually, in early adolescence." Whew! A critic of mine once wrote that, contrary to the diplomatic example of Dale Carnegie, my first book on atheism should have been titled *How to Lose Friends and Alienate People*. He was probably right, since most of my critics employed *ad hominem* attacks on *me*—and on my supposed lack of ethics—rather than pointing out any factual or logical errors within the text of what I'd written.

The *New York Times* published a poll (August 15, 2003) showing that "Americans believe, 58 percent to 40 percent, that it is necessary to believe in God to be moral." By contrast, only 13 percent of Europeans agree with the U.S. view. The same poll also revealed that "Americans are three times as likely to believe in the Virgin Birth of Jesus (83 percent) as in evolution (28 percent)."

The Pew Forum on Religion and Public Life conducted its 2008 U.S. Religious Landscape Survey and found that almost 70 percent of Americans believe that "angels and demons are active in the world" and nearly 80 percent believe that "miracles still occur today as in ancient times." A 2005 Gallup poll found that belief in the existence of the devil has soared 27 percent since 1990, and more than 40 percent of Americans believe "that people on this earth are sometimes possessed by the devil."

So this naturally brings me, an atheist, to a relevant question: For whom is this book intended? Am I trying to convert the followers of Pat Robertson and James Dobson and Bill Bennett and Rush Limbaugh and Bill O'Reilly and Ann Coulter? Does this book strive to make atheists out of the religious right-wingers on the radio talk shows? No. That's not the purpose. Nor, in my opinion, is it even possible to change the religious views of those who perceive themselves as ethically superior because they belong to the one "true" religion. Their ears and eyes and minds are closed forever. No amount of science or logic will make any difference to them. They know in their hearts that God is on their side, and that anyone who disagrees with them is evil.

Instead, this book is intended for the 40 percent of Americans who, according to the *New York Times* poll, do recognize that there are good people (and bad people) in all religions—and with no religion. This book is written for open-minded readers who are not afraid to learn—in fact, who are eager and fascinated to learn—about the many conflicts and controversies between science and the Christian Bible.

Many previous books have been published about science and religion; but most of them were written so as not to offend anyone and to leave the very false impression that science and Scripture coexist in perfect peace and harmony. That's how to sell the greatest number of books: try to please everybody by saying nothing offensive or specific. That's how the politicians do it too: win a popularity contest by avoiding the tough issues. Even purely secular science books that directly rebut the arguments of so-called Creation Science usually wimp out in the end, criticizing only the Genesis account of Creation, without going further to show that religion as a whole—any and all religion—is an unscientific mirage.

But this book will not avoid the tough issues. There is no information in this book that is not readily accessible in your local library. But at your library, this information is scattered about, sugarcoated, camouflaged, hidden away, and watered down just enough to guarantee that most readers do not appreciate that the material they've just read flatly contradicts and disproves a tenet of their own Christian religion. This book will put all the pieces together for you and clearly articulate why, in my opinion, all science and all logic indicate that we live in an Atheist Universe.

A study published in *Nature* (July 23, 1998) revealed that, of the membership of the prestigious National Academy of Sciences, only 7 percent of its leading scientists believed in a personal God (in any form) and even fewer in the religious theories of "Creation Science" or "Intelligent Design." The religious right's greatest success therefore has been in duping the news media and the general public into believing that there is a widespread and growing controversy raging among scientists over God's role in Nature. As we shall see, there is no scientific controversy at all over this bogus proposition. The "controversy" is entirely social and political.

For the most part, the chapters in this book are independent and self-contained. Many people who read books—and a sensitive group they are!—feel slightly guilty if they skip around from chapter to chapter in a disorganized way. When reading this book, you won't be disadvantaged by such hopscotching. If one chapter sounds most interesting to you, then dive into that chapter first, wherever its location in the book. Once you select a chapter to read, however, I might suggest that you do read it from the beginning, since there is usually a logical progression of ideas building and expanding throughout the individual chapters.

Chapter 1, "Interview with an Atheist," is a fun-filled give-and-take, in laymen's conversation, covering almost every aspect of atheism. This chapter actually represents the compilation of three separate interviews, with redundant material excised. Since these were broadcast interviews, the answers I provided were short and to the point. Not all facets of atheism, however, lend themselves to short answers. So the remainder of the book provides a meatier discussion than is presented in Chapter 1.

Chapter 2, "Origin of the Universe: Natural or Supernatural?" is certainly the most complex chapter in the book, due to the nature of the subject matter. If you can follow the material in this chapter—as I'm sure you can—the rest of the book should be easy, though it is *not* necessary to read Chapter 2 in order to enjoy and benefit from the chapters thereafter, which should be straightforward, pleasurable and self-explanatory when you arrive.

Before we begin, I'd like to offer a few brief comments on writing in general. Mortimer Adler, the former editor-in-chief of *Encyclopaedia Britannica*, stated many years ago that "writing should be clear without being plain, and elevated without being obscure." In the mid-1970s, I published a pamphlet that drew a reader response. Familiar with Adler's prescription for good writing, the respondent wrote, "Contrary to Mortimer Adler's suggestions, Mr. Mills, your writing was plain without being clear, and obscure without being elevated." I'm embarrassed to admit that my critic was correct in her assessment of the ill-fated pamphlet. From that point on, I realized that clarity—above all else—is what counts in writing. You may disagree with my message; but you, as the reader, shouldn't have to struggle to discern what that message is.

Another priceless tip for good writing was handed down to us by Thomas Jefferson himself. In a letter to John Adams, Jefferson wrote, "I apologize to you for the lengthiness of this letter, but I had no time for shortening it." Jefferson meant that a skillful writer uses as few words as possible to communicate his message. If I can successfully convey my thoughts to you using a 12-word sentence, then I am wasting your time—and watering down my message—by stretching the sentence to 13 words or to 30. Concise writing saves time and effort for the reader, but demands more time and effort of the writer, as Jefferson pointed out. In writing this book, I did devote the time necessary to shorten each sentence to its minimum length.

I will share a secret with you that is closely guarded by authors and publishers. Most books, you should know, contain a maximum of two or three meaningful ideas. Authors and publishers sell you mammoth volumes, however, by cleverly reiterating their two or three main ideas throughout the entirety of the book. Authors sometimes write as if they are being paid a penny a word. Yet, substantively, they say little. After reading this book, you may find yourself in complete disagreement with every word. You may be offended by some material. But you will not believe that this book had little to say.

Whenever you finish school, you usually forget immediately everything you ever learned about history, language, math and science. But when it comes to the more esoteric subjects—like philosophy and religion—you tend to remember *just enough* to screw you up forever. This book strives to liberate you from your holy ghosts and demons of the past.

David Mills

Huntington, West Virginia
March, 2009

1

Interview with an Atheist

"I have never seen the slightest scientific proof
of the religious theories of heaven and hell,
of future life for individuals, or of a personal God."
—THOMAS EDISON (1847–1931), in *Columbian* magazine

"By simple common sense I don't believe in God, in none."
—CHARLIE CHAPLIN (1889–1977), actor and comedian

"Neither in my private life nor in my writings
have I ever made a secret of being an out-and-out unbeliever."
—SIGMUND FREUD (1856–1939), in a letter to Charles Singer

INTERVIEWER: You openly refer to yourself as an "atheist." What exactly does that mean?

MILLS: Essentially, an atheist is a person who rejects the concept of god. The word "atheist" is derived from the Greek word *theos*, which means "god" or "gods." The word *theology*, for example, refers to the "study of god." When the negative prefix *a* is added to *theos*, the derivative form becomes *atheist* and simply means "without god," just as *asexual* reproduction means reproduction without sex.

INTERVIEWER: But doesn't the word "atheist" really mean a lot more than that? You don't believe in life-after-death either, do you?

MILLS: No, I don't. And I think you're quite correct that the word "atheist" can be extrapolated to mean a rejection of *all* supernatural beings and phenomena that are normally associated with the idea of god. Atheists, for example, do not believe in Heaven, Hell, devils, angels, miracles, holy ghosts, or rising from the dead. Bishop Fulton Sheen, unwittingly speaking the truth, once defined an atheist as "a man who has no invisible means of support."

INTERVIEWER: So when you die, you're dead like a dog?

MILLS: That's hardly an attractive or appetizing way to phrase it; but, yes, that is what I believe.

INTERVIEWER: What's the difference between an atheist and an agnostic?

MILLS: The words *atheist* and *agnostic* have totally disparate origins. But the real answer to your question is guts. It is more socially acceptable to be an agnostic than an atheist. While the two philosophies overlap to a considerable degree, atheism, it seems to me, represents a more specific and firmly held position than agnosticism, which, in current usage, can mean a hundred different things.

INTERVIEWER: I'm sure that you're familiar with public opinion polls which consistently show that 94 to 96 percent of all Americans believe in God. Is everybody else wrong but you?

MILLS: No. If the United States has a current population of approximately 280 million people, and if, let's say, 5 percent are atheists, then that's 14 million atheists in the U.S. alone. So, like it or not, there are plenty of us out there. Most atheists, however, tend to be less vocal in espousing their beliefs than members of various evangelical religious denominations. It's easy therefore to underestimate the number of atheists. I am somewhat dismayed when people tell me that I'm the only atheist they ever met. That's nonsense, of course—they've certainly met hundreds. But few atheists ever speak up to be counted.

INTERVIEWER: Does that indicate that atheists might be ashamed of themselves?

MILLS: Not at all. There's an old saying that "If you want to keep your friends, then you should never discuss politics or religion." Atheists recognize that their philosophical position is misunderstood by many people. Most atheists see no reason therefore to deliberately piss off their friends and to bring upon themselves an unwanted and very unfair social ostracism. If some atheists fear to speak up, it's more of an indictment against the religious bigotry they encounter than it is an indication of "shame" in affirming the atheist position.

INTERVIEWER: In looking at all the wonders of the universe, how can you possibly say there's no God? Even the Bible says, "The fool hath said in his heart 'There is no God.'"

MILLS: Whenever someone quotes that Bible verse to me, I usually recite to them another Bible verse, Matthew 5:22—"But whosoever shall say 'Thou fool' shall be in danger of hell fire."

INTERVIEWER: And what do Christians think of an atheist quoting the Bible?

MILLS: They're unprepared. Christians imagine that I, and other atheists, know nothing about the Bible or its history. When you respond in kind, they tend to be taken aback. I was on a talk show in the late 1970s and a woman stood up in the audience and quoted the verse "The fool hath said in his heart 'There is no God.'" When I humorously quoted Matthew 5:22, which threatens eternal damnation for calling someone a fool, she angrily retorted that "Even the *devil* can quote the Bible, and I think *you* are the devil." The fact is that most Christians know next to nothing about the Bible which they carry proudly to church every Sunday. I would be happy and confident to take a standard Bible-knowledge test against any churchgoer you might arbitrarily pluck from a pew next Sunday morning.

> "Properly read, the Bible is the most potent force for atheism ever conceived."
> —ISAAC ASIMOV (1920–1992), scientist and writer

INTERVIEWER: But let's get back to my fundamental question. *Why* don't you believe in God?

MILLS: Clarence Darrow, the famous trial attorney, once remarked that "I don't believe in God because I don't believe in Mother Goose." Until about ten years ago, I was of the opinion that, in order to qualify as an "official" atheist, a person had to intimately familiarize himself with the multitude of specific arguments for and against God's existence. Indeed I've written three full-length books devoted to thrashing out these arguments myself in great detail. But I now believe that it is a perfectly acceptable philosophical position to dismiss the god idea as being self-evidently ridiculous as Darrow quipped. Christians instantly disregard the Greek gods as being figments of an overactive imagination, and so I view the Christian god in the same way that the Christians view the Greek gods. Remember that when the Romans threw Christians to the lions, the Romans shouted "Away with these atheists" because the Christians did not accept the local Roman gods. But to answer your question directly, I am an atheist because no more evidence supports the Christian god than supports the Greek or Roman gods. There is no evidence that God—as portrayed by any religion—exists.

> "As for myself, I do not believe that such a person as Jesus Christ ever existed; but as the people are inclined to superstition, it is proper not to oppose them."
>
> —NAPOLEON BONAPARTE (1769–1821)

INTERVIEWER: But can you prove God *doesn't* exist?

MILLS: It's fairly easy to demonstrably prove that the Genesis accounts of Adam and Eve, and Noah's worldwide deluge, are fables. It's easier to prove these stories false because, unlike the notion of God, the Creation account and Noah's flood are scientifically testable. Science may explore human origins and the geologic history of Earth. In this regard, science has incontrovertibly proven that the Book of Genesis is utter mythology. So while, on esoteric philosophical grounds, I hesitate to claim absolute proof of a god's nonexistence, I will claim proof that the Bible is not "The Word of God" because much of it has been shown by science to be false.

Again, there is no more reason to believe in the Christian god than to believe in the Greek or Roman gods. Can I absolutely prove Zeus nonexistent? No. Do I believe that Zeus exists? No. Remember that the rules of logic dictate that the burden of proof falls upon the affirmative position: that a god *does* exist. Atheists have no obligation to prove or disprove anything. Otherwise—if you demand belief in all Beings for which there is no absolute *dis*proof—then you are forced by your own twisted "logic" to believe in mile-long pink elephants on Pluto, since, at present, we haven't explored Pluto and shown them to be nonexistent. The idea of the Christian god only seems more rational than the pink elephants or the Greek gods because we've been brainwashed into accepting the Christian god by repetitive parental and societal propaganda.

INTERVIEWER: But why do so many people believe in God?

MILLS: Because, again, they were taught to believe as small children and because almost everybody they know believes in God also. We should recognize that all children are born as atheists. There is no child born with a religious belief. The Jesuits used to have a saying: "Give us a child until he's 5 years old and we'll have him for life." In a similar mode of thought, Bertrand Russell once observed that "A man's religion, almost without exception, is the religion of his community." Few adults—and literally no children—have the independence of mind to dismiss the prevailing majority opinion as being total nonsense. I certainly believe that democracy is the best form of government ever devised. But, on matters of religion or philosophy or even science, truth is not discerned through democratic means.

INTERVIEWER: How could the universe have been created without there being a God?

MILLS: Leaving aside your presumptuous use of the word "created"—that line of reasoning is known as the Aquinas cosmo-

> "I cannot believe in God when there is no scientific evidence for the existence of a supreme being and creator."
>
> —JODIE FOSTER, actress and director, in an interview in the *Calgary Sun* (July 10, 1997)

logical argument. Thomas Aquinas, who lived during the 13th century, argued that everything needs a cause to account for its existence. Aquinas believed that if we regress backward in time through an unbroken chain of causation, then we would eventually arrive at the cause of the universe itself. Aquinas argued that this "First Cause" could be nothing other than God Himself.

This so-called "First Cause" argument, however, is a textbook illustration of *ad hoc* reasoning. For if "everything needs a cause to account for its existence," then we are forced to address the question of who or what created God? If God always existed, and therefore needs no causal explanation, then the original premise of the cosmological argument—that everything needs a cause—has been shown to be erroneous: something can exist *without* a cause. If everything *except* God requires a cause, then the "First Cause" argument becomes *ad hoc* [i.e., inconsistent and prejudicially applied] and is thus logically impermissible.

If we can suppose that God always existed—and thus requires no causal explanation—then we can suppose instead that the mass-energy comprising our universe always existed and thus requires no causal explanation. Many people, including some atheists and agnostics, misinterpret Big Bang theory as proposing that mass-energy popped into existence *ex nihilo* [i.e., out of nothing] before the universe began its current expansion. This something-from-nothing belief is not only false, but flagrantly violates the law of the conservation of mass-energy.

I recently published a scientific paper on this very question. The subject is complicated and technical. But let me summarize by saying that the "First Cause" argument not only begs the question logically and is scientifically bankrupt, it also fails to address *which* god is supposedly proven existent by the argument! In other words, Zeus or Allah has just as much claim to being the "First Cause" as does Jehovah or Jesus. Additionally, new discoveries in quantum theory, as well as research done by Stephen Hawking and his colleagues, have demonstrated that matter can and does arise quite spontaneously from the vacuum fluctuation energy of "empty" space. [See Chapters 2 and 11 for a more thorough explanation.]

INTERVIEWER: How, then, do you explain Nature's beauty and order?

MILLS: There is some degree of beauty and order within Nature. But each year, Nature also cruelly victimizes millions of perfectly innocent men, women and children through natural disasters: earthquakes, hurricanes, tornadoes, floods, lightning, fires, drought, starvation and epidemic disease. Cancer is, for the most part, a naturally occurring *dis*order, which all-too-frequently afflicts, and prematurely kills, innumerable animal and plant lifeforms. Did you know that plants suffer cancer too? So while Nature is at times beautiful and purposeful, it is just as often vicious and chaotic. For every new baby "miraculously" born in the maternity ward, there is, down the hall, a lonely old man dying a torturous death in the cancer ward.

Christians are masters of *selective observation*—or "counting the hits and ignoring the misses." Anything Christians perceive as attractive or orderly is counted as evidence for God's existence. But anything Nature offers that is grotesque or in disarray is never counted against God's existence. Any theological conclusions based upon such selective observation are therefore meaningless.

Moreover, science has provided richly satisfying explanations for the portions of Nature that *do* display true organization, such as the human body. [See Chapter 5.] There is nothing difficult to understand or to accept about biological evolution. The reason why Christians view evolution as such an absurdity is that their only exposure to evolutionary theory has been through absurd caricatures and harebrained misrepresentations offered by pulpit-pounding evangelists. For example, most Christians continue to believe that evolutionary theory teaches that man evolved from modern apes [sic].

INTERVIEWER: Don't you think that religion offers great comfort to people?

MILLS: Occasionally it does. But more often, religion is a source of overwhelming guilt and anxiety. You have this unbelievably nosy voyeur in the sky, allegedly watching your every move and monitoring all your private thoughts. If God detects any "sin" in your life, then He threatens to roast you eternally in a fiery torture chamber. This belief is hardly comforting.

Moreover, religious believers mistakenly view their own guilt and anxiety as proof of the Holy Ghost's existence. They believe that, through instilling these emotions, the Holy Ghost is "convicting them of their sins" in an effort to motivate repentance. Likewise, when a religious follower does, as you say, feel comforted by his beliefs—such as when he imagines that he will someday be reunited with his beloved dead mother—then he perceives his own internal emotions to be "the Holy Ghost's bringing peace to his soul." So regardless of whether a person is comforted or anxiety-stricken as a result of his religious beliefs, he invariably views these emotions as proof of the Holy Ghost's actual existence. I dubbed this psychological tendency as "Holy Hypnosis" in a book of that title, which I authored in the late 1970s.

INTERVIEWER: If you don't believe in God or life-after-death, what, then, is the meaning of life?

MILLS: I think that we make a serious error to speak of *the* singular meaning of life. From a purely biological frame of reference, the purpose of life appears to be reproduction and survival. But I believe that your question seeks a more philosophical response. The only realistic answer to meaning-of-life questions is that 500 different people will have 500 different meanings to their lives. What I personally find deeply meaningful and satisfying may be of little interest to you. Similarly, the things you cherish most in life may bore me to tears. Generally speaking, however, I would say that most people, including myself, find family relationships to be among life's most meaningful aspects. But I respect others who might disagree with my opinion and believe that sculpting magnificent statues or racing automobiles is more meaningful. The error in searching for *one* meaning of life is to assume that every human being holds identical values. In reality, every individual is different, and has a perfect right to be different.

INTERVIEWER: How do you respond to the charge that atheism is a completely negative philosophy? We know what you're against, but we don't know what you're for. Aren't you just trying to rain on someone else's parade, yet offering no alternative?

MILLS: No. I've always considered atheism to be a very positive philosophy in that, by eliminating a very burdensome obligation to appease a nonexistent God, an individual thereby gains maximum freedom to choose his own goals and ideals for a satisfying life. Atheism doesn't have any kind of stiff, ritualized credo. You're right. But that's why it's so appealing. Atheism is synonymous with freedom and freedom of thought, which, in my opinion, are highly positive and desirable.

> "I'm an atheist, and that's it. I believe there's nothing we can know except that we should be kind to each other and do what we can for each other."
>
> —KATHARINE HEPBURN
> (1909–2003), actress, in *Ladies' Home Journal* (October 1991)

INTERVIEWER: Let's assume for a moment that you're correct in your beliefs: there's no God, no Heaven, and no Hell. If you're right about that, then you have nothing to gain. But if you're wrong, then you've lost your soul for eternity. On the other hand, if a person believes in God, then he has everything to gain and nothing to lose. If he's right in his beliefs, then he'll go to Heaven. If he's wrong about there being a God, then he'll at least have looked forward to going to Heaven even if he merely rots in the ground beside you.

MILLS: That argument is known as Pascal's Wager, because it was first articulated by Blaise Pascal, a 17th-century French philosopher. There are several fallacies in the argument. But the most obvious is that the same argument can be applied to any religion—not just to Christianity. For example, I could say that, since we have everything to gain and nothing to lose by converting to Islam, we should all become Muslims. Or since we have everything to gain and nothing to lose by being Hindu, we should all adopt Hinduism. Christians never stop to consider that they are in just as much danger of going to the Muslim hell as I, an atheist, am in danger of going to the Christian hell.

Pascal's Wager is also flawed in its premise that a person has everything to gain, and nothing to lose, by converting to a religion. The fact is that, whether we like it or not, our earthly life is the only life we're ever going to experience. If we sacrifice this one life in doormat subservience to a nonexistent god, then we have lost everything!

INTERVIEWER: Could we both agree at least that, whether you view Him as God or man, Jesus Christ was an admirable figure?

MILLS: No, I disagree completely. I think it's quite evident from reading the New Testament that Jesus believed in a literal hell, where those who rejected His teachings were to be sadistically tortured, akin to being dowsed with gasoline and set ablaze with a match. Not only is this teaching not "admirable," it is thoroughly disgusting and, in my view, should never be taught to young children, who understandably become upset and horror-stricken at the ghastly imagery. Parents are *so* eager to teach their children that happy little prayer " . . . If I should *die* before I wake, I pray Thy Lord my soul to take." How inhumane can you possibly be!

> "The Bible is full of interest. It has noble poetry in it; and some clever fables; and some blood-drenched history; and some good morals; and a wealth of obscenity; and upwards of a thousand lies."
>
> —MARK TWAIN (1835–1910), in *Letters from the Earth*

There is a pronounced dissimilarity between the popularized "loving" version of Jesus we hear about in church and the Jesus as actually quoted in the New Testament. No wonder His followers are so intolerant. They are only following Jesus' declarations that anyone who disagrees with their religious beliefs deserves eternal incineration. The Bible—both Old and New Testaments—is filled with instances in which God, in various incarnations, supposedly orders people and armies to be murdered or to commit murder.

Another reason why I don't find Jesus admirable is that He squandered His alleged supernatural powers on frivolous nonsense. Instead of bringing mankind a cure for heart disease and cancer, He used His magic to curse a fig tree. Instead of ending birth defects and infant mortality, He filled pigs with demons. Instead of ending world hunger and illiteracy, He conjured up a jug of wine. What an incredible waste of omnipotence!

INTERVIEWER: Even though you don't believe that He was God, do you believe that Jesus Christ, the man, lived on Earth?

MILLS: Probably not. If He did actually live, then He was almost certainly illiterate, since He left no writings of his own—at least none that we know about. At the time that He supposedly lived, however, most people *were* illiterate, so I don't mean to be critical of Him on this point. I too would have been illiterate. But it *is* curious to ponder an illiterate God.

INTERVIEWER: But aren't there secular historical references to Christ? Even if you totally disregard the Bible, how do you explain the fact that writers and historians of the time—*non-Christian* writers—detailed the life of Jesus?

MILLS: You're correct that there are secular historical references to Jesus. For example, Josephus, Tacitus, Lucian, Seutonius, Pliny, and Justin Martyr all make reference to "Christ" or "Jesus Christ" in their historical accounts. But there is one monumental flaw in this argument: Not one of these secular writers was born until decades after Jesus' alleged crucifixion. Thus, none of these writers could possibly provide firsthand knowledge of anything having to do with the life of Jesus. Their historical references to Jesus do provide evidence that the Christ *legend* was extant during the period in which they wrote. But that's about it. Moreover, many of these secular sources who allude, decades afterward, to the life of Jesus also detail the lives and folklore of numerous other "miracle workers" completely apart from Jesus. Tales of mystical hocus-pocus were widespread in the ancient world and were incorporated into the holy books of many different religions. Such credulity naturally provided fertile ground for the acceptance and growth of Christianity as well.

INTERVIEWER: What about secular writers who lived as Christ's contemporaries?

MILLS: There is not a single reference to a "Jesus" or to "Jesus Christ" written by any secular source who lived during the years in which Christ supposedly walked the earth. To me, this fact is very revealing, since these years represent one of the most thoroughly documented periods of antiquity. Wouldn't Jesus' miracles have drawn the attention of hundreds of contemporary writers and record-keepers? Why is there no mention at all of Jesus' existence? Why is there no historical record of Herod's alleged Slaughter of the Innocents [plagiarized directly from Exodus] or of Matthew's assertion that, following Jesus' death, living corpses from nearby cemeteries were strolling the streets of Jerusalem? Were these "facts" too humdrum to be noted by historians of the day? To summarize my position on the "historical" Jesus, I once wrote a poem:

> "My earlier views of the unsoundness of the Christian scheme of salvation and the human origin of the scriptures have become clearer and stronger with advancing years and I see no reason for thinking I shall ever change them."
>
> —ABRAHAM LINCOLN (1809–1865), to Judge J. S. Wakefield, following Willie Lincoln's death in 1862

Today some say that Jesus died,
And still remains quite dead.
But these who speak have surely lied.
The real truth is, instead,
That Jesus Christ, Whose blood was spilled,

Is *no* corpse, I insist!
For how could someone have been killed,
Who never did exist?

INTERVIEWER: [Groans] . . . Here I don't think you're being objective. I'm sure you believe that George Washington was the first President of the United States. You believe that *he* existed, even though you have no firsthand knowledge of that fact. You accept, without question, the word of others regarding the life of George Washington; whereas you immediately dismiss the word of others regarding the life of Jesus. You're revealing your anti-religious prejudice!

MILLS: Not at all. Here are the distinctions: The life of George Washington was documented by innumerable dispassionate observers who lived during Washington's own lifetime. This was decidedly not the case with Jesus, Whose existence was attested by *no* secular writer of His time. Moreover, Washington himself left us a wealth of his own writings. Jesus left no writings—period.

But there is a third distinction that, to me, is the most significant: Although Washington certainly led an unusually eventful and productive life, there is no historical claim that Washington stood the laws of physics on their head. For example, no one ever claimed that Washington rose from the dead or walked on water. "Extraordinary claims," said Carl Sagan, "require extraordinary evidence." So while I might accept someone's word that George Washington was born in Virginia, I would not believe someone's assertion that Washington was born of a virgin. The more far-fetched the claim, the more overwhelming and irrefutable the evidence must be. Since none of Christ's contemporaries even bothered to mention His name in their historical accounts, the level of proof necessary to document His "miracles" is woefully inadequate. In fact, it's absolutely nonexistent.

Finally, I'm willing to bet that many of the "facts" we know—or think we know—about George Washington are likewise mythology. The cherry tree story, and "I cannot tell a lie," and Washington's throwing a silver dollar across the Potomac River are probably as factual as Christ's placing a curse on a fig tree.

INTERVIEWER: So how was the stone rolled away in front of Jesus' tomb? Wouldn't such a feat require supernatural power, especially with Roman guards on duty to thwart such an effort?

MILLS: This is precisely the type of argument that Christian apologists so adore and that so dazzles the naive Fundamentalists. The obvious flaw is that the argument begins by presupposing that 99 percent of the Bible is true. It isn't difficult therefore to logically "prove" the remaining 1 percent. If you assume (1) that Jesus existed, (2) that He lived under Roman jurisdiction, (3) that He was crucified, (4) that His body was laid in a tomb, (5) that a large stone was placed before the tomb's entrance, (6) that Roman guards were stationed outside the tomb, (7) that the stone was later dislodged, and (8) that the body was absent after the third day, *then*, perhaps, one may construct a possible scenario in which supernatural forces were at work—although hundreds of other explanations would continue to be more plausible. But to blindly accept on religious faith that these eight biblical "facts" are true is to assume *a priori* the accuracy of the very book whose veracity is being debated. Then Christian apologists have the gall to claim that this "proof" of Jesus' resurrection is deduced through logic, rather than based upon Scripture!

By analogy, let's say that I believe in four bad witches: Witch 1, Witch 2, Witch 3 and Witch 4. I am wondering which of the four witches cast an evil spell on my dying vegetable garden. An enchanted gremlin informs me that Witches 1, 2 and 4 were out of town when the spell was cast. I therefore claim "proof" that Witch 3 cursed my vegetables.

Now, there is not a person on Earth who would believe that such logic proves anything, except that I had taken leave of my senses. I have not proven that Witch 3 cursed my garden because all of the premises of my argument are entirely fictitious. Yet equally vacuous "logic" is routinely proffered by Christian apologists, and is gullibly swallowed by millions, who are comforted that their religious beliefs have been "proven" to be so logical.

INTERVIEWER: A few minutes ago, you mentioned Carl Sagan. He believed that intelligent life might exist elsewhere in the universe. Do atheists acknowledge that possibility? Do you personally believe in UFOs?

MILLS: Yes and no. I definitely believe that life—and probably intelligent life—is fairly common throughout the universe. But, no, I don't believe that our planet has ever been visited by alien spacecraft. The flying saucer stories are total nonsense because a spacecraft traversing vast interstellar distances could not be physically designed in the shape of a small, flat saucer. The lunar module, by the way, looked nothing like a flying saucer, because the design necessary to accomplish an extraterrestrial landing would not permit such a configuration. While I personally don't believe in UFOs, atheism is not necessarily incompatible with a belief in flying saucers, since our alien visitors are alleged to be highly advanced beings, who better harness the laws of physics, rather than supernatural gods, who violate the laws of physics. Carl Sagan was himself a resolute atheist.

INTERVIEWER: But don't you think that, whether it's UFOs or God or something else, people need to believe in something in order to be happy?

MILLS: I think that people generally need interests or hobbies outside of themselves to be maximally happy. But there's no reason that such outside pursuits must take the form of a crackpot religion. A person may become creatively absorbed into literally millions of different activities, pastimes, relationships, arts or sciences—any one of which may provide deep fulfillment and happiness for the particular individual. Religious leaders, though, very cleverly try to recruit converts by preaching that you need

> "I do not believe in the divinity of Christ, and there are many other of the postulates of the orthodox creed to which I cannot subscribe."
>
> —WILLIAM HOWARD TAFT (1857–1930), in a letter to Yale University

their brand of religion in order to be contented. Without Jesus or Allah or Buddha, you'll supposedly lead a wretched and calamitous existence. Advertisers use this identical psychological ploy to sell their products: they'll convince you (1) that you have a problem, (2) that you need their product to solve your "problem," and (3) that other, competing products will leave you in despair.

Ironically, if you truly believe that your happiness requires a particular religion—or a chocolate sundae or a sports car or a certain bed partner—then you'll obviously create a self-fulfilling prophecy, making yourself unnecessarily miserable until your so-called "needs" are satisfied. As Eric Hoffer noted, "the aim of a religious movement is to inflict a malady in society, then offer the religion as a cure." Because of this religious propaganda—that is, "no religion, no happiness"—most Christians imagine that non-believers lead meaningless, empty lives wallowing in depression. In reality, virtually all of the atheists I've known have been dynamic, highly optimistic men and women who enjoyed life to the hilt, partially because they were liberated from the morbid, guilt-ridden, religious ball-and-chain around their necks. By contrast, I've known scores of Christians who led very unfulfilling lives, praying endlessly for "miracles" that never occurred or waiting pitifully for Jesus' oft-delayed second coming.

INTERVIEWER: In 1963 Madalyn Murray O'Hair persuaded the U.S. Supreme Court to remove prayer from America's public schools. I'm sure you supported that Court decision. But don't you think that it's unfair in a democratic society for the majority who want to pray in school to be denied the opportunity by a tiny minority who object?

MILLS: As long as there are algebra tests, students will continue to pray effusively in the public schools. The 1963 decision prohibited *mandatory* prayer, in which students of diverse religious backgrounds were forced, under penalty of expulsion, to mumble a prayer reflecting the religious beliefs of the local schoolboard. There is no law in any state that prohibits voluntary prayer in America's public schools. Let's remember that Jesus warned the

Pharisees not to pray publicly, because such prayers were usually pretentious, insincere efforts to showboat.

INTERVIEWER: Because of her part in that Supreme Court decision, Madalyn O'Hair was often called "the most hated woman in America." Did you ever meet her?

MILLS: Yes, three times. We also exchanged letters occasionally, and I spoke with her by phone perhaps half a dozen times over the years. We're also pictured together on the dust jacket of my first book, *Holy Hypnosis*.

INTERVIEWER: What was your impression of her?

MILLS: People don't like to hear this, but she truly was a woman of extraordinary intelligence and ability. She obviously held her viewpoint unwaveringly, and didn't hesitate to correct you in front of others if she thought you were mistaken about a particular point or way of doing something. My own observation was that she was ordinarily very gentle and pleasant to be around, despite her ogre-like image. Even some atheists say that she sometimes exhibited a hard edge to her personality. But let's remember that she received literally hundreds of death threats during her lifetime and, in the end, was in fact kidnapped, robbed and murdered in cold blood. *All* movements—be they religious, anti-religious, political, military, or whatever—are led by men and women with extremist views and extremist personalities. That's why they're the leaders. That's also why the Democratic nominee for President is usually more liberal than the general public, while the Republican nominee is more conservative than the average voter.

> "In the experiences of a year of the Presidency, there has come to me no other such unwelcome impression as the manifest religious intolerance which exists among many of our citizens. I hold it to be a menace to the very liberties we boast and cherish."
>
> —WARREN G. HARDING (1865–1923), in a presidential address (March 24, 1922)

INTERVIEWER: Didn't Madalyn's son become a born-again Christian?

MILLS: Bill Murray [Madalyn Murray O'Hair's son] is suffering from Stockholm Syndrome, the psychological malady in which hostages become emotionally attached and sympathetic to their terrorist captors, who, in Bill's case, were the mean-spirited Christians he encountered throughout his life. Like Madalyn, Bill Murray received many death threats from Christian fanatics across the United States. He eventually snapped from this pressure, became an alcoholic, a drug abuser, then a notorious fugitive. After thoroughly destroying his marriage and family, he suddenly announced that he was becoming a traveling Christian evangelist [sic].

I'm not saying that Bill Murray is insincere in his embrace of Christianity. But he *is* traveling the country making factually inaccurate statements about his own family history. Because of his unique background, he understands better than most other preachers how to press the buttons of Christian Fundamentalists when passing the collection plate. Religion is infinitely more profitable than atheism, and nobody knows this fact better than Bill Murray. Though I've never met Bill Murray, I assure you that Madalyn's other children, Jon and Robin, whom I did meet before their tragic murder, were strongly atheistic.

> "The memory of my own suffering has prevented me from ever shadowing one young soul with the superstitions of the Christian religion."
>
> —ELIZABETH CADY STANTON (1815–1902), feminist leader, in *Eight Years and More*

INTERVIEWER: You have a young daughter of your own. Are you going to force atheism on her?

MILLS: Of course not. But if I *were* inclined to force atheism on her, here's what I would do: I would absolutely insist that she attend church several times a week, whether she wanted to or not. I would force her to read the Bible for two hours a day; and I would demand that she pray every night for at least another hour. I would remind her often that she might burn in Hell for disobeying Jesus. And I would absolutely forbid her to date or wear cosmetics until she is 21 years old. By using all these techniques of Christian parenting, I would certainly lead her to look favorably upon atheism.

INTERVIEWER: You're obviously joking. But if she really wanted to go to church, would you try to discourage her?

MILLS: No. I would be happy to take her to church, or to attend church with her myself if that's what she wanted. But I wouldn't hypocritically pretend to believe in the religion myself. And I would occasionally express my thoughts to her that science, rather than mysticism, is the key to understanding the universe and ourselves. I realize, of course, that despite my willingness to aid my daughter in whatever path she chooses in life, many Christians nonetheless consider me an "unfit" parent for exposing her to a healthy diversity of opinion. It is the Christians, not the atheists, who routinely pressure their children into adopting a belief system. It is the Christians who punish their children for deviating from their parents' religious ideals.

INTERVIEWER: Feelings of love, such as those you feel toward your family, cannot be seen or detected through any type of scientific or laboratory experiment. Yet you admittedly believe strongly that they exist. Since God is said to be love, why do you accept the "unprovable" existence of family love, but not of God's love?

MILLS: The love that a person feels for his family is a vital and wonderful function of human psychology. If you wish to argue that, like family love, God is a function of human psychology, then I agree with you: God certainly "exists" within the psychological framework of millions of people. But the popular religious belief is that God also exists apart from, and independent of, human psychology. If everyone on Earth died tomorrow, the Christian Church believes that God would nonetheless continue to rule over the universe in our absence. By contrast, my love for my family "exists" only so long as I remain alive and have a cognitive function. Saying that love exists independently from our brains is like saying that digestion exists independently from our stomachs. The longing for human love to transcend our mortal limitations is no doubt a primary reason why myths of an afterlife were originally invented and readily believed.

The Bible does indeed say that "God is love" (1 John 4:8). It also says that "Love is not jealous" (1 Corinthians 13:4). Then we are told that "I, the Lord thy God, am a jealous God" (Exodus 20:5). "God is love" when He is not torturing billions of non-Christians in Hell or ordering the Israelites to "keep the virgins for yourselves" but massacre all the innocent men, women and male children in the confiscated Promised Land (Numbers 31:18).

INTERVIEWER: How do you respond to the charge that atheism is just another religion?

MILLS: It seems to me that any religion worthy of the name must include some form of belief in a god or gods and some type of belief in the supernatural. Otherwise, the "religion" would be indistinguishable from atheism. Atheism is the opposite of religion in that a belief in God and the supernatural is rejected. If, however, you define "religion" to mean any form of philosophical system, then I suppose you could label atheism a religion. But such all-inclusive, watered-down definitions soon become altogether meaningless and only lead to confusion. By such a loose definition, for example, I, a devout atheist, could be called a devoutly religious man. On the other hand, I do agree that the devoted Christian and the devoted atheist share more in common psychologically than they do with a person who doesn't give a damn one way or another. I've always found it intriguing, though, that Christians attempt to slander atheism by calling it a "religion." Christians seem to be saying, "Look, you atheists are just as irrational as we are!"

> "I would love to believe that when I die I will live again, that some thinking, feeling, remembering part of me will continue. But as much as I want to believe that, and despite the ancient and worldwide cultural traditions that assert an afterlife, I know of nothing to suggest that it is more than wishful thinking."
>
> —CARL SAGAN (1934–1996), Pulitzer Prize–winning astronomer, in *The Demon-Haunted World*

INTERVIEWER: Isn't it true that some famous atheists have recanted on their deathbeds?

MILLS: No. There are lots of bogus stories to that effect circulated by dishonest TV evangelists. But none of these accounts is rooted in fact. Let me provide one clear example of how absurd these recantation stories are. Thomas Paine, who played an integral role in the American Revolution, wrote a famous attack on Christianity titled *The Age of Reason*. Despite his being a true American hero, the Christian community of the time despised Paine because of his anti-religious sentiment. Following Paine's death, Puritans started a rumor that he had suddenly recanted on his deathbed, renouncing all of his anti-religious writings.

This fabricated tale of Paine's recantation was simply an effort by the Puritans to dissuade people from reading his influential writings. If Paine himself disavowed *The Age of Reason*, then you should too, went the story. The reality, however, was that Paine had written *The Age of Reason* while awaiting the guillotine! He had been falsely imprisoned and believed that he was going to be beheaded. During what he thought to be his last days, Paine wrote *The Age of Reason*. So, far from turning to religion as death approached, Paine wanted to create a lasting testimony to his unbelief. Fortunately, Paine was later released from prison. But shameless Puritans nevertheless spread the tale, years later, that Paine, fearing death, recanted his anti-religious beliefs at death's door.

Most Christians find it utterly inconceivable that someone could genuinely disbelieve their holy doctrines. Christians imagine that atheists and agnostics harbor a latent belief in God and in life-after-death—an underlying belief that supposedly springs to the surface in times of crisis or impending death. "There are no atheists in foxholes." But the only individuals who sincerely turn to religion during such times of crisis are individuals who sincerely believe in an afterlife. Atheists, by definition, are excluded from this group. My own observation is that those most terrified of death are not atheists, but believers, uncertain whether they are going to Heaven or Hell. I routinely receive email from atheists in the military, many of whom have seen direct combat in Iraq or Afghanistan.

INTERVIEWER: Are *you* afraid to die?

MILLS: I'm afraid to die in that I want to continue living. I don't want my life terminated. I'm also afraid to die in that I don't want my wife to become a widow and my daughter to be fatherless. And I certainly don't want to suffer an agonizing or slow and painful death. But I'm not afraid of death in the sense of roasting in some kind of hell. That's mythology.

INTERVIEWER: You obviously believe that all religions were human inventions. But you haven't presented any kind of explanation as to why people would deliberately invent and promulgate myths that they themselves knew to be false.

MILLS: I don't believe that ancient man suddenly decided one day to cook up a false religion. That's not how it happened. Primitive man comprehended very little about himself and the world around him. He didn't understand why it rained, why his crops failed, why his children fell sick and died, why the seasons changed. So the idea of there being superhuman gods in charge of these various elements seemed the only plausible explanation.

Moreover, I think that religious worship and ritualism probably evolved as man sought to persuade these gods to treat him kindly. A person might have thought, for example, that if he abstained from sexual pleasures and asked the Potato God to improve his crop, then his sexual abstinence would somehow galvanize the Potato God into action as a compensatory reward. In other words, by controlling a small part of his own private life, primitive man hoped to indirectly gain control over larger areas, such as managing the weather or curing illness through imploring the gods. The specifics of these rituals and self-sacrifices varied enormously among the diverse primitive cultures. But all religions share one commonality: someone must suffer before God will forgive "sin" and bless mankind. To a considerable degree, therefore, religion is a form of masochism: pain must be inflicted before one may guiltlessly enjoy life.

INTERVIEWER: Do you believe that religion encourages moral conduct?

MILLS: If we're talking about the Christian religion, the United States is indisputably the most religiously devoted nation on Earth. The United States also suffers one of the world's highest crime rates. By contrast, in the more secular nations of Europe—where fewer than 10 percent of the people attend church on a regular basis—the crime rate is a minuscule fraction of the U.S. total. Per-capita contributions to charity are likewise much higher in secular European nations than in "Christian" America. So there seems to be an *inverse* correlation between a nation's religious devotion and its moral conduct.

> "Say what you like about the Ten Commandments, you must always come back to the pleasant fact that there are only ten of them."
>
> —H. L. MENCKEN
> (1880–1956), editor and critic

If you carefully study the Ten Commandments, you will be stunned to discover that only three of the ten prohibit unethical treatment of other individuals, for example, killing, stealing, bearing false witness. The majority of the Commandments merely prescribe accepted methods of religious ritual, such as keeping the Sabbath, no graven images, no other gods, no taking the Lord's name in vain.

To the extent that a religion strives to promote ethical conduct, I support those efforts wholeheartedly. But too often, religions define morality in terms of whether a person belongs to the "correct" religion, rather than in terms of whether an individual treats others fairly and compassionately. Protestant Fundamentalists believe, moreover, that non-Christians are necessarily ethically inferior to Christians. Such "thinking" leads inevitably to bigotry, prejudice and Holy War.

The bloody history of Christianity would lead any objective person to conclude that religion in general—and the Christian religion in particular—has been a moral abomination to mankind. The Crusades, the Inquisition, the witch burnings, the torture of "infidels" were all carried out in the name of the Christian God. While it is unfair to hold Christianity responsible for perversions of its teachings, it is nonetheless indisputable that, historically, more people have been slaughtered in the name of the Christian religion than for any reason connected to atheism.

For 1500 years, the Christian Church systematically operated torture chambers throughout Europe. Torture was the rule, not the exception. Next to the Bible, the most influential and venerated book in Christian history was the *Malleus Maleficarum* [Hammer of Witches], which was a step-by-step tutorial in how to torture "witches" and "sorcerers." Each year, the Christian Church in Europe tortured to death tens of thousands of people, including children as young as two years of age. The only restriction was that the instruments of torment had to be blessed by a priest before their initial use. Most Americans think of witch burning as having occurred only during a brief period in Colonial New England. The fact is, however, that witch burning ended in Colonial America after a gruesome 1500-year reign of terror throughout Europe.

Today, the average Christian goes to church every week or so—shakes hands with a few Christian friends and says "God bless you"—listens to a gentle sermon and a few quiet hymns— then goes home feeling the "peace of God" in his heart. Because the Christian Church now conducts itself in a relatively civilized manner, a false perception is created that religion has always been a tranquil force for good. That is not the case. Aside from the wholesale extermination of "witches," the Christian Church fought bitterly throughout its history—and is still fighting today—to impede scientific progress. Galileo, remember, was nearly put to death by the Church for constructing his telescope and discovering the moons of Jupiter. For centuries, moreover, the Church forbade the dissection of a human cadaver, calling it "a desecration of the temple of the Holy Ghost." Medical research was thereby stalled for almost a thousand years. It is no coincidence, therefore, that Christianity's longest period of sustained growth and influence occurred during what historians refer to as the *Dark Ages*.

I'm genuinely afraid that, unless we start teaching some real science in our miserable public schools, we may find that 21st-century America suffers an intellectual climate resembling that of the Dark Ages. We tend to believe that, once knowledge has been acquired and technology developed by man, these gains are "locked in" and the future will only build upon these past achievements. But history argues forcefully against such an optimistic assumption. The ancient Greeks and Egyptians, for example, made amazing scientific discoveries and wrote detailed scientific analyses that the Christian Church later destroyed and suppressed for centuries. A mob of religious zealots deliberately burned the greatest library of the ancient world, at Alexandria, Egypt. And it was not until Renaissance scholars emancipated Europe from religious shackles that these scientific principles were rediscovered 1500 years later.

Fifteen-hundred years of progress were therefore stifled by the Christian Church. Were it not for religious persecution and oppression of science, mankind might have landed on the moon in the year A.D. 650. Cancer may have been eradicated forever by the year A.D. 800. And heart disease may, today, be unknown. But Christianity put into deep hibernation Greek and Egyptian scientific gains of the past.

Historically, the Church fought venomously against each new scientific advance. But after fruitlessly criticizing each new scien-

> "I regard monotheism as the greatest disaster ever to befall the human race. I see no good in Judaism, Christianity or Islam—good people, yes, but any religion based on a single, well, frenzied and virulent god, is not as useful to the human race as, say, Confucianism, which is not a religion but an ethical and educational system."
>
> —GORE VIDAL, writer, in *At Home* (1988)

tific achievement, the Church soon flip-flopped its position and embraced the new discovery as a "gift from God to mankind." The Catholic hierarchy even opposed the invention of the printing press because copies of Scripture could be easily mass produced and placed in the hands of those who might misinterpret or criticize "God's Word." Before the printing press, Scripture had been read and deciphered only by Catholic priests.

The Church angrily denounced the introduction of medicines, antibiotics, anesthesia, surgery, blood transfusions, birth control, transplants, *in vitro* fertilization and most forms of pain killers. Supposedly, these scientific tools interfered with nature and were therefore against God's will. Today, the Church is fighting stem-cell research, cloning technology and genetic engineering. But when cloning laboratories provide an unlimited supply of transplant tissue for dying children, and when genetic engineering cures all forms of cancer, Church leaders will once again forget their initial opposition and hail these achievements as evidence of God's love for mankind. Today, science is prevailing, but throughout most of recorded history, religion strangled scientific inquiry and often tortured and executed those who advocated the scientific method.

> "One is often told that it is a very wrong thing to attack religion, because religion makes men virtuous. So I am told; I have not noticed it."
>
> —LORD BERTRAND RUSSELL (1872–1970), British Nobel Laureate, mathematician, philosopher and peace activist, in *Why I Am Not a Christian*

Unless we drastically improve our educational system, it is not inconceivable that scientific ignorance will once again become so ubiquitous that ultra-conservative Fundamentalists seize control of our government and resurrect book burning and witch burning. Five hundred years from now, the hot topic of debate in scientific circles may be whether the Earth is round or flat. This frightening scenario is not likely, but it is far from impossible.

INTERVIEWER: Has anyone ever threatened *you* because of your religious views?

MILLS: Only the local police.

INTERVIEWER: Are you serious?

MILLS: Yes. Back in the late 1970s, I organized a protest demonstration against a charlatan faith healer whose Miracle Crusade rolled through town once a year. While I absolutely supported his constitutional right to promulgate his religious beliefs, I did feel that our local community needed to exercise caution. This "man of God" frequently told diabetics to throw away their insulin; and he often instructed cancer patients to forgo their chemotherapy and trust God for a miracle.

Several months before the faith healer's next scheduled visit to our city, a child was born in a local hospital with an enlarged opening between the chambers of his heart. Normally, this birth defect is fairly easy to repair, and the child can lead a normal, healthy life. The mother in this case, however, refused surgery for the child, waiting instead for the faith healer's return. Tragically, the child died of complications from the unrepaired birth defect while waiting to be miraculously cured. Since none of the local news media reported this sad story, I decided to speak out myself by organizing a protest against the faith healer's next Miracle Rally.

Along with a few like-minded friends, I painted some placards imploring the community to "Donate money to medical research, not to religious fraud." We planned to carry these signs near the tent meeting in hope of discouraging financial contributions to the faith healer's bulging coffers. He routinely asked that the thousands of people in attendance donate $100 per person, per night, "to show God how much we trust Him."

I was worried, however, about two potential dangers of staging a protest. First of all, the followers of this traveling faith healer were not the most sophisticated people in the world. And I was concerned that they might physically assault my friends and me as we peacefully carried our signs near the Miracle Rally. Second, I wanted to be extremely careful that our protest did not violate any technicality of the law, such as trespassing or blocking entrance to a public facility, for which the police might break up our demonstration.

Because of these two fears, I did an incredibly stupid thing: I drove to the local police station to ask law-enforcement authorities for information and for police protection against potential threats from religious zealots during our protest march. The first police official with whom I spoke asked, "Is you gonna protest fir him or 'gin him [i.e., the faith healer]?" When I responded "Against him," the official said that he himself planned to attend the Miracle Rally and would not hesitate to spit directly in my face as he walked past our demonstration.

I thought, perhaps, I'd better speak with someone else. The next police official I encountered at the station said that if any trouble broke out during our protest, he would arrest me. I replied that I was not a person inclined to physical violence since I had never been in a fight in my entire life. The policeman said that he didn't care who *started* a fight. If any of the faith healer's people confronted us violently, then the police would be delighted to arrest *me*, since I was trying to interfere with God's work. He said that he personally "would love to throw my ass in the county jail."

Disgusted, I went home and telephoned the police station in hope of speaking to men of greater rationality than those I had encountered face to face. I was finally connected to a police sergeant who said, "To hell with you, buddy. No policeman wants to protect a goddamned atheist. I hope somebody bloodies you up good." In total that day, I spoke with about seven or eight police officials, either in person or by telephone. None of them was helpful, and most of them threatened me, directly or indirectly, with violent reprisals of their own if we conducted our perfectly legal protest. These were unquestionably the most intellectually challenged "professionals" I've ever dealt with.

INTERVIEWER: Did you go ahead with the protest?

MILLS: Yes, and there was no trouble at all. Not even the police were unruly. Most importantly, we got significant television coverage airing our position that this faith healer was collecting money under fraudulent pretenses and endangering public health through his bogus medical advice. But I'm certain that he collected a fortune in donations anyway.

This Sunday morning, I invite you to spend about four hours watching your local TV preachers and faith healers. Then ask yourself this question: Would an omnipotent God truly select and permit *these* men to be His spokesmen?

INTERVIEWER: [Laughs] . . . Has being an atheist affected your social life?

MILLS: Not especially. Although I've written quite a lot about religion and atheism, I almost never bring up the subjects in conversation unless someone asks me a specific question about my beliefs. I do feel, however, that I have a thorough appreciation of what it's like to be black or Hispanic or gay in America. You do face bigotry sometimes from unsophisticated people who misunderstand you and who believe that you are immoral just because you are a minority of some kind. It's sad that, whenever I've engaged in give-and-take dialogue on radio call-in shows, the phone-in questions frequently force me to offer responses such as "No, I don't believe that murder is okay."

INTERVIEWER: How *do* atheists define morality then? Since you don't believe in God, do you believe in a right and wrong?

> "The Good Book—one of the most remarkable euphemisms ever coined."
>
> —ASHLEY MONTAGU (1905–1999), British anthropologist; Harvard and Princeton science professor

MILLS: Of course. I'm willing to bet that if you seated beside me the most ultra-conservative preacher in town, he and I would probably agree 95 percent of the time on whether certain behavior is "right" or "wrong." I do believe, though, that the terms "right" and "wrong" usually lack a clear, unbiased definition when employed by most speakers. Personally, I prefer to label behavior as either "considerate" or "inconsiderate" of someone else's rights. Those terms, I feel, tend to clarify the issues, rather than to obscure them.

If an act deliberately and needlessly impinges upon someone else's rights, then I consider that act wrong and abstain from that activity. Murder, robbery, assault and battery—and almost *all* crimes—would fit into this category. Lawyers call these activities *malum in se* [i.e., bad in themselves]. Again, a Baptist minister and I would have few, if any, disagreements over what behaviors qualify as *malum in se*.

The minister and I would undoubtedly have ethical disputes, however, over behavior that is *malum prohibitum* [i.e., bad because it is prohibited]. An example of a *malum prohibitum* violation would be inadvertently leaving your car parked until 5:30 p.m. in a space that was supposed to be vacated by 5 p.m. Here, there is nothing intrinsically evil or necessarily injurious about your actions, but you did foolishly violate a statute. Ethical disputes between atheists and Christians almost invariably center around *malum prohibitum* conduct—usually sexual conduct. The atheist would argue that two consenting, unmarried adults who used proper disease and pregnancy prevention could engage in sexual intercourse without being "unethical" or "immoral." The Christian, however, would necessarily label this sexual tryst as "wrong" because it was prohibited, supposedly, by God.

Masturbation is another example. If a teenage male enjoys fantasizing about his female classmates, and privately and harmlessly masturbates himself to orgasm, then the atheist would probably say "enjoy yourself." The Christian, by contrast, would view such activity as "wrong" because Jesus, supposedly, never masturbated and has prohibited such "disgraceful" conduct. To summarize, then, I consider a behavior "wrong" when it genuinely harms someone, rather than because "The Lord Thy God has spoken."

Merely because I'm an atheist, I've been criticized on issues of "family values" by Christians

> "The Old Testament is responsible for more atheism, agnosticism, disbelief—call it what you will—than any book ever written."
>
> —A. A. MILNE (1882–1956), creator of Winnie the Pooh

whose own personal lives and behavior were thoroughly scandalous. I've never raised my voice to my daughter, never smoked a cigarette, never written a bad check, never gotten a speeding ticket, never been in a fight, and never lied on an income tax form. Except for the tiny fact that I'm an atheist, I lead a good "Christian" life! [Laughs]

INTERVIEWER: But doesn't the fact that everyone agrees, for example, that murder is "wrong" indicate that we all share a common conscience guided by one God?

MILLS: I frequently hear this [C. S. Lewis–inspired] reasoning from Christians, but the argument is entirely definitional rather than substantive. Murder, by definition, is an unjustified killing. Of course everyone agrees that an unjustified killing is wrong. We're simply agreeing that an unjustified killing is unjustified. But what constitutes an unjustified killing? Here, we'll face heated debate. Is abortion murder or a sometimes-prudent medical procedure? Is euthanasia murder or a humane and compassionate way to end pointless suffering? Is the death penalty a state-sponsored murder, or justice served? Like many Americans, I'm pro-choice, pro-euthanasia and anti-death-penalty, but few Christians agree with these positions. So where's our "common conscience"? It exists only by wordplay.

INTERVIEWER: But don't you think there has to be some kind of ultimate justice for human beings? People who do wrong are not always punished in this world, and good is not always rewarded. Don't these injustices require an afterlife to redress the imbalance: where good is ultimately rewarded and evil punished?

MILLS: You're undeniably correct that there is often grave injustice in this world. But that sad fact argues against, rather than for, God's existence. There is no reason to believe that the injustice we perceive in daily life is not typical of how the universe as a whole operates.

For example, suppose that a deliveryman places a large crate of oranges on your doorstep. You open the crate and discover that every single orange you see on top of the box is rotten. Would you then conclude that the remaining oranges on the bottom of the crate must be good? No. You would conclude that the rotten oranges you see on top are probably quite representative of the shipment as a whole. Likewise, the injustice we perceive in our world is evidence that we unfortunately live in an unjust world, rather than that justice is waiting "just beyond sight."

INTERVIEWER: How do you explain that many of the Bible's prophecies have been fulfilled?

MILLS: The same way I explain that your daily newspaper horoscope is always "fulfilled" and that millions of Americans swear by the predictions of The Psychic Friends' Network. In all these instances, the prophecies are so incredibly vague as to mean practically anything. Bertrand Russell once remarked that "the Bible is known for many things, but clarity is not among them."

When I was a devout believer back in the early 1970s, I was absolutely convinced that Jesus' second coming was at hand. I read all of Hal Lindsey's doomsday books foretelling the end of the world based on Old and New Testament prophecies. It wasn't until years later that I studied Church history and realized that every generation for 2000 years has believed that Jesus' second coming was imminent, because Bible prophecies allegedly foretold events of their generations also. I always like to state that, in my opinion, the individuals who wrote the Bible had a non-prophet organization!

INTERVIEWER: So you used to believe in God?

MILLS: Yes. I was "saved" and baptized when I was nine years old. For the first fifteen years of my life, I regularly attended church and Sunday school and was a typical believer in the Baptist faith. Then, during my first year of high school, I began associating with some friends who were highly charismatic and exuberant about their "relationship with the Lord." Their enthusiasm soon rubbed off on me. I myself became a glassy-eyed religious fanatic, parading around high school distributing pamphlets titled *What Must I Do to Be Saved?* I preached the Gospel to any lost soul who would listen, and I felt deep satisfaction whenever someone called me a "Jesus freak," since I considered that label to be a badge of high honor.

INTERVIEWER: So what happened that turned you against God?

MILLS: It's amazing how many people believe that atheists must have suffered some horrible trauma in their lives that shocked them into rebellion against God. Actually, I had an exceptionally happy childhood, and have enjoyed a remarkably carefree and pleasurable adult life as well, thanks largely to having marvelous parents and a wonderful family of my own. The most traumatic thing that ever happened to me as a child was probably having my tonsils out while in elementary school. That's it. I think what you're really asking is "Why did I become an atheist?"

INTERVIEWER: Yes.

MILLS: Again, I refer to my high school days as a proselytizing born-again Christian. Whenever I shared the Gospel or read Scripture to an "unsaved" student, he or she would ordinarily listen politely and say little. But occasionally I would confront someone who asked for proof that my religious beliefs were true. I recall in particular a friend of mine named Doug, who was Jewish by family heritage but was, in practice, a religious skeptic. So Doug was not about to blindly accept my every assertion about Jesus, the miracle-working Messiah. Doug said that he would happily become a Christian if I could only prove the Christian faith true. I told Doug that Jesus bore witness in my heart that He was real, but Doug sought proof of a more scientific nature.

So in order to better serve the Lord and to become a more effective witness to others, I began studying Christian apologetics. Apologetics is the branch of Christian theology that strives to defend the Bible through logic or science, rather than relying solely on blind faith. But the more I learned about Creation "science" and Christian "logic," the more disenchanted I became. At first, Christian apologetics seemed impressive and highly sophisticated to me. The language used by Christian-apologist writers is deliberately obscure and jargon-filled to create the facade of intellectual respectability. But I soon realized that their lofty theological arguments all boiled down to this: "We know the Bible is true because it's the Bible." In other words, despite Christian pretensions and insistence to the contrary, there was quite literally nothing in logic or science to confirm Christian dogma. Christianity is instead embraced by the masses for emotional reasons: because Christians "feel the Holy Ghost in their hearts."

> "I have recently been examining all the known superstitions of the world, and do not find in our particular superstition (Christianity) one redeeming feature. They are all alike, founded upon fables and mythologies."
>
> —THOMAS JEFFERSON
> (1743–1826), in a letter
> to Dr. Woods

After making these discoveries, I did not immediately turn to atheism, however. I still felt that Christianity was supposed to be accepted by faith, rather than because of scientific proof. So the absence of evidence to support Christianity had little effect on my beliefs. What finally turned me toward atheism was my realization that science not only could not confirm Christian teachings, but offered powerful evidence against the Bible as well. For example, the Genesis accounts of Creation, Noah's flood, and the age of the Earth are provably false, as are numerous other Old and New Testament fables.

INTERVIEWER: So how do you explain the Shroud of Turin?

MILLS: You have cited a perfect illustration of how religious belief absolutely paralyzes the critical reasoning of Christian apologists and Creation "scientists." Back in 1988, the Shroud was tested in three separate laboratories using radiocarbon dating techniques. All three laboratories, in Arizona, Oxford and Zurich, reported independently that the Shroud dates back only to the Middle Ages. This radiometric timeframe for the Shroud's origin coincides precisely with the first historical references to the Shroud, which likewise first appear during the Middle Ages. Any rational person would therefore conclude that the Shroud had its origins during the Middle Ages, not during the time of Christ.

But no. Defenders of Christianity abandon all rationality in their zeal to offer the Shroud as evidence of Jesus' existence. For example, a team of Creation "scientists" in Colorado Springs, Colorado, claims that all of the radiocarbon tests performed on the Shroud were inaccurate because the Shroud was once in close proximity to a neighborhood fire! The fire, they say, must have altered the nuclear structure of the Shroud's atoms, thus skewing the test results. Notice that whenever scientific tests contradict their religious beliefs, Creation "scientists" never concede that their religious beliefs may be erroneous. It's always the scientific tests that are wrong. Despite their haughty charade, Creation "scientists" are thus religionists to the core, blindly dismissing any science that "grieves the Holy Ghost."

So here we have genuinely intelligent, learned individuals deluding themselves that a common house fire can generate sufficient energy to produce a nuclear reaction within the Shroud of Turin—a nuclear reaction necessary to upset the results of radiometric dating techniques! Any "scientist" who seriously proposes such slapstick buffoonery should be fired from any academic position he holds, because he has obviously relinquished all scientific objectivity and is governed slavishly by religious dogma and raw emotion.

Christians sometimes try to defend their beliefs through "appeals to authority," claiming that "highly intelligent people often believe in God." But highly intelligent people, like the rest of us, are frequently guided by their emotions, personal biases and family traditions, particularly in areas of personal religious affiliation. Debate surrounding the Shroud of Turin is a prime example of intelligent people who fail to use their intelligence, relying instead on "gut feelings."

Another such example is the alleged discovery of Noah's Ark atop Mount Ararat in eastern Turkey. Wood fragments, supposedly broken off the Ark, have been tested repeatedly in various labs around the world, including the University of California at

Los Angeles, Riverside and La Jolla. The wood has been proven to be slightly over 1200 years old—or 3500 years too young to have composed part of Noah's Ark. Yet many creationists continue to believe that the Ark is, today, poised high on Mount Ararat "just beyond view." Again, emotion usually overrides logic and lab reports even among Christians of high intelligence.

INTERVIEWER: But hasn't science occasionally labeled ideas as false that, later, turned out to be true?

MILLS: Only rarely. What happens far more frequently is that ideas popularly believed to be true are shown by science to be false.

INTERVIEWER: Do you celebrate Christmas?

MILLS: Atheists celebrate the Winter Solstice, which has been recognized since ancient times as the shortest day of the year—December 25th by the Julian calendar. The ancients celebrated this day because they realized that they had "rounded the corner" and, soon, the days would grow longer and longer, and their crops would once again provide sustenance.

During the early days of Christianity, believers tried to persuade the ruling authorities to establish a legal holiday to commemorate Jesus' birth. But the governing authorities refused. So the Christians decided that "if you can't beat 'em, join 'em" and thereafter celebrated Jesus' birth on an already-established holiday: the Winter Solstice, December 25th. Pope Gregory XIII later revised the ancient Julian calendar; and so the calendar we use today—the Gregorian calendar—moves the Winter Solstice

> "In the realm of science, all attempts to find any evidence of supernatural beings, of metaphysical conceptions, as God, immortality, infinity, etc., thus have failed, and if we are honest, we must confess that in science there exists no God, no immortality, no soul or mind as distinct from the body."
>
> —CHARLES PROTEUS STEINMETZ (1865–1923), electrical engineer and inventor, in the *American Freeman* newspaper (July 1941)

back a few days to December 21st for astronomical reasons, whereas Christmas continues to be celebrated on the 25th.

Every Christmas season, I hear ministers preaching sermons about how we have forgotten the "true" meaning of December 25th. I agree! We have forgotten that December 25th had nothing to do with Jesus' birth. It was an ancient celebration of the Winter Solstice. Easter is likewise a Christian hijacking of an ancient pagan holiday, the Vernal Equinox, a day when darkness and light are equally divided. Even today, the date of Easter is set each year by calculating the first Sunday after the first full moon after March 21st, the Vernal Equinox.

To answer your question on a more practical level, though, our family does erect a tree and does happily exchange gifts. But again, these customs originated from pagan celebrations, not from the birth of Jesus, lest anyone think I'm being hypocritical. Our daughter, like all children, loves the sights and sounds of the season, and looks forward to receiving an overabundance of presents.

INTERVIEWER: One of the most rudimentary laws of physics is that matter and energy cannot be destroyed. Since we're all composed of matter and energy, doesn't that scientific principle lend credibility to a belief in eternal life?

MILLS: In an extremely esoteric sense, yes, it does—but not in the Christian sense that your "soul" will live forever in Heaven or Hell. It's quite accurate to say that the atoms composing your body will survive your death and may someday be incorporated into other lifeforms or inanimate objects. In that sense, you might live forever. But when most people use the phrase "eternal life," they generally mean "eternal consciousness"—that your current "self" or "ego" or "soul" will exist forever intact and will be conscious of its existence. Such a transcendental belief is in no way bolstered by the law of the conservation of mass-energy.

The reason why humans and other animals experience consciousness is that they possess sense organs and, more importantly, brains to process these inflowing nervous impulses. When an organism dies, the cells that constituted its sense organs and brain die also, though the individual atoms within the cells remain essentially unaltered. If the brain and the sense organs die, and therefore cease to function entirely, then it is difficult to see, from a scientific point of reference, how "consciousness" can be maintained by this dead organism.

A good analogy is that of a computer, which is "conscious" of a few external events, such as which key you're pressing on the keyboard or whether you're clicking the mouse button. The computer thinks very rapidly, but in a relatively primitive way when compared to human beings. Now, if you take a sledgehammer and smash this computer into a thousand little pieces, all of the individual atoms within the computer will indeed survive the ordeal. But the computer will no longer function, and will no longer be conscious of keyboard activity or mouse clicks.

The point here is that a change in structure invariably brings a change in function. If human consciousness is a function of the brain and sense organs, then the death of the brain and sense organs will obviously bring a cessation of consciousness. We lose consciousness when we sleep. We lose consciousness after a blow to the head. Is it really so difficult to accept that we lose consciousness after our brains and bodies are totally destroyed?

Moreover, the law of the conservation of mass-energy states that mass-energy can be neither destroyed nor created. If life-after-death—or "consciousness after death"—is allegedly supported by this law, then so is "consciousness before conception" since the mass-energy conservation law would prohibit creation of consciousness, at birth or conception, as well as forbid its annihilation after death. Yet the same people who believe that they will be conscious twenty years after their deaths do not simultaneously believe that they had consciousness twenty years prior to their births. Their application of the mass-energy conservation law is therefore *ad hoc*. Belief in eternal life is thus unfailingly rooted in religious doctrine, rather than scientific law.

If we believe that eternal life is proven by the mass-energy conservation law, then logic forces us to believe that every cockroach, every gerbil and every mosquito will also "inherit the Kingdom of Heaven" because they are, like humans, composed of mass-energy.

INTERVIEWER: Does it make you uncomfortable that communist nations espouse atheism, whereas capitalist, freedom-loving nations encourage religious belief?

MILLS: Christian Fundamentalists have been devilishly successful in their propaganda campaign that all communists are atheists, and all atheists are communists. But these "facts" are altogether erroneous. First, I strongly challenge the assumption that communism is a truly atheistic philosophy. It seems to me that the omnipotent, omniscient and omnipresent god of Christianity is simply replaced by the omnipotent, omniscient and omnipresent god of the State. Under the communist system, the State is supposedly allwise, all-good and all-powerful. Communism is therefore just as nutty as religion in its unrealistic, utopian fantasies and pie-in-the-sky promises.

> "As a historian, I confess to a certain amusement when I hear the Judeo-Christian tradition praised as the source of our present-day concern for human rights . . . In fact, the great religious ages were notable for their indifference to human rights."
>
> —ARTHUR SCHLESINGER, JR., historian, in a speech at Brown University (1989)

Undeniably, some communist nations, such as Stalinist Russia and Maoist China, have been guilty of horrible human rights abuses. No atheist I ever met defends such political repression! Not even the current leaders of Russia and China defend the barbaric actions of their predecessors. But these past human rights abuses invariably stemmed from the leadership's power-mad political ambitions, rather than from an academic or philosophical conviction that religion contradicted the laws of physics. Atheists believe in both freedom of religion and freedom from religion, as each individual chooses. If atheism is hypothetically responsible for political repression in China, then Christianity is certainly responsible for the atrocities of the Inquisition, the Crusades and witch burnings. Is it really fair to condemn a school of thought for perversions and abuses of its teachings?

Most of the criticism you hear regarding "communist suppression of religion" is voiced by politically conservative Christians who never set foot in a communist nation. These Christians have been duped by the shameless fund-raising scams of television evangelists, who endlessly beg for money to supposedly "send Bibles to Russia and China." As someone who actually lived in communist Poland for a time during the height of the Cold War and martial law authoritarianism, I will tell you firsthand that there was absolutely no religious repression of any kind in that country.

My ex-wife's mother, who still lives in Poland, is a devoutly religious woman, and I've happily accompanied the family to church dozens of times during visits. Not once did the "secret police" trail us or threaten to ship us to Siberia for going to church. Pope John Paul II, a Polish native, expressed grief that, since Eastern Europe emancipated itself from communist rule, church attendance has fallen drastically, probably because the Church is no longer needed or used as a rallying point for government opposition.

INTERVIEWER: Finally, let's suppose that you're dead wrong. There is a God and you're brought before Him on Judgment Day. What would you say?

MILLS: I would probably point out that, during my lifetime, I read the Bible more than most of His followers. I studied Church history, I thought more, read more and wrote more about religion than most Christians. *And I didn't even believe in Him!* Therefore, I should get double credit! [Laughs]

2

Origin of the Universe: Natural or Supernatural?

"God was invented to explain mystery.
God is always invented to explain those things
that you do not understand. Now, when you finally
discover how something works, you get some laws
which you're taking away from God;
you don't need him anymore."

RICHARD FEYNMAN (1918–1988), Nobel Prize–winning physicist

In 1919, a thoughtful young scientist named Edwin Powell Hubble joined the ambitious staff of the Mount Wilson Observatory in California. Focusing their 100-inch telescope on the darkened sky, Hubble soon made a profound and startling observation. Hubble detected on his carefully prepared photographic plates that light emitted from distant galaxies was shifted appreciably toward the red end of the spectrum. Hubble discovered, moreover, that the farther away the galaxy was from Earth, the more red-shifted it appeared. These two astronomical observations, later confirmed by independent scrutiny, came to be known as *Hubble's Law.*

Edwin Hubble's most exciting and enduring contribution to astronomy, however, lay in his explanation of the observed redshift. Hubble reasoned that the perceived shift in color (i.e., wavelength) was due to the relative motion, away from Earth, of the distant galaxies. Since Hubble knew that the red-shift in a galaxy's spectrum increased in proportion to the galaxy's distance from Earth, he concluded that the farther away the galaxy was, the faster was its motion. Regardless of where in the sky Hubble pointed his optical instruments, he found that all galaxies—or, to be more precise, all galaxy clusters—were quickly receding from the Earth, and from each other as well.

Through one additional step of logic, Hubble realized that, if the galaxies are receding—that is, if, yesterday, they were closer to us (and to each other) than they are today—then, at sometime in the very distant past, all the matter in the universe must have been squeezed together into a contiguous area of tiny volume and extremely high density. The observed expansion of the universe, then, must have resulted from some kind of initial propulsive force or explosion. This theoretical explosion of the universe was soon lightheartedly dubbed the *Big Bang*.

Evidence supporting Big Bang cosmology is not limited to Hubble's red-shifted galaxies and logical deductions. In 1965, Arno Penzias and Robert Wilson, working for Bell Telephone Laboratories in New Jersey, detected faint microwave background radiation pervading the universe in all directions. This microwave radiation later proved to be an electromagnetic "fossil" of the Big Bang—and provided powerful, independent evidence to substantiate the theory of an expanding universe.

In early 1992, NASA's COBE satellite (*Cosmic Background Explorer*) recorded slight asymmetries in this background radiation. These slight variations, long sought by cosmologists, are necessary to explain why matter in the universe is not evenly distributed. If the Big Bang had been a perfectly symmetric explosion, the universe could not show, as it now does, vast regions virtually devoid of matter, coexisting with regions of high mass-density. The COBE observations, therefore, not only provide additional confirmation of Big Bang theory, but also harmonize beautifully with the observed asymmetric distribution of matter throughout the known universe.

Even before Hubble's discoveries, Einstein's original equations in general relativity predicted that the universe should be expanding. Interestingly, however, Einstein later inserted into his equations an arbitrary "cosmological constant" to negate the necessity of cosmic expansion. Einstein later described his cosmological constant as "the biggest blunder of my life." It is incredible to contemplate that, in addition to his other extraordinary contributions to science, Einstein could have provided theoretical evidence for the Big Bang before any experimental or observational evidence suggested its occurrence. Unfortunately, Einstein was influenced by the popular belief of his time that the universe was more or less static. Einstein, like those of us of lesser ability, could hardly display more intellectual independence than his time permitted.

A number of science historians speculate that even Isaac Newton, who lived during the 17th century, must have pondered the theoretical necessity of an expanding universe. For if Newton's own laws of universal gravitation were to be believed, then a non-expanding, static universe would have long since collapsed upon itself. In this first decade of the 21st century, we may therefore conclude, with reasonable and open-minded confidence, that a Big Bang did indeed galvanize the universe into its current expansion approximately 14 billion years ago.

Pre–Big Bang

If we proceed under the assumption that Big Bang theory is at least partially descriptive of our true cosmic history, then we immediately face a perplexing question. All "bangs" and "explosions" that we observe on Earth and in deep space involve the violent dispersion of physical matter. Bombs, volatile liquids or gases, volcanoes, supernovae all create explosive reactions, and all are composed of physical materials. So, if the universe, as we know it today, began with a giant bang or explosion, how did the exploding physical matter come into existence? Or, as the contemporary philosopher Mortimer Adler is fond of asking, "Why is there something, rather than nothing?"

Regarding this difficult question, a number of scientists currently take one of two positions: 1) They ignore the question entirely; or 2) They state that such questions are beyond the purview of scientific inquiry and must be left to the philosophers and theologians.

Philosophers and theologians are more than happy to speculate on such brain-teasing questions. From the time of Thomas Aquinas in the 13th century—and probably long before—many ecclesiastical thinkers endorsed a *First Cause* explanation of universal origins. Although most of these theologians believed themselves in the Genesis account of Divine, instantaneous creation *ex nihilo* (i.e., out of nothing), these churchmen nonetheless strove to participate in, and hopefully rebut, secular cosmological discourse.

The traditional First Cause argument goes as follows: We observe in the universe a Law of Cause-Effect. Everything requires a cause to account for its existence. Each cause, in turn, is itself an effect that demands a preceding causal antecedent. If, therefore, we regress indefinitely through this chain of causation, we would ultimately arrive at a First Cause, to Whom we give the name "God."

Historically, secular-minded philosophers countered the First Cause argument by asking, "What caused God?" When churchmen responded that "God always existed," secularists usually offered two points of rebuttal: 1) If we can suppose that God always existed, then why not suppose instead that physical matter always existed? After all, this non-supernatural assumption is far simpler than presupposing a highly complex series of Divine Creation miracles; 2) The ecclesiastical argument—that God always existed—contradicts the original premise of the First Cause argument—that the "Law of Cause-Effect" can be consistently applied. If everything *except* God is governed by the "Law of Cause-Effect," then the First Cause argument becomes *ad hoc* and therefore logically impermissible. In other words, we're right back where we started, having advanced neither our logical arguments nor our understanding of universal causation.

These age-old arguments, both for and against a First Cause, are genuinely absorbing, but are mainly philosophical and theological in nature, rather than being strictly scientific. For this reason, many contemporary scientists, as mentioned above, hesitate to engage in such non-scientific speculation, and happily pass the buck to the philosophers and theologians.

In this chapter, my goal is to demonstrate that such cosmological buck passing is unnecessary for today's science-minded individual. Through extrapolating a long-established law of physics, science can successfully describe an elemental pre–Big Bang universe. My intention, in other words, is to communicate that the origin of physical matter is a question that science has actually long-since answered but has usually failed to explain comprehensibly to the general reading public.

The Laws of Physics

Today, creationist writings and lectures abound with references to "physical law." Creationists adore using technical jargon and hope that such a lofty vocabulary bestows upon them a mantle of academic respectability. Yet, when carefully examining their "scientific" books and pamphlets, two significant facts become clear: 1) creationists misunderstand, misuse and rewrite the established laws of numerous scientific disciplines; 2) creationists, on a more basic level, do not appear to grasp what modern science means by the term "physical law." Before proceeding, therefore, I must define what science does, and does not, mean by the term "physical law."

Simply defined, a scientific or physical law is a human description of how the universe consistently behaves. For example, Isaac Newton, after studying the behavior of celestial bodies, proposed his law of universal gravitation, detailing and predicting, with mathematical precision, the orbits of the nearby planets.

Gregor Mendel, breeding various species of plant life, established the framework for a law of genetic inheritance, predicting with accuracy the reproductive results of crossbreeding. Both these laws, Newton's and Mendel's, were expanded and refined by later scientists, whose experimental observations were more precise and informed. The important point here is that scientific or physical laws are human descriptions, based upon human observation, and are therefore subject to future revision—or even outright rebuttal.

Ignoring this definition, creationists often claim that the laws of physics govern the behavior of the universe—that the law of gravity, for example, causes objects to fall earthward, or that the laws of chemistry control molecular interaction. Such a claim— i.e., that physical laws govern the physical universe—reflects a fundamental misperception of science among the creationists. Fearnside and Holther, in their book, *Fallacy: The Counterfeit of Argument,* provide an illuminating and relevant analogy. Suppose that a newspaper reporter is sent to cover a high school football game. The reporter sits in the press box and writes a newspaper article about the game he has just witnessed. It would be absurd to believe that this reporter's written account of the game's outcome *caused* the game's outcome. Likewise, it is absurd to state that the laws of physics, which are likewise written accounts of human observation, cause the outcome of the observed phenomena.

Creationists loathe to admit that physical laws are human in origin. Instead, creationists believe that the laws of physics exist

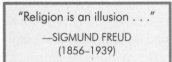

"Religion is an illusion . . ."
—SIGMUND FREUD
(1856–1939)

independently from man and therefore require a "Lawgiver," a Divine Power Who, through these laws, "governs" the behavior of the universe. If the laws of physics are human inventions, then the concept of a Divine "Lawgiver" becomes unnecessary: Man himself is the "lawgiver."

To recognize that mere scientists are the "lawgivers" is not to suggest, however, that the behavior of the physical universe does not have underlying causal antecedents. No true scientist would ever suggest that the universe behaves in a completely arbitrary, unpredictable fashion. Indeed, the entire purpose of science is to discover and understand the regularities and causal relationships at work throughout the universe.

But, by believing that the laws of physics *cause* the behavior of the universe, creationists overlook the need for pursuing *genuine* causal explanations. For example, if I ask why a rock thrown skyward soon falls back to Earth, it would be meaningless to respond, "It's the law of gravity." "Gravity" or "the law of gravity" is simply the name and description we assign to the observed phenomenon. The true, underlying reason why all objects in the universe attract each other is, to this day, a baffling enigma. True, Einstein showed that massive objects distort space-time and produce gravitational effects. But why do massive objects distort space-time? Such questions are still unanswered, and are by no means addressed by saying "It's just the law of gravitation." A physical law, then, is a man-made description, rather than a causal explanation, of how the universe consistently behaves.

The so-called "Law of Cause-Effect," often employed by creationist writers and speakers, is a philosophical and theological plaything, rather than an established law of the physical sciences. Likewise, the "Law of Cause-Effect" provides no explanation to *any* scientific problem or question. Suppose, for example, that my car fails to run properly, and I have it towed to a garage for repair. I ask the service technician why my car will not operate. If the service technician replied, "It's just the law of cause-effect again," I would certainly feel that he was giving me the run-around, and that his "explanation" was totally empty. A realistic scientific explanation might be that my spark plugs are disconnected; that the gasoline therefore cannot be ignited; that the engine therefore cannot rotate the drive shaft; that the rear axle, attached to the drive shaft, cannot be rotated; and that the wheels, connected to the axle, have no current means of forward propulsion. A genuine scientific explanation, then, incorporates specific mechanistic relationships and interactions. Any argument, thus, that appeals blindly to the "Law of Cause-Effect," without filling in the blanks, is likewise an argument totally empty of scientific content.

The Conservation of Mass-Energy

Now that we have discussed what is, and what is not, meant by the term "physical law," let me re-state my thesis: that a long-established law of physics may be extrapolated to construct a rudimentary pre–Big Bang cosmology. The scientific principle to which I refer is the *law of the conservation of mass-energy.*

During the 19th century, the law of the conservation of mass-energy was still divided into two disparate laws: the law of the conservation of mass, and the law of the conservation of energy. The law of the conservation of mass stated that mass (matter) cannot be created or destroyed, but can be changed from one form of matter into another. For example, a piece of coal has a specific mass—a given amount of material of which it is composed. If this piece of coal is burned, it becomes carbon-dioxide gas, water vapor, and ash. But, according to the law of the conservation of mass, the combined mass of the resulting byproducts— i.e., the total amount of material present after the coal is burned— is precisely the same as the original piece of coal. Mass can be neither created nor destroyed.

The law of the conservation of energy was essentially the same, but is more difficult to visualize. There are many different forms of energy: chemical energy, electrical energy, solar energy, heat, energy of motion, electromagnetic radiation and various other overlapping forms of usable and unusable energy. The energy-conservation law similarly stated that energy cannot be created or destroyed, but can be changed from one form into another. For example, a chemical reaction might occur in which energy appears to be lost. But if careful measurements are made of the resulting heat (a form of energy) or the resulting light or electrical byproducts (likewise forms of energy), the total amount of energy present remains unchanged after the chemical reaction. Energy can be neither created nor destroyed.

In the last decade of the 19th century, however, a French scientist named Antoine Henri Becquerel was studying uranium in his laboratory. In the vicinity of this element, energy seemed to appear out of nowhere, while uranium mass seemed to simultaneously disappear into thin air. Becquerel had discovered natural radioactivity (i.e., nuclear energy). Within two decades following Becquerel's discovery, Albert Einstein proved that mass from radioactive elements does not actually disappear, and that the energy generated therefrom does not arise *ex nihilo* (out of nothing). Einstein showed that mass and energy are, in reality, the same thing, expressed by nature in two different ways. In his famous equation $E=mc^2$ (i.e., energy equals mass times the velocity of light squared), Einstein fused together the two conservation laws into a single, comprehensive principle: the law of the conservation of mass-energy. This more-inclusive law states that mass may be changed into energy (as in the case of uranium), and that energy may be changed into mass. Mass may change its form; and energy may change its form. But when all factors are considered and combined, mass-energy cannot be created or destroyed: the total amount of mass-energy in the universe always remains constant. Moreover, all material objects—you, me, the earth, the stars and the smallest atoms—are literally made of mass-energy in its various forms. Since the time Einstein published his theories over 90 years ago, all careful empirical observations have completely confirmed his law of the conservation of mass-energy. Unless or until future evidence reveals this law to be in error, today's science-minded individual is obligated to accept its description of the universe.

During the last twenty years, astrophysicists and cosmologists—led by Cambridge University's Dr. Stephen Hawking—have expanded even further our understanding of mass-energy and have explained how mass-energy's seemingly bizarre properties actually solve the riddle of cosmic origins. Hawking and others have described a naturally occurring phenomenon known as "vacuum fluctuation," in which matter is created out of what appears to be perfectly empty space—i.e., out of a perfect vacuum. Scientists have discovered that even in a perfect vacuum, in which all traditionally understood forms of matter and energy are absent, random electromagnetic oscillations are present. These oscillations actually represent a form of energy now called vacuum fluctuation energy, which can be converted into matter in complete harmony with the mass-energy conservation laws. In other words, the "nothingness" of a perfect vacuum in empty space can and does spontaneously produce matter in full agreement with Einstein's long-established laws.

EXTRAPOLATION

If mass-energy cannot be created or destroyed, and if the universe is entirely composed of mass-energy, then the law of the conservation of mass-energy may be extrapolated to this startling conclusion: the universe, in one form or another, in one density or another, always existed. There was never a time when the mass-energy comprising our universe did not exist, if only in the form of an empty oscillating vacuum or an infinitely dense theoretical point called a singularity, consisting of no volume whatsoever.

At the Big Bang, the universe was incredibly dense and unimaginably hot. The elementary particles, which now constitute the chemical elements, could not exist under such extreme conditions. Immediately following the Big Bang, therefore, the rapidly expanding universe is believed to have been composed solely of energy, with matter condensing later, after further expansion allowed for cooler temperatures. Regardless of its form, however, the universe—which is the sum of all mass-energy—could not, according to the mass-energy conservation law, come into existence *ex nihilo* in the way demanded by creationism. According to this well-confirmed scientific principle, our universe of mass-energy was never created, and cannot be annihilated. To believe in "scientific" creationism, therefore, is to overlook or dismiss the law of the conservation of mass-energy. If creationists possess empirical evidence to contradict the law of the conservation of mass-energy, let them share such information with the general scientific community. Otherwise, the fundamental doctrine of creationism—that the universe was created by God out of literally and absolutely nothing—must be recognized as theological rather than scientific. The term "Creation science" is therefore a self-contained contradiction in terms.

Objections

But what about Mortimer Adler's question: "Why is there something, rather than nothing?"

I hesitate to criticize Adler because I admire his writings and respect his outstanding contributions to education and to contemporary philosophy. So, in Adler's defense, let me point out that he has always claimed to speak as a philosopher, never as a scientist. Adler's question, however—"Why is there something, rather than nothing?"—assumes that there is supposed to be nothing: that the "natural" state of the universe is nonexistence. The fact that there obviously *is* something, then, is viewed by Adler as a miracle requiring a supernatural explanation. The perceived "mystery" of Adler's question lies, not in a supernatural answer, but in his presumptive formulation of the question itself. Adler's question is similar to presuming that grass is supposed to be red, then claiming that its undeniably green color is evidence that a Divine miracle has occurred.

From a scientific perspective, though, the question is: Why *shouldn't* there be something rather than nothing? What law of science claims that the universe is not supposed to exist, or that nonexistence is the "natural" condition of the universe? There is no such law. On the contrary, the law of the conservation of mass-energy leads to a radically different conclusion: that the mass-energy which now constitutes our universe always existed, though the universe, as we *observe* it today, did indeed have a beginning at the Big Bang.

Stated in terms of the First Cause argument: For something to exercise a causal influence within or upon the universe, this causal agent must itself already exist. In other words, something nonexistent cannot possibly serve as any type of causal agent within or upon the universe. The entire concept of causation, therefore, assumes previous existence. But instead of recognizing that causation assumes existence, creationists espouse a perverse backward "logic" that existence (of the universe) assumes causation—i.e., that the universe was created out of nothing and thus requires a supernatural causal explanation. No scientist argues that a universe created by God out of nothing would *not* require a supernatural explanation. Creationists miss entirely the relevant questions, which are: 1) What evidence is there that the universe emerged *ex nihilo*? 2) What evidence is there that mass-energy—which constitutes the universe—always existed? Answer: We have no evidence that mass-energy appeared *ex nihilo*; and we have well-confirmed empirical observations that mass-energy cannot appear *ex nihilo*. If we adhere rigorously to the scientific method, therefore, we are led to one conclusion: Our universe of mass-energy, in one form or another, always existed.

The only way creationism could qualify as a scientific explanation for the existence of the universe would be for creationists to detail the precise mechanism or the means by which nothing was transformed by God into something. Absent such an explanation, creationism ceases to be science and reverts to being religious dogma. Proclaiming that "Creation is a Divine mystery" or that Creation resulted from the "Law of Cause-Effect" is decidedly not a scientific explanation.

Mathematically absorbed theoretical physicists may object that, before the Planck Era—or the first microsecond after the Big Bang—our current laws of physics break down. Some may further argue that, since space-time itself came into being at the Big Bang, we proffer a logically absurd and contradictory question when asking: What existed or happened prior to the Big Bang?

I would respond that the "collapse of physical law" prior to the Planck Era involves the disharmony between General Relativity and Quantum Theory, neither one of which contradicts or challenges the laws of mass-energy conservation. Either General Relativity or Quantum Theory—or both—will eventually be replaced or be shown to have "broken down" in the early moments of the universe. But this fact is irrelevant to the question of mass-energy conservation. In the entire history of science, no real-world experiment has ever been conducted—and no serious theory has ever been proposed—that invalidates or threatens to invalidate the conservation of mass-energy under any circumstances. Moreover, a true falsification of the mass-energy conservation laws would obviously bolster a secular cosmology, since an *ex nihilo* appearance of mass-energy would no longer require a supernatural explanation.

Speaking in terms of pure theoretical physics, it is indeed a contradiction to ask: "What existed or happened prior to the Big Bang?" because the emergence of space-time—and therefore the concepts of "before" and "after"—are obviously inextricably linked to the presence and expansion of mass-energy. How could you possibly measure time without the presence and motion of matter? But in a practical debate, cosmologists, in my view, should not object too strenuously to our asking what existed or happened "before" the Big Bang, because prohibiting this question is perceived by the average person as an avoidance of the issue. "You don't have an answer, so you're disallowing the question." While we should not produce junk science just to placate the uninformed, neither should we overlook that, even if permitted this "off-limits" question, our current laws of physics nonetheless provide a very satisfying answer to universal origins without invoking the supernatural.

If we are truly barred from questioning what existed or happened prior to the Big Bang, then this restriction imposed by physics would once again support a secular cosmology, because the necessity of a prior-existing god could not even be taken into scientific consideration, much less be proven through scientific means as creationism aspires to do.

Psychological Roadblocks

That the universe's building blocks always existed is, for most of us, a difficult and mind-boggling idea to accept. In our day-to-day affairs, all material objects certainly seem to have a beginning and ending to their existence. The new car we purchased today did not exist before the auto manufacturer designed and built the car last autumn. The vegetables we eat today did not exist a few short months ago, before the planting season. A human being appears to be created inside the mother's womb. The embryo begins as a single cell, yet, at birth, the child's body consists of billions of cells, all of which seem to have come into existence for a carefully designed purpose.

It is no wonder, therefore, that our "common sense" tells us that the universe itself must have had a beginning, and so must have been created by God. Our "common sense" is formulated by our observations of locally occurring events, and virtually everything we observe on Earth does indeed seem, at one point, to come into existence and, later, to disappear forever into nothingness. Yet, when considering the existence of the universe, let us recall two relevant facts: 1) Our observation of locally occurring events does not necessarily establish within our minds a "common-sense" judgment that can be applied to the universe as a whole; 2) A careful observation of locally occurring events will show that terrestrial objects do not truly emerge *ex nihilo* as "common sense" tells us.

Science, by its very definition, disregards "common-sense" notions and relies solely upon experimental data to construct scientific law. It is wholly irrelevant whether we feel comfortable with the results of our experiments. These experimental results, if repeatable and independently verifiable, must be accepted, regardless of our cherished "common-sense" theories to the contrary.

Suppose, for example, that a man is standing in the middle of a vast plain. Six feet above the ground, at eye level, he points a handgun in a perfectly horizontal attitude across the plain—not angled up, not angled down, but perfectly horizontal in aim. In his other hand, likewise at eye level, the man holds a fifteen-pound bowling ball. Suppose now that, at the same precise instant, the man both fires a bullet horizontally across the plain and drops the bowling ball straight down to the ground. According to your common-sense judgment, which object will touch ground first: the bullet or the bowling ball?

Do you predict that the bowling ball touches ground before the bullet does? Most people are surprised to learn what Galileo discovered centuries ago: that all objects accelerate to earth at the same rate, regardless of their differing weights or their simultaneous propulsion toward the horizontal. In other words, if there are no external intervening factors, the bullet and the bowling ball will touch ground at the same instant. Whether our "common sense" feels comfortable with this conclusion is of no concern to science. The experimental results must be accepted. Likewise, a science-minded attitude requires us to accept the cosmological implications of the mass-energy conservation law whether or not we feel comfortable with those conclusions.

Very often, our "common sense" will lead us astray if it is utilized to formulate scientific law. Many pre-Renaissance scholars thought it was common sense that the Earth was flat and motionless. If Einstein's special and general theories of relativity had been tested by common sense, Einstein would have been committed to a psychiatric hospital. Where, may I ask, is the common sense in Einstein's time dilation or in his proposition that empty space can be bent? Ideas based only upon "common sense" are of little use to science.

Moreover, as we have discussed throughout this chapter, the law of the conservation of mass-energy shows that, upon careful observation, locally and universally occurring events do not and cannot produce matter or energy *ex nihilo*. Strictly speaking, it is scientifically incorrect to say that the Ford Motor Company creates automobiles, for, clearly, pre-existing raw materials go into the manufacturing process. We may state, more accurately, that the Ford Motor Company *assembles* automobiles from component parts, which themselves were refined from raw materials already existing on Earth. Science teaches us, further, that the higher elements which now compose our bodies were built up from primordial hydrogen in the internal nuclear reactions of stars. In the words of Carl Sagan, you and I are made of "star stuff." In a very real sense, then, you and I, like our universe of mass-energy, always existed, though in a strikingly different form.

Summary

What may we summarize, then, about a pre–Big Bang universe?

According to the current laws of physics, mass-energy, which began its current expansion at the Big Bang, existed prior to the Big Bang. NASA's COBE satellite has collected data that tend to support a so-called "inflationary model" of the Big Bang. Among other theoretical implications, the inflationary model suggests that the mass-density of the universe—that is, the amount of matter scattered throughout space—may be sufficient to eventually stop, through gravitational attraction, the current expansion of the universe. The universe would then begin to collapse upon itself, also due to gravitational gathering. Eventually, all mass-energy would return to a single, contiguous point, in a backward rerun of the Big Bang. Scientists have dubbed this massive collision the *Big Crunch*.

At the moment of the Big Crunch, many scientists speculate that our universe of mass-energy would rebound and explode in the form of another Big Bang. This theory—that a tightly squeezed universe would rebound—is partially based upon our understanding of supernovae, which, after collapsing upon themselves, do indeed "bounce back" and explode violently. Whether supernovae provide a good analogy for the universe as a whole is uncertain. Other, more recent theoretical models seem to indicate that the universe may continue expanding forever and never collapse. My own opinion, for what it's worth, is that until cosmologists provide more satisfying descriptions of the nature and quantity of the so-called "dark matter" and "dark energy"—which may constitute over 90 percent of all mass-energy in the universe—no scientist has the right to arrogantly boast that he knows the "final" answer to this riddle. At present, the universe may be experiencing its first period of expansion, or it may have expanded and collapsed billions of times before. At the dawn of the 21st century, we do not yet know. But we may conclude, based upon our current laws of physics, that our universe of mass-energy is infinitely older than its current period of expansion.

3

God of the Gaps: Does the Universe Show Evidence of Design?

> "Surely the ass who invented the first religion
> ought to be the first ass damned."
>
> —MARK TWAIN (1835–1910), handwritten
> in the margin of Twain's newspaper

From nowhere, a magician appears on stage in a puff of smoke. A child in the audience cheers excitedly. The magician recruits a female volunteer, then slices her in half before the child's startled eyes. Next, a parakeet is pulled from a top hat and placed in a large, cloth-covered box. Presto, the bird reappears as a man-eating tiger. A magic wand then transforms itself into a dozen roses. The child is amazed, dumbfounded, flabbergasted. What miracles this magician performs! What supernatural powers he possesses!

Magic tricks, when skillfully performed, do appear to be miraculous, supernatural acts. The child believes these "miracles" because he doesn't see and understand all that is actually occurring on stage (and back stage). He doesn't notice the hidden door, the trick prop, or the two-way mirror. The "miracle" is created within the child's mind by his own failure to comprehend how the trick is performed. There are gaps in his understanding of the illusion's cause-effect.

When the miracle-believing child learns the mechanical nuts-and-bolts of how a magic trick is performed, the miracle dies instantly in his mind. He is disappointed by the simple mechanics of the illusion. The magic is gone. He preferred the previous gaps in his cause-effect understanding, because those gaps created the "miracles" he enjoyed so much.

▲ ▼ ▲

Creationists, by definition, believe in the "Miracle of Creation." Citing their "First Cause" argument, creationists posit that the mere existence of physical matter proves supernatural intervention at the Big Bang. "Matter cannot create itself," say creationists. "Therefore the universe must have been created by a supernatural Power, unconstrained by the limitations of physical law."

In the preceding chapter, we enumerated the unstated, false assumptions and inaccurate "scientific" conclusions of the "First Cause" argument. The most charitable comment available is that the "First Cause" argument begs the question (i.e., If God created the universe, then who created God? If God always existed, then why couldn't the mass-energy of the universe have always existed?). A less charitable comment might be that the "First Cause" argument reflects ignorance of the scientific method, in that theological philosophizing is offered as a substitute for independent, empirical verification of one's scientific conclusions.

Creationists do not surrender their beliefs, however, after unsuccessfully postulating a "First Cause." More "evidence" of the supernatural is brought forth. According to creationists, the universe is governed by physical laws—laws that they believe were purposefully designed and engineered by a miracle-working God. Creationists claim that these physical laws reveal an underlying order and regularity of the universe. The universe, they say, is like the intricate mechanism of a highly accurate pocket watch: Just as the watch requires a skilled watchmaker to account for its design and reliable function, so too the intricacy and predictability of the universe, as revealed by the laws of physics, require a "Divine Watchmaker." Surely the exquisite heavenly clockwork of planetary motion does not result from blind chance or from the mindless chaos of "brute" matter. The universe is magnificently organized, we are told, and this order can flow only from God.

Are creationists right? Does our universe show evidence of supernatural design and governance?

The unequivocal answer to this question is no, the universe shows no evidence at all of miraculous design or supernatural management. In the chapters that follow, we shall explore why creationists routinely perceive miracles where none exist. We shall see how creationists, like children at a magic show, create their own miracles by failing to observe and understand scientific cause-effect relationships.

One of the most important skills a magician tries to perfect is his ability to misdirect the audience's attention. While he directs the audience's eyes toward a flashing red light, the magician secretly removes a scarf from his sleeve. While a leggy blonde struts by in a bikini, the magician lifts a rabbit into his top hat. No one notices how the trick is performed. Attention was focused elsewhere by the illusionist—and another bit of "magic" appears to have occurred onstage. If we selectively observe only part of the scene, miracles seem to abound.

Like the magician, creationists try to focus our attention on flashy distractions while ignoring any scientific cause-effect interactions that expose the "miracle" as the mundane. Because of their misunderstanding, misuse and frequent ignorance of many well-established scientific laws, creationists perceive a universe overflowing with miracles, almost all of which fall into three broad categories: (1) The Miracle of Planetary Clockwork (which refers to the regularity of planetary and celestial motion); (2) The Miracle of Life on Earth (which invokes the complexity of human anatomy and that of other biological systems); and (3) Miracles of Christian Perception (which refer to highly positive, statistically improbable events occurring in the believer's own life).

Historical Background

Historically, whenever primitive man lacked scientific understanding of an observed event, he created a "God of the Gaps" to fill the intellectual vacuum. A sailor who knew nothing of astronomy would interpret an eclipse of the sun as a sign from the Almighty. A mother, unaware of the existence of viruses and microorganisms, would ascribe her daughter's illness to the wrath of God (or perhaps the devil). A 14th-century farmer, knowing nothing of soil chemistry, would attribute crop failures to the sins of his family. Unaware of biological evolution, medieval man considered the complexity of his own anatomy to be evidence of Divine Creation. The wider the gaps in scientific understanding, the greater the historical need for a miracle-working "God of the Gaps."

> Why does it rain? God makes it rain.
> Why does the wind blow? God makes the wind blow.
> Why is the sky blue? God made the sky blue.
> Why does the sun shine? God makes the sun shine.

All of these questions have precise scientific answers. But pre-Renaissance man lived during a period when superstition overshadowed rational thought, and when those who proposed scientific explanations were often tortured to death by religious authorities. Galileo narrowly escaped a death sentence imposed by the Catholic Church for his telescopic observation that Jupiter's moons orbited Jupiter instead of Earth, birthplace of Jesus and presumed orbital hub of the universe.

> "The Christian system of religion is an outrage on common sense."
>
> —THOMAS PAINE (1737–1809), American Revolutionary hero

Throughout most of recorded history, God was seen as an omnipresent force, intimately involved in the smallest detail of human affairs. During the past fifty years, however, creationists have abandoned their historical position that God is a hands-on participant in all cosmic and earthly events. God is now portrayed as more passive in His supervision of Nature—often watching from the sidelines as Nature operates on Her own. Earthquakes and hurricanes, for example, are now seen by creationists as natural, rather than supernatural, disasters. It has become offensive to call such catastrophes "Acts of God," since thousands of innocent people, including many children, may have perished horribly. Even though creationists believe that God retains power to forestall such natural disasters, God can never be criticized or blamed for allowing these tragedies to happen. "God works in mysterious ways."

Initially, we may applaud modern creationism for finally accepting the occurrence of natural events. It is no coincidence, though, that creationism altered its position on natural phenomena at the precise historical moment that science itself began to provide concrete, verifiable explanations of these same natural events. Unfortunately, this revision in creationist doctrine was motivated not by a newfound acceptance of science, but by an attempt, within an increasingly educated society, to reconcile (A) natural catastrophes with (B) a God of "infinite love and mercy." By accepting natural phenomena, creationists absolve God from direct responsibility for anything disorderly or tragic that Nature inflicts upon humanity. "It isn't God's fault." If, on the other hand, Nature is more agreeable—providing a beautiful spring day, instead of a killer earthquake—then God still gets the credit.

As a general historical observation, each step forward taken by science has further distanced the hand of God from perceived intervention into natural events. As humanity's gaps of knowledge were slowly replaced by scientific understanding, a "God of the Gaps" found fewer and fewer caverns of intellectual darkness in which to live.

4

■ The "Miracle" of Planetary Clockwork

"Extraordinary claims require extraordinary evidence."
—CARL SAGAN (1934–1996), Pulitzer Prize–winning astronomer, in
*Billions and Billions: Thoughts on Life and Death
at the Brink of the Millennium*

The current advocates of Creation Science and Intelligent Design remind me of the creative theologians of ancient Greece, whose vivid imaginations led them to believe in gods who guided the planets in their orbits. Today, Christian apologists maintain the hallowed tradition of ascribing to supernatural Powers control of all celestial objects. In this chapter, I'd like for us to travel back in time and observe the close parallel between the "science" employed in ancient Greece and the "astronomy" of today's Christian defenders.

In ancient Greece, a hunter draws his bow and launches an arrow toward his prey. The arrow speedily and mercilessly traverses the distance to the doomed animal, providing dinner for the hunter's family.

Citizens of ancient Greece were quite perplexed by the observed flight of such an arrow. Which god, they wondered, kept the arrow moving toward the target? The bow obviously provided the initial propulsion, but once out of direct, physical contact with the bow, why didn't the arrow instantly fall to earth? Which god, they pondered, kept the arrow aloft, at least temporarily? Which supernatural Being was responsible for the arrow's continued forward motion?

The true answer to this Greek riddle was to be found centuries later in Newton's familiar first law of motion (also called the Law of Inertia): "An object in motion has a tendency to remain in motion, in a straight line, at a constant speed, unless acted upon by an outside force." Newton showed that, once the arrow was set into motion by the bow, no Greek god need be posited to explain the arrow's continued motion. Inertia keeps the arrow going, until an outside force—such as the intended target, or the pull of gravity—stops the arrow's forward progress.

Newton's first law of motion is best demonstrated in deep space, where outside forces are virtually nonexistent—i.e., no gravity, no wind resistance, no objects to collide with. In such an undisturbed environment, an arrow shot from a bow (perhaps by a spacewalker) will literally travel forever without slowing down or altering trajectory. If the arrow leaves the bow traveling 100 miles per hour, the arrow will travel eternally at that speed (or until the universe itself collapses.) No eternally perpetuating force, however, is required to sustain the arrow's continued motion. The arrow's own inertia does the job.

As you read these words, the *Voyager 2* spacecraft is speeding over 35,000 miles per hour through interstellar space. *Voyager* is not followed by a contrail of fire and smoke belching from the spacecraft's engine nozzles. *Voyager* is coasting "in a straight line, at a constant speed" and will do so forever. No propulsive force is needed to maintain *Voyager*'s regularity and constancy of motion.

It is essential to recognize that inertia itself is not a force; inertia represents the absence of a force, in much the same way that the numeral zero (0), when used alone, represents the absence of something, rather than the presence. Newton defined a force as anything that speeds up, slows down or changes the direction of an object's motion. If an object travels "in a straight line, at a constant speed," then there are no forces acting upon it, according to Newton's first law.

Regularity or constancy of motion therefore denotes the absence of an external force.

▲▼▲

It is easy to ridicule the ancients for believing that Greek gods perpetuated flying arrows. Yet the Greeks, unlike the Romans and Byzantines who followed, were at least curious about these questions and spent considerable time in philosophical contemplation of Nature's behavior. The main shortcoming of Greek science was that it was almost entirely philosophical, virtually devoid of real-world experimentation. All experiments were "thought experiments"—exercises in mental imagery—rather than "laboratory tests." But thought experiments are often instructive, so let's go back to ancient Greece and perform a thought experiment of our own:

When the Greek hunter shoots an arrow toward an animal, the arrow does not travel "in a straight line, at a constant speed." Instead, the arrow is "acted upon by an outside force"—Earth's gravity, which causes the arrow to curve downward in a parabolic arc. The shape of this arc is determined by the speed of the arrow. A slow-moving arrow produces a rounder arc than a fast-moving arrow. But the fast-moving arrow travels a greater distance from the bow before touching ground, when compared to the slow-moving arrow. The faster the arrow travels, the farther from the bow it lands.

Suppose, as part of our thought experiment, that we have a particularly energetic hunter using a particularly powerful bow. Arrows shot from this bow travel 17,500 miles per hour. Question: If the hunter launches an arrow directly toward the horizon at 17,500 miles per hour, how far will the arrow travel before touching ground?

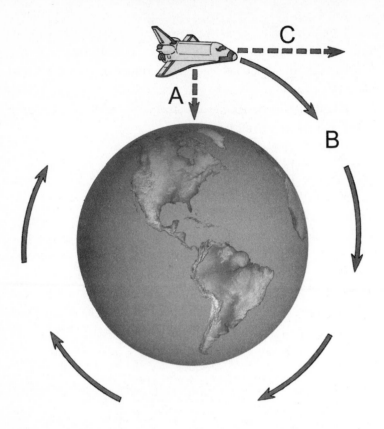

All objects in orbit—Shuttles orbiting Earth, moons orbiting planets and planets orbiting suns—are in a state of continual free fall. The degree of orbital arc (B) is simply a compromise between the strength of the gravitational attraction (A) and the orbiting object's inertia (C).

The answer is that the arrow will never touch ground. Why not? Because the Earth is round, not flat, and curves away from the arrow as the arrow curves toward the Earth. In other words, the arc of the arrow's flight path matches the arc of the Earth's surface, thus placing the arrow into low Earth orbit. The arrow continually drops toward Earth as Earth continually drops out from under the arrow.

The above scenario may sound fanciful,[1] but we have precisely described how the Space Shuttle[2] maintains its Earth orbit.

After a powered ascent through and above most of Earth's atmosphere, the Shuttle terminates all thrust and coasts around the planet at 17,500 miles per hour. Thereafter, the Shuttle, and the astronauts aboard, are in a continual state of free fall—falling toward Earth's horizon as Earth's horizon continually falls away from the Shuttle.

Many television and print journalists, when reporting news of Space Shuttle flights, erroneously state that "the astronauts are orbiting beyond Earth's gravity and are therefore weightless aboard the Shuttle." To these journalists, I pose the following question: If the moon, 239,000 miles from Earth, is held in orbit by Earth's gravitational field, then how can the Shuttle, orbiting 100 to 300 miles in altitude, be "beyond Earth's gravity"? The answer is that the Space Shuttle and its astronauts are not beyond Earth's gravity. In fact, there is relatively little difference between the gravitational attraction at, say, 200 miles in altitude and the gravitational attraction exerted on an object at Earth's surface. The force of gravitation, as Newton calculated, is equal to the product of the masses (of the two objects, such as Earth and Shuttle) divided by the square of the distance separating them.

If you want to know what "weightlessness" feels like, then imagine yourself being on a runaway elevator as it falls freely down the elevator shaft. If you are standing on a bathroom scale inside the elevator as it falls, you will literally weigh nothing by the scale's measure. In fact, you may find yourself floating in mid-air above the scale as if you were an astronaut in orbit. Einstein himself pointed out that an object in free fall is immune from the effects of a gravitational field in the sense that the object becomes weightless. So if you're interested in learning the exact weight of the entire massive Earth as it orbits the sun, the correct answer is 0 pounds, 0 ounces, because the Earth, like all objects in orbit, is in a gravitationally induced free fall.

Returning to our imaginary friend, the Greek hunter: I suspect that many of the animals that he pursues are annoyed by having to dodge arrows all day. Let's suppose that these disgruntled animals stampede and butt the meddlesome hunter over a cliff. The hunter falls 1000 feet to his death. Now, conferencing at the bottom of the cliff is a group of Greek theologians, hotly debating which particular god it was that transported the hunter from the top of the cliff to the bottom. Sure, the animals knocked the hunter over the cliff's edge. But only an atheist would suggest that no Greek god was involved in the hunter's subsequent downward spiral. It couldn't be—could it?—that simple gravity, unaided by supernatural Beings, transported the hunter to the bottom of the cliff.

So, what's the moral of this story? And how does it relate to modern creationism and the alleged "Miracle of Planetary Clockwork"?

▲▼▲

Creationists argue that the regularity and predictability of planetary orbits are evidence of supernatural governance of the universe. In other words, creationists believe, in direct opposition to Newton's first law, that constancy and regularity of motion are evidence not only of an external force, but of a supernatural external force. I submit to you that this creationist claim—of a miraculous Power guiding the planets—is identical in every sense to the ancient Greek belief in god-propelled arrows or god-assisted plunges to the bottom of a cliff. Let us recall that "regularity or constancy of motion denotes the *absence* of an external force." If gods are unnecessary to explain the continued motion of a hunter's arrow, then the gods are unnecessary to explain the continued motion of celestial objects. If gods are unnecessary to explain the hunter's downward plunge off a cliff, then they are unnecessary to explain other gravitational fields as well. For, as Isaac Newton discovered, the same gravity that pulls an apple (or a hunter) to the ground is the same gravity that holds the moon and planets in their orbits. There is no difference—except perhaps to those who, for emotional reasons, strive to see miraculous visions and omens in the night sky.

▲▼▲

Creationists of Fundamentalist persuasion disagree vehemently that planetary motion is a wholly natural phenomenon. It's far more intriguing and emotionally inspiring for them to believe in "Divine Watchmakers" than to accept the mundane, mathematical explanations of science. A minority of creationists, however, raise few, if any, objections to the conclusions drawn thus far in this chapter. This minority will readily accept that inertia and gravitation are not supernatural forces, and that routine planetary motion is simply the merging of gravity with inertia. Put another way, a small group of creationists do accept (in this instance, at least) the scientific principle known as Ockham's Razor, which states that the simplest reasonable explanation is usually the most accurate.

Ockham's Razor further requires us to "slice off" any unnecessary assumptions built into our scientific explanations. For example, if planetary behavior can be explained thoroughly and provably by simple gravity and inertia, then Ockham's Razor prohibits us from arbitrarily inventing highly complex, miracle-working gods to do the job. The needless addition of supernatural forces to our cause-effect explanations is fat that must be trimmed—creationist fat that must be liposuctioned from all scientific and rational discourse.

A minority of creationists, as noted, do not believe that God is currently hand-shepherding the planets around the solar system. Instead, they believe that a Supreme Being initially set the planets into motion, and thereafter stepped aside, allowing the laws of physics to govern the universe without further supernatural aid. Such a philosophy is called *Deism*.[3]

All creationists—both Fundamentalist and Deist—believe that only a miracle-working God could have originally designed the solar system and started the planets along their initial orbital paths. Indeed, if we use the Space Shuttle as an analogy, the spacecraft's orbital path must be carefully engineered by highly skilled scientists. The Shuttle does not stumble accidentally into the proper orbit. There is conscious design and thoughtful planning to each flight; nothing is left to "blind chance." If the Shuttle flies too slowly, it crashes to Earth. If it flies too quickly, it escapes Earth's orbit and drifts, lost forever, into interplanetary space. Achieving a stable orbit, therefore, reveals intelligent design and conscious planning on the part of NASA scientists.

Why, then, doesn't the solar system itself reveal evidence of intelligent design? After all, the nine planets all follow stable orbits. Was this a lucky accident? An incredibly fortunate coincidence? Wouldn't the odds be astronomical (no pun intended) against blind chance's establishing one—much less nine—stable orbits around our sun?

To answer these questions competently and satisfyingly, we must achieve a clear understanding of how our solar system formed. Our solar system, like hundreds of billions of others, was originally an amorphous cloud of dust and gas called a nebula.[4] Because we possess, within our solar system, the heavier elements—such as iron, gold and uranium—we know that this nebula was the remnant of a preceding supernova explosion. A supernova is the grand finale of a dying star, whose supply of nuclear fuel has been exhausted. After literally running out of gas, a supernova collapses upon itself, then rebounds in an unimaginably powerful explosion. During this explosion, the heavier elements are formed and blown randomly back into space, forming another nebula of gas and dust. The fact that our solar system contains samples of these heavy elements means that at least one generation of stars—and perhaps two—preceded the formation of our own solar system 4.5 billion years ago.

Following this supernova explosion, the remnant cloud of dust and gas began to condense or pull together, due to simple gravitational attraction. As this gravitational gathering occurred, the dust and gas began to spin rapidly around a central orbital hub. This same effect is observed when you pull the stopper out of your kitchen sink. Because of gravity, water is attracted to the center of the sink, but spins rapidly before disappearing down the drain.

Within this spinning cloud of dust and gas are randomly scattered regions of high mass-density and low mass-density. The regions of high mass-density possess a stronger gravitational field than the regions of low mass-density. This stronger gravitational field thus attracts still more material, which, in turn, produces an even more powerful gravitational attraction. Over millions of years, original areas of high mass-density become runaway successes at collecting matter, while original areas of low mass-density are eventually swallowed up by the more powerful gravitational fields of high-density regions. These circling lumps of dense, accumulated matter are what we see today as the planets.

> "In those days, in Far Rockaway, there was a youth center for Jewish kids at the temple . . . Somebody nominated me for president of the youth center. The elders began getting nervous, because I was an avowed atheist by that time . . . I thought nature itself was so interesting that I didn't want it distorted by miracle stories. And so I gradually came to disbelieve the whole religion."
>
> —RICHARD FEYNMAN (1918–1988), Nobel Prize–winning physicist, in *What Do You Care What Other People Think?*

The central orbital hub of this system possesses much more material—and thus a much stronger gravitational field—than any of the fledgling planets that circle it. Most of the would-be planets eventually succumb to the powerful attraction of the central region and themselves become part of the central hub. (In our own solar system, the sun contains more than 99 percent of all material in the system.) When the central hub finally collects enough material, its growing mass produces the extreme pressures and temperatures needed to start and sustain hydrogen fusion. This nuclear fusion releases incredible amounts of energy in the form of heat and light. A star—or sun—is thus born in the center of the planetary system, which then becomes a "solar system."

Material orbiting the sun "too slowly" eventually collides with the sun, adding to the solar mass. Material orbiting "too quickly" escapes the sun's gravitational field and leaves the solar system forever. Material orbiting at an "in-between" speed establishes a stable orbit, which creationists perceive to be miraculous. "Logically," therefore, creationists posit a "God of the Gaps" to "explain" these orbiting "miracles."

These planetary "miracles," like all miracles, are faulty perceptions based upon gaps in cause-effect understanding. In this case, the creationist gap in understanding takes the form of a crude statistical miscalculation: creationists imagine that only a tiny number of orbital-speed-orbital-distance combinations result in a stable planetary orbit around the sun. Supernatural Powers must be responsible, we are told, for successfully establishing these statistically improbable orbits.

This "planetary-miracle" argument falls apart quickly in two ways: First, mathematical calculations—first performed by Johannes Kepler in the early 1600s—reveal that the number of successful orbital-speed-orbital-distance combinations is virtually unlimited, rather than minuscule. Second, a telescopic examination of the night sky allows us to directly observe, with our own eyes, celestial motion that flatly contradicts the creationist position. In other words, creationists cannot reasonably argue that the number of successful orbital-speed-orbital-distance combinations is tiny, when we directly observe, throughout the universe, orbital-speed-orbital-distance combinations in the hundreds of millions.

It is interesting to note here that Kepler was a deeply religious man, striving for years to prove his theory of "Divine Geometry" in which the planets moved in perfect circles around the sun. Finally, Kepler was forced to abandon his theory because the observed motion of the planets contradicted the theory's predictions. Three hundred years later, "modern" creationism still maintains that the solar system obeys Divine Geometry.

Here, briefly, are a few other examples of creationist error on the subject of astronomy. These summary examples were gleaned from creationist books, audio tapes, and speeches, and from my personal correspondence and conversation with numerous creationists over the years. I do not mean to suggest that all creationists hold the following erroneous views. But many creationists do often incorporate these mistakes into the premises of their "miracle-proving" arguments. Needless to say, if an argument's premises are flawed, then the argument's conclusion—i.e., that the universe is miraculous in design—is flawed as well.

Creationist belief: Earth and the other planets travel in perfectly circular orbits around the sun.

Scientific fact: No planet travels in a perfectly circular orbit. Each planet's orbit has a different shape from all the other planets', and no planet even maintains a constant distance from the sun. Moreover, the sun is not at the center of any planet's orbit.

Creationist belief: Earth and the other planets travel around the sun at a constant speed.

Scientific fact: No planet travels around the sun at a constant speed. All planets vary their orbital speeds, sometimes dramatically, during their revolutions around the sun.

Creationist belief: Earth and the other planets retrace their identical orbit around the sun each year.

Scientific fact: No planet repeats the same orbit twice.

Creationist belief: Earth must be precisely situated in its current orbit to support life.

Scientific fact: Earth could support life (as we know it terrestrially) from an orbital position halfway to Venus all the way to the orbit of Mars.[5] It is not miraculous that life flourishes where the environment supports it. (God overlooked the best opportunity to demonstrate a true miracle: He could have established life on Venus, where surface temperatures are hot enough to melt lead.)

The Earth is not situated in its current orbit because life exists; rather, life exists because Earth's orbit lies within a vast region known as the Zone of Habitability.[6] Mars also lies within this region and, very likely, once supported life too, as NASA scientists have studied. Did God create Martian microorganisms as well?

Creationism maintains that God created Earth primarily as a home for mankind. For what purpose, then, did God create the other planets and stars? Creationists sometimes respond that God created the heavens to attest His majesty and to provide man with a beautiful night sky. Such an argument—already highly dubious—disintegrates further when we consider that *all* planets and stars visible to the naked eye are located within our own Milky Way galaxy. Of what benefit to mankind are the other hundred-billion galaxies?

Creationist belief: If one of the planets were eliminated from our solar system, then the entire arrangement would collapse.

Scientific fact: Newton's laws of universal gravitation disagree that a "missing planet" would collapse our solar system.

Creationist belief: The regular, predictable cycles of Earth—such as day and night, and the four seasons—reveal supernatural design.

Scientific fact: Day and night cycle because of Earth's rotation, which is continually slowing down, due to the tidal drag of the oceans against the continents. Billions of years ago, a day was less than thirteen hours in duration.

The seasons cycle because of the tilt of the Earth's axis. The current tilt of 23.5 degrees is temporary and variable, and will shift our planet into a new Ice Age within a few millennia. The seasons, as we know them today, will be unrecognizable, as during the last Ice Age, which ended 11,500 years ago.

Surprisingly, even the Earth's magnetic field is shifting and changeable. Sea-floor spreading at the bottom of the Atlantic Ocean has locked into volcanic rock a history of Earth's ever-changing magnetic field. This underwater geologic record reveals that only a few thousand years ago, your compass would have pointed South.

Our planet's magnetic field—like all of Earth's other properties—has undergone continuous and radical change during the past 4.5 billion years. What seems, during a human lifetime, to be immutable and eternal, soon disappears or changes into something vastly different on the geologic timescale. The "regularity" of Nature, cited by creationists, is usually a false premise based upon short-term, short-sighted data.

Creationist belief: Scientists' theories about how our solar system formed are blind speculation and completely untestable.

Scientific fact: Using the Hubble Space Telescope and Earth-based observatories, scientists now have photographic evidence documenting each stage in the formation of a solar system: (1) photographs of gas-and-dust nebulae, (2) photographs of nebulae condensing into hydrogen-burning stars, (3) photographs of stars surrounded by their own orbiting planetary systems like our own, and (4) photographs of supernovae explosions, which destroy solar systems and provide raw material for the formation of new systems. Modern telescopes allow us to actually witness the births (and deaths) of other solar systems in our region of the Milky Way. Science, moreover, has a very clear understanding of how these solar systems naturally develop. Why, then, should we arrogantly presume that our own solar system arose in a radically different and miraculous way?

▲▼▲

Because, in past decades, I have written critically on the subject of creationism, I have received considerable feedback over the years from the Christian community. One of the most common rebuttals they pose is a famous quotation from Albert Einstein: "God does not play dice with the universe." Creationists interpret this quotation to mean: (1) Einstein believed in the biblical God, (2)

Einstein believed that the universe was orderly, and (3) Einstein believed that God was responsible for this order.

Einstein penned his oft-repeated phrase about God in a 1926 letter to Max Born, who, along with Danish physicist Niels Bohr, fathered the study of quantum mechanics. Bohr had claimed that the behavior of subatomic particles was often chaotic and unpredictable. Bohr argued that our everyday notions of structure, order and cause-effect do not apply at the atomic level. Einstein refused to accept such a whimsical view of Nature, claiming instead that "God does not play dice with the universe." The Bohr-Einstein debate raged for over a decade.

Ultimately, Bohr and Born emerged victorious in this dispute, their evidence prevailing. Einstein was admittedly wrong. So, on the atomic level at least, God does indeed play dice with the universe. Subatomic particles do in fact behave at times in random, unpredictable ways—thwarting completely our common-sense expectations, and even those of Albert Einstein.

The question of whether Einstein believed in God depends on your definition of "God." If you define "God"—as the creationists do—as a supernatural Being Who created the universe, Who hears your prayers and Who decides whether you go to Heaven or Hell, then the answer is no. By the traditional definition of God, Einstein was an atheist. Einstein himself said, "It was, of course, a lie what you read about my religious convictions, a lie which is being systematically repeated. I do not believe in a personal God and I have never denied this but have expressed it clearly. If something is in me which can be called religious then it is the unbounded admiration for the structure of the world so far as our science can reveal it."[7]

Regarding life-after-death, Einstein said, "I cannot imagine a God who rewards and punishes the objects of his creation, whose purposes are modeled after our own—a God, in short, who is but a reflection of human frailty. Neither can I believe that the individual survives the death of his body, although feeble souls harbor such thoughts through fear or ridiculous egotism."[8]

Einstein's statement that "God does not play dice with the universe" was a reference to the philosophy of *pantheism*. Rather than proposing a miracle-working, personal Deity, pantheism accepts the supremacy of the laws of physics. Thus interpreted, Einstein's statement would read "The laws of physics do not permit Nature to behave randomly or chaotically." As we noted, however, even this "translated," non-mystical expression of Einstein's statement turns out to be false, as Niels Bohr and Max Born demonstrated.

Another famous scientist frequently cited by creationists is Stephen Hawking, often called the greatest scientific genius since Einstein. In 1988 Hawking published a fascinating book, *A Brief History of Time*. This outstanding bestseller explains the current, popular theories describing the Big Bang origin of our universe. Quite open-mindedly, Hawking also analyzes the creationist claim that supernatural Powers are necessary to explain the existence of the universe. Hawking concludes that no such Powers are required, and that our universe was and is entirely natural, rather than supernatural, in origin and operation.

Inexplicably, however, creationists—and, to an even greater extent, the news media—have portrayed Hawking's book as endorsing creationism because he uses the word "God" throughout the text when critiquing creationist arguments. Never mind that the entire thesis of Hawking's book flatly rejects creationism. Never mind that Hawking is openly atheistic (by any standard definition of the word). Never mind that Hawking divorced his wife, Jane, in part because she became a creationist. Hawking used the word "God" in his book, so he must be a creationist too.

The ABC newsmagazine *20/20* ran an over-hyped, ratings-boosting special proclaiming that a newly published book (i.e., Hawking's) provided a scientific basis for religious faith. Television and radio evangelists often cite Hawking as proving that God created the universe. This vulgar misrepresentation—often deliberate—of *A Brief History of Time* reflects a very sad, profoundly disturbing aspect of American society: Science illiteracy is so ubiquitous, and religious dogma so firmly ingrained, that legions cannot read a well-written science book without hallucinating the supernatural on every page.

▲▼▲

Two facts provide overwhelming evidence that our solar system formed entirely through natural means. If you forget everything else we've discussed in this chapter, remember the following two facts: (1) All planets in our solar system travel the same direction around the sun; and (2) All planets travel on the same orbital plane, which also corresponds to the plane of the sun's equator.[9]

Why do I find these obscure facts so convincing? Because these are the facts that we would expect to observe if the solar system formed naturally. Recalling our previous analogy of water being sucked down an open drain: All the water within this flow naturally spins in the same direction as it is drawn toward the center. None of the water revolves in an opposing direction. Likewise, all newly forming planets, as they are drawn in by the central hub's massive gravitational field, naturally begin orbiting in the same direction. The fact that all planets orbit in the same direction, on the same plane—and over the sun's equatorial plane—is powerful, convincing evidence of the planets' natural formation.

By contrast, a miracle-working Creator could have kick-started the planets in numerous directions and orbital inclinations around the sun. Some planets could have been assigned West-to-East orbits, while others received opposing East-to-West assignments from the Creator. Still other planets could have been assigned polar orbits, traveling around the sun from North to South and back again. The Creator could also have established orbits with a middle-of-the-road 45-degree inclination, or any combination in-between. An almost unlimited array of orbital trajectories was available to the Creator. Why, then, was the Creator so strikingly uncreative in His choice of planetary orbits? Why did the Creator so camouflage his miraculous orbital designs as to precisely mimic naturally occurring orbits?

▲▼▲

Without appealing to the supernatural, let us suppose momentarily that the laws of physics by themselves are sufficient to explain the formation and operation of our solar system and the universe. Question: Even though the universe, let us assume, behaves entirely naturally, rather than miraculously, couldn't the Creator be *using* the physical laws He invented to govern the universe?

On the surface, this question appears to be quite reasonable, suggesting a possible reconciliation between science and creationism. Yet the very posing of the question itself is a concession of absolute defeat for creationism. Why? Because if one concedes that the universe shows no evidence of the miraculous, then one has conceded that no evidence supports creationism. Let us recall that the entire thrust of the creationist argument is that the universe reveals evidence of the supernatural. If that evidence is conceded to be absent, then creationism is left with no argument at all.

If the laws of physics alone do the job and perform all the work within our universe, then a Miracle Worker is left with nothing to do. Ockham's Razor thus demands that this idle Power be eliminated from our scientific explanations.

Returning for a final visit to ancient Greece: Suppose that the citizens finally concede that no Greek gods are perpetuating the arrow's motion, and that no gods are transporting the hunter to the bottom of the cliff. The citizens concede, in other words, that physical laws fully explain Nature's behavior. Suppose, however, that the citizens, instead of proposing direct, miraculous intervention by their gods, now insist that their gods are simply using the laws of Nature: The Greek gods are using inertia (to keep the arrow moving) and using gravity (to bring the hunter to the ground).

After conceding that physical laws sufficiently explain Nature's behavior, we may wonder why the citizens continue to insist so dogmatically that the Greek gods exist at all. What evidence is left to substantiate the gods' existence? None. We may wonder whether psychological or emotional attachment to the gods may be clouding the citizens' scientific judgment. Likewise, modern creationism, in the end, has little to do with science, and everything to do with human psychology and emotion.

5

The "Miracle" of Life on Earth

"Today, the theory of evolution is an accepted fact
for everyone but a fundamentalist minority,
whose objections are based not on reasoning
but on doctrinaire adherence to religious principles."

—JAMES WATSON, Nobel Prize–winning biologist
and co-discoverer of DNA's structure

"Evolution, as such, is no longer a theory for a modern author.
It is as much a fact as that the earth revolves around the sun."

—ERNST MAYR (1904–2005), Harvard science educator, in
Impact Press (December 1999–January 2000)

"Which is it: is man one of God's blunders,
or is God one of man's blunders?"

—FRIEDRICH NIETZSCHE (1844–1900), in *Twilight of the Idols*

Creationists believe devoutly that the presence of life on Earth—
and the beauty and complexity of that life—are incontrovertible
evidence of conscious, purposeful design by the Creator. Regarding the scientific theory of evolution, creationists hold two contradictory and tormented views:

Creationist View #1: Evolution is a total myth. Animals may
adapt slightly to their environments but never evolve beyond their

"kind." Millions of fossils that supposedly document large-scale evolutionary progress are either fakes or have been fraudulently misrepresented by science. There is a mass conspiracy among scientists—inspired originally by the devil—to cover up the Truth of Creation by spreading the Lie of Evolution.

Creationist View #2: Major evolutionary progress may have occurred in many species. But there is no necessary conflict between the Bible and the theory of evolution.

Let's thoughtfully and open-mindedly examine both creationist views of evolution. First we'll ask, "Is evolution a myth?" Later, in Chapter 6, we'll debate the question, "Can Genesis be reconciled with modern science?"

Is Evolution a Myth?

My father often plays the state lottery, hoping against all odds to match six numbers out of forty to become an instant millionaire. You won't be surprised to learn that he's never hit the jackpot. He's never come close. About half the time, Dad matches only one of the six winning numbers. Occasionally he'll match two—and, just once, he matched three. Many weeks, however, Dad matches no numbers at all. Personal experience tells us that lotteries are practically impossible to win because the odds are stacked against us, millions-to-one.

The reason why the winning jackpot is so elusive is that you must simultaneously match all the numbers. You can't play "carry-over" from one lottery card to another, or from one week's contest to the next. Dad once joked that if he could only *accumulate* six winning numbers, then he'd be a jackpot winner for sure.

Let's suppose that Dad's "carry-over" wish came true. This week, let's say, he matches one number. Next week, he matches another, for a total of two. A month later, he matches two numbers on the same card, for a running total of four. Within a few months at most, Dad would accumulate six winning numbers and collect the jackpot. And so would everyone else!

▲▼▲

Creationists have thoroughly and effectively portrayed the theory of evolution as a "lottery of life"—a random biological lottery in which blind chance and mindless circumstance allegedly produce highly developed organisms. We know in a lottery that the odds are against us. We know that it's almost impossible to win. So creationists want us to believe that the odds are similarly stacked against evolution, millions-to-one. To believe in evolution is to believe the impossible, according to creationist doctrine.

Creationists often cite the human eye as evidence of God's design. We are told (quite accurately) that the human eye is more complex and advanced than the most modern digital camera. Rhetorically we are asked, "If the camera requires a designer, then how could the human eye, which is far more sophisticated, arise by random accident?"

The answer is that the human eye did *not* "arise by random accident." Nor did any evolutionary biologist ever make such a claim. Creationism thrives by setting up and knocking down evolutionary strawmen—i.e., self-evidently ridiculous assertions about evolution that no scientist proposed in the first place. It's easy to topple an argument erected specifically for demolition.

Producing an eye by "random accident" is even less likely than winning the lottery jackpot. But is this an accurate analogy? Does evolution more closely resemble a simultaneous matching of lottery numbers, or an accumulation of them over an extended period, as Dad wished to do?

Evolution, by definition, is a gradual accumulation of functional adaptations. Evolution has only three essentials for success: (1) time, (2) genetic variety among offspring and (3) a mechanism for preserving only beneficial variation. Such a mechanism is called natural, or cumulative selection, and was first proposed by Charles Darwin in 1859.

First, let's repair a creationist misunderstanding of the phrase "theory of evolution." Creationists would have you believe that evolution is called a "theory" because scientists are unsure whether it's a fact. Such a misunderstanding of the term "theory" reflects creationism's total estrangement from the scientific community.

Scientists use the term "theory" to mean "explanation." We have Cell Theory, which explains the structure and function of living cells. Yet no scientist doubts that cells exist. We have Atomic Theory, which explains the behavior of atoms. Yet no scientist doubts that atoms exist. We have Gravitational Theory, which explains how celestial objects are attracted to each other. Yet no scientist doubts that gravitation is real. Evolutionary Theory, therefore, explains evolution—its subtleties and processes. As we shall see, science considers evolution as undeniable as cells or atoms or gravitation. And the evidence for evolution is just as solid.

What, then, is the evidence for evolution? And what do creationists have to say about it?

▲▼▲

Many people think of evolution as something that may have occurred millions of years ago. "Evolution" brings to mind a dusty museum filled with rickety old bones of animals long since extinct. Yet the theory of evolution need not look to the distant past for confirmation. We may observe its mechanisms operating today, literally evolving new plant and animal characteristics before our eyes.

Farmers, for example, fight a never-ending battle against the rapid evolution of insects, which feed off their crops. To combat the insect infestation, farmers routinely apply insecticides to their fields. Most of the insects are killed by this insecticide, and so never produce another generation of offspring. But because of wide genetic variation among insects, a few withstand the insecticide and live to produce further offspring. These offspring will thus inherit their parents' tolerance of insecticide.

If the farmer then reapplies the same insecticide to his crops, more insects will survive the second application than survived the first. In turn, this growing number of survivors will produce an even larger generation of offspring, which likewise inherit a tolerance of the farmer's insecticide. Soon, the insecticide does little or nothing to protect the farmer's crops. He must switch to a different poison because insect evolution has rendered his insecticide useless.

When isolated from creationist propaganda and distortion, the Theory of Evolution by natural selection is easy to understand and easy to accept. In many ways, evolutionary theory is a case of stating the obvious. Moreover, it is not hypothetical speculation that insects evolve rapidly. It is a fact. In the real world, farmers do regularly change their insecticides for just this reason. Companies marketing insecticides must often reformulate their products to keep pace with insect evolution.

Although insect evolution is bad news for farmers, let's consider for a moment the insects' point of view. Suppose that you are among the tenth generation of grasshoppers to live in a farmer's field. You have inherited an almost total immunity to the farmer's brand of poison. Knowing nothing of your species' recent evolution, nor of the near extermination of your forefathers, you marvel that the complex chemistry of your body is perfectly suited to resist insecticide. You ponder the unlikelihood that "random accident" designed your chemistry so precisely and efficaciously. You conclude that the only reasonable explanation for your highly developed state is the existence of a supernatural Creator. You scoff at, or even despise, your fellow grasshoppers that propose evolutionary theories explaining your immunity to insecticide. You consider the evolutionists to be immoral, lacking any basis for a system of ethics or grasshopper family values. You may even quote Scripture, "The fool hath said in his heart, 'There is no God.'"

When we, like the grasshopper, suffer gaps in our understanding of events, we summon our "God of the Gaps" to fill the void.

The fast pace of modern evolution is often frightening. Many of our most powerful antibiotic weapons against disease are now wholly ineffective against evolving microorganisms. Whenever you read on a medicine bottle to "Finish Taking *All* of This Prescription," you are being warned against the very real danger of bacterial evolution. If you stop taking your antibiotic before all the bacteria are killed, then you permit the reproduction of the remaining, most-resistant organisms. When these most-resistant organisms start to multiply, you may become sicker than ever. Because of bacterial evolution, doctors sometimes encounter infections that actually thrive on the antibiotics designed to kill them. Treatment in these cases consists of simply withdrawing the antibiotic.

We tend to view bacterial evolution as irrelevant and divorced from the debate between creationism and evolution. Yet even today, the vast majority of life on Earth is too small to be seen without a microscope. Bacteria were the dominant lifeform on Earth for three billion years. And, like it or not, many of your direct ancestors were simple colonies of bacteria.

Let's look at one more quick example of modern evolution at work. In the early 1800s, light-colored lichens covered many of the trees in the English countryside. The peppered moth was a light-colored insect that blended in unnoticeably with the lichens. Predators had great difficulty distinguishing the peppered moth from its background environment, so the moths easily survived and reproduced.

Then the Industrial Revolution came to the English country-side. Coal-burning factories turned the lichens a sooty black. The light-colored peppered moth became clearly visible. Most of them were eaten. But because of genetic variation and mutation, a few peppered moths displayed a slightly darker color. These darker moths were better able to blend in with the sooty lichens, and so lived to produce other darker-colored moths. In little over a hundred years, successive generations of peppered moths evolved from almost completely white to completely black. Natural selection, rather than "random accident," guided the moth's evolutionary progress.

Many creationists grudgingly admit that evolution by natural selection—or "survival of the fittest"—is clearly evident in the reproduction of bacteria or farm insects or peppered moths. But creationists rarely concede that evolution by natural selection also applies to human beings. Again, we are asked, "How could evolution account for the human eye?"

To explain such complexity in Nature, Charles Darwin observed that virtually all species exhibit a strong tendency toward overpopulation. Competition is therefore extremely intense within the species for limited nutrients and for other scarce essentials of life. Any members of the species that possess even the slightest advantage in competing for these essentials will likely survive to produce offspring, which inherit this tiny advantage.

Any awareness of the environment provides a tremendous competitive advantage. If light, for example, could be sensed by skin cells, a lifeform could: (1) orient itself vertically, (2) be aware when a possible source of nutrition eclipsed the light source, and (3) be aware when predators cast a shadow.

A lifeform without eyes produces offspring without eyes. But suppose that a few of the offspring possess a small number of light-sensitive skin cells. (Human skin cells vary widely in their sensitivity to light.) These offspring would enjoy a competitive advantage and would perpetuate this characteristic throughout the species. Suppose now that a few offspring begin concentrating these light-sensitive cells into a single location, thus amplifying their sensitivity. Again, this competitive edge would quickly spread throughout the species. Offspring that did not display this characteristic would die without contributing to the gene pool.

Next, let us suppose that a tiny percentage of offspring are produced with a slightly concave shape to their light-sensitive regions. This rounder shape would allow the lifeform to better discern the direction from which light was emanating, again providing a reproductive advantage. Finally, let's recall that cells are filled with semi-transparent liquids. So it wouldn't be too surprising if this liquid occasionally found itself within the concave surface of the light-sensitive region. The liquid would thus serve as a very primitive lens, helping to focus light.

In this manner, step by step, millennia after millennia, natural selection accumulates beneficial adaptations while discarding the remainder. "What is impossible in a hundred years, may be inevitable in a billion," said Carl Sagan. The human eye required almost four billion years to evolve.

Regarding the evolution of bodily organs and appendages, creationists often ask, "What good is half an eye?" or "What good is half a wing?" In other words, until such body parts are fully functional, they produce no survival advantages. Natural selection therefore would not perpetuate an eye or wing that was "under construction" or "on the verge of working." Creationists believe thus that conscious, end-result planning and design were necessary to produce functional organs and appendages.

Nature herself, however, flatly contradicts the creationists' all-or-nothing argument. For within Nature, we find eyes in all stages of development. We find lifeforms with: (1) no eyes at all, (2) eyes that sense only the presence or absence of light, (3) eyes that focus light extremely poorly, such as the mole's, (4) eyes that cannot see more than a few feet, (5) eyes that cannot see color, such as most dog breeds, (6) eyes that are humanlike, and (7) eyes that are far superior to human eyes, such as the bald eagle's. Within Nature, we find a smooth and unbroken continuum of visual capabilities among the various animal species.

What good is 50 percent of an eye? It enjoys a decided advantage over 49 percent or 37 percent or 8 percent in the struggle for survival. The creationist argument—that partially developed anatomical structures produce no survival advantage—ignores the real-world diversity of Nature. Moreover, the terms "fully developed" and "partially developed" are relative. Bald eagles may pity human beings for their "partially developed" eyesight and wonder how natural selection perpetuated such "unfinished" organs.

Likewise we find winged animals ranging from the falcon (a superb flier) to the pigeon (an average flier) to the chicken (a poor flier) to the flying squirrel (a downhill-only glider) to the ostrich and penguin (which cannot fly at all). Natural selection evolves traits and bodily structures to fit the species' own particular environment. Virtually all animal species continue to be "under construction" because environmental pressures continue to be exerted.

But what if genetic variation or mutation does not produce the beneficial adaptations upon which natural selection may act?

In such a case, the species would show no evolutionary progress, and would likely become extinct. Extinction is as much a part of evolution as natural selection. Looking back over Earth's geological history, over 99 percent of all animal species have failed to adapt successfully to their environments—and have therefore fallen victim to extinction. If creationists want to believe that all lifeforms were carefully and purposefully designed by a Creator, then they must accept the Creator's abysmal 99 percent failure rate. Any watchmaker whose product similarly failed would be dismissed as incompetent.

Because we humans currently live outside the environment in which we evolved, we sometimes feel psychologically disinclined to accept Evolutionary Theory. The circumstances under which human beings emerged and developed bore no resemblance to today's modern industrial society. Today, the "struggle for survival" usually means paying the mortgage on time, or saving enough money to send your children to college. Most of us,

> "Truth, in matters of religion, is simply the opinion that has survived."
>
> —OSCAR WILDE (1854–1900), writer, in The Critic as Artist

fortunately, have no firsthand experience in true life-or-death combat. And it is precisely because of our total estrangement from "survival of the fittest" that, psychologically and emotionally, we are highly skeptical whether human beings evolved at all.

Moreover, because of technological advances that overcome human genetic imperfections, human evolution is now moving backward rather than forward. My own eyesight, for example, is extremely poor, requiring a -5.75 correction in each eye. If I had been born one million years ago, I would never have survived to father children. Today I simply wear contact lenses or glasses, and enjoy no less opportunity to reproduce than a person with naturally perfect vision. My daughter, however, may inherit my poor vision, and so may her children. A technologically advanced society therefore may largely neutralize the progress of natural selection—thereby creating the illusion that natural selection was never operative in the evolution of the species.

▲▼▲

Thus far, we have cited a few instances of evolution in action. I hope that these examples have illustrated both the simplicity and the elegance of Darwin's theory of natural selection. But suppose that you're the kind of person who isn't impressed much by theories or philosophical discussion. After all, the history of science is replete with grand theories that turned out to be nonsense. Suppose that you're the kind of person who, before accepting a scientific claim, requires direct, clear, visible evidence.

Fortunately, evolution quite literally gave us rock-solid evidence to attest its progress—from single-celled organisms all the way to human beings. This rock-solid evidence is known as the *geologic column*. The geologic column refers to our planet's accumulated layers of sedimentary rock. The geologic column amassed its layers from bottom to top, just as water collects in a pail from bottom to top. The oldest layers of the geologic column therefore lie at the bottom, whereas the newest layers are uppermost.

A freshly painted lawnchair provides a good analogy to the geologic column. If you observe wet orange paint covering the entire surface of a lawnchair, you may be confident that the orange layer was also the most recent layer of paint applied. If you scrape off the outer layer of orange, you may discover a weather-worn layer of green paint underneath. You may safely conclude that the green layer is older than the orange layer. Likewise a red layer found under the green would indicate that red paint was applied first, followed by green, and finally orange. New layers of paint may be applied over old layers, but never *under* old layers.

Similarly, sedimentary rocks that compose the geologic column are layered on top of each other. This stacking of sediments, layer upon layer, means that the oldest rocks are lowest on the column, while the newest rocks are highest. Simple logic pre-

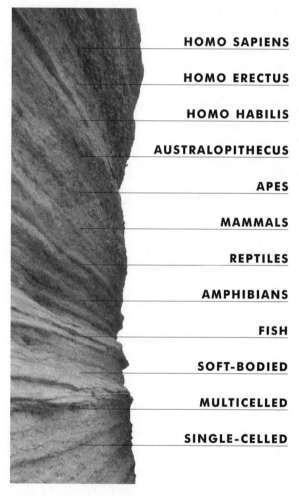

HOMO SAPIENS

HOMO ERECTUS

HOMO HABILIS

AUSTRALOPITHECUS

APES

MAMMALS

REPTILES

AMPHIBIANS

FISH

SOFT-BODIED

MULTICELLED

SINGLE-CELLED

The sedimentary rock layers of the geologic column reveal, from bottom to top, the chronological order in which various lifeforms first appeared on Earth.

cludes any other conclusion. In order for the lower-lying rock layers to be younger than the higher rock layers, Nature would have to somehow: (1) lift up an entire mountain, (2) remove the lowest, underlying layer of ancient rock, (3) replace the ancient rock with modern rock, (4) place the ancient rock on top of the modern rock, and (5) set the mountain back down on top of the newly arranged stack. Such a scenario is beyond the absurd.

More realistically, erosion may weather-away the geologic column's top layer of rock, which may later be replaced by new sedimentary deposits. The result is that contiguous layers of the column do not always represent uninterrupted time periods. But the point to remember is that the column always amasses from bottom to top—from oldest to newest.

Radiometric dating techniques also confirm the chronological order of the geologic column. Radioactive elements such as uranium, potassium and rubidium decay at precise and constant rates. Uranium decays to lead; potassium decays to argon and rubidium decays to strontium. By measuring the ratio of parent-to-daughter isotopes (i.e., one of two or more atoms having the same atomic number but different mass numbers), geologists can establish the age of rocks containing these radioactive elements. Without being told where a particular rock was discovered within the geologic column, a scientist may independently ascertain the answer using radiometric dating. The chronology of the column may therefore be established both by logical and radiometric methods—both of which confirm and reinforce each other.

Why is the geologic column important to evolutionary theory? Because the oldest fossil-bearing layers of rock—3.5 billion years old—contain fossils only of simple, one-cell organisms, which lived in the oceans. Layers slightly higher on the column hold the remains of tiny multicellular organisms. Moving upward, these multicellular lifeforms evolve into soft-bodied creatures, such as corals, sponges and worms. Continuing our ascent, we first encounter primitive fish in layers dating back 600 million years.

A few species of fish then evolved into amphibians, capable of surviving both in water and on land. Amphibians first appear in the geologic column in layers 405 million years old. Climbing higher, we discover that amphibious creatures evolved into reptiles approximately 310 million years ago. Reptiles, as all children know, grew in size and became the mighty dinosaurs. The first dinosaurs appear in rock layers dating back 225 million years. Small mammals also appear in these layers.

> "How can any woman believe that a loving and merciful God would, in one breath, command Eve to multiply and replenish the earth, and in the next, pronounce a curse upon her maternity? I do not believe that God inspired the Mosaic code, or gave out the laws about women which he is accused of doing."
>
> —ELIZABETH CADY STANTON (1815–1902), feminist leader

Dinosaurs suddenly disappear from the column in layers younger than 65 million years. The small mammals, however, continue to develop, both in size and complexity. A very primitive form of ape first appears in rock layers dating 40 million years. Ape evolution progresses to *Australopithecus* (southern ape) still higher on the column. *Australopithecus* was our species' direct ancestor.

We're now approaching the uppermost sedimentary layers of the geologic column. *Australopithecus* is followed first by *Homo habilis*, then by *Homo erectus*. Finally, at the very top of the column—and only at the top—*Homo erectus* evolves into *Homo sapiens*, our own species. The oldest known fossils of *Homo sapiens* are found in rock layers only 275,000 years old.

Leaving aside for a moment the findings of radiometric dating, the geologic column establishes the chronological order in which various lifeforms first appeared on Earth: (1) single-celled, (2) multicelled, (3) soft-bodied, (4) fish, (5) amphibians, (6) reptiles, (7) mammals, (8) apes, (9) *Australopithecus*, (10) *Homo habilis*, (11) *Homo erectus*, (12) *Homo sapiens*.

Creationism's most sacred doctrine is that God created all life-forms, including man, during a single, brief period known as "Creation Week." Dinosaurs and human beings walked the earth simultaneously, as did gorillas and trilobites. All animal "kinds" are the same age, give or take a few days.

If this biblical doctrine were true, then all "kinds" of animal fossils would appear simultaneously, side-by-side, in the same layers of the geologic column. Rather than a gradual progression from simple to complex lifeforms, the column would reveal an instantaneous appearance of all animal "kinds." But the scientific facts simply do not support the creationist position. Creationism is therefore unscientific at its core, and should be viewed appropriately as a religious dogma.

Answering Creationist Objections to Evolution

Creationists staunchly defend their beliefs as science-based, rather than solely Bible-based. Christian Fundamentalists work feverishly to persuade local school boards to include creationism as part of the science curriculum. Below, then, let's examine creationist objections to evolutionary science. In doing so, let's continually ask ourselves one question: Is the objection to evolution based upon issues of science or passages of Scripture?

Creationist argument: The geologic column reveals the Cambrian Explosion, a sudden appearance of many diverse lifeforms.

Answer: Apparently, creationists want to believe that the Cambrian Explosion actually represents Creation Week, as depicted in Genesis. Such an interpretation of Earth's geology is flawed for the following reasons:

(1) Cambrian rock layers do indeed reveal the sudden appearance of many lifeforms. However, when geologists and paleontologists use the word "sudden" in describing the Cambrian Explosion, they are referring to a timespan of

tens of millions of years, which, on the geologic scale, is a very brief period. Creationists read the word "sudden" in the scientific literature and misinterpret it to mean "instantaneous."

(2) The reason why Cambrian rock layers show a dramatic increase in fossil remains is that soft-bodied, Precambrian lifeforms did not easily fossilize. It was not until hard shells, bones and teeth evolved that fossilization could readily occur. The Cambrian Explosion actually represents the evolution of fossilizable body parts.

(3) Despite the difficulty and rarity of soft-body fossilization, the geologic column nonetheless contains many Precambrian fossils, which antedate the Cambrian Explosion by billions of years. If the Cambrian Explosion is supposed to represent Creation Week, how do we explain the previously existing lifeforms? Since the Christian God was preceded historically by the Greek gods, did they create the pre-existing lifeforms?

(4) The Cambrian Explosion occurred 570 million years ago, rather than 6000 years ago as creationism demands.

(5) Cambrian rock layers contain fossils of neither mammals nor reptiles. Again, this disproves the notion that all lifeforms appeared simultaneously.

Creationist argument: The many gaps found in the fossil record contradict evolutionary theory.

Answer: Here again we encounter the now-familiar "God of the Gaps." This time, He becomes "God of the Fossil Gaps," Whose existence is asserted to "explain" any absentee fossils within the geologic column. A few comments:

(1) The Theory of Evolution does not predict the fossilization of *any* species. Fossilization occurs for wholly independent reasons of geochemistry—not because of evolutionary theory. So fossil gaps in no way contradict evolutionary science. The geologic column is a fortunate coincidence of Nature that attests biological evolution.

(2) Even under ideal circumstances, fossilization is an extraordinarily rare occurrence. Until the early 1900s, for example, tens of millions of passenger pigeons flew throughout North America. Their past existence is documented both by photographic evidence and by millions of eyewitnesses. Yet, to date, scientists have discovered no fossilized passenger pigeons. We shouldn't be surprised therefore if many other species likewise left no fossilized remains.

(3) Gaps found within the fossil record do not relate to the direct evolution of *Homo sapiens*. Because our species is found only at the top of the geologic column, and because scientists devote more effort to finding our own ancestors than those of other species, the fossil record of recent human ancestry is rich and incontrovertible. The difficulty of chronicling the evolution of *Homo sapiens* is not fossil gaps, but fossils so closely related that it is difficult to classify where one ancestral species ends and another begins.

(4) When scientists present intermediate fossils documenting the transition of one species into another, creationists are never satisfied. For example, if Fossil #1 is argued by science to be a close ancestor of Fossil #2, creationists invariably claim that a gap exists. "What we need," say creationists, "is an intermediate specimen" (let's call it Fossil #1.5). If scientists possess, or later discover, Fossil #1.5, creationists then lament that *two* gaps now exist— one gap between Fossils #1 and #1.5, and other gap between Fossils #1.5 and #2. As paleontologists unearth each new intermediate lifeform, creationists find two newly created gaps to be filled.

(5) I have received many letters from Christian Fundamentalists who refer to a so-called "missing link." Most of these letters allege that this "missing link" is a fossil gap

separating human beings and modern apes. I am told that, since the missing link is missing, there is no evidence that humans evolved from apes.

A "missing link" will always exist between humans and modern apes because they are not our ancestors, having evolved on a separate branch of the primate tree. Scientists are currently searching for a distant ancestor common to both humans and modern apes—and this research seems to be the source of much confusion among creationists and the general public. But there is no "missing link" raising doubts about the evolution of *Homo sapiens* from *Homo erectus*.

Creationist argument: Scientists have proposed contradictory theories of evolution. Since both sides of a contradiction cannot be true, evolutionary theory must be partially or completely wrong.

Answer: Creationists love to point out that various scientists espouse differing theories on how biological evolution has progressed throughout geologic history. Charles Darwin initially proposed that species evolve gradually to fit their environments. This position is known as *gradualism*. More recently, some scientists—led by Harvard's Stephen Jay Gould—have posited that evolution sometimes progresses in fits and starts: long periods of little or no evolution are interrupted by quick evolutionary bursts. This theory is called *punctuated equilibrium*.

A few thoughts as to whether these diverse theories lend credence to creationism:

(1) Here again, creationists are failing to clearly differentiate the "theories" of evolution from the facts of evolution. By analogy, when Einstein published his Theory of General Relativity in 1915, it conflicted slightly with the established gravitational theory previously set forth by Isaac Newton. Would creationists propose that conflicting theories of gravitation mean that gravitation is a myth? The current debate

is how—not whether—evolution occurred. Stephen Jay Gould, by the way, was one of the leading scientists who fought to keep creationism out of the public schools.

(2) Gradualism and punctuated equilibrium are complementary, rather than contradictory. The geologic column reveals that some species evolved in a steady but gradual manner, whereas others evolved more rapidly and erratically. The speed of evolution is closely tied to external pressure exerted by the environment. During periods of swift ecological change, species either evolve rapidly or become extinct. By contrast, sharks, which thrive in a stable ocean environment, have shown almost no evolutionary change in millions of years.

(3) When scientists openly discuss and debate gradualism versus punctuated equilibrium, all members of the scientific community view such discourse as beneficial, challenging, invigorating, and as a great strength of the scientific method. Creationists, however, view scientific debate and disagreement as signs of weakness. Creationism therefore ridicules open-mindedness and scoffs at the free exchange of ideas so essential to a democratic society and to the scientific method itself. To question one's own opinion is sinful for the creationist, who is not permitted the luxury of healthy skepticism. All contrary opinion is instantly dismissed as foolishness, because the Lord Thy God has spoken.

(4) Creationists have demonstrated themselves to be not scientists, but literary critics. They carefully scan the scientific literature for any hint of disagreement among paleontologists studying human origins. When they inevitably find a diversity of opinion on various aspects of human origins, creationists leap to the *non sequitur* that such diversity substantiates creationism. I know of very few instances in which a team of creationists actually sponsored or partici-

pated themselves in an archaeological dig. They are too busy writing literary reviews.

Creationist argument: Even if one believes that all life evolved from a single cell or cells, a Creator is still necessary to explain the origin and complexity of cellular life.

Answer: Earlier, we discussed how creationists point to highly evolved organs, such as the human eye, and claim that the organ's complexity reveals supernatural design. The fallacy of this argument is to assume that "blind chance" or "random accident" guides evolutionary progress. Moreover, the argument falsely demands a lottery-like instant winner, rather than a gradual accumulation of adaptations through natural selection.

Never tiring of repeating the same mistakes, creationists trot out their "random accident" strawman to preach the unlikelihood of cell evolution. Creationists detail the complex structure and inner workings of a single cell—with its DNA, RNA and various organelles that perform so efficiently their complicated tasks. Then creationists pose a question: "Since the first cell, or group of cells, could not benefit from the accumulated advantages of previous natural selection, how could such intricate structures originate without God's intervention?"

The answer is that *ancient* cellular life did not contain the complex nucleic acids and organelles found within *modern* cells. As with the human eye, creationists cite a modern example—the result of four billion years of cellular evolution—then ask, "How could such an elaborate structure randomly pop into existence?" The answer is that it couldn't—and no scientist claimed that it could.

The first cells contained no nucleus at all, and were bare structures consisting mainly of an exterior membrane. Biological membranes form easily and spontaneously from a mixture of water and simple lipids. Hundreds of books have detailed at length the now-legendary Miller-Urey experiment performed at the University of Chicago in 1953. As a brief summary: Stanley Miller and Harold Urey found that amino acids—the building blocks of cell proteins—form readily from a mixture of ammonia, methane, water and hydrogen gas, all of which were present in abundance on the primordial Earth. In other words, Miller and Urey discovered that the molecules of life naturally assemble themselves from a few basic, easily available ingredients. The origin of life required only organic molecules, water and, most importantly, millions of years to develop. Moreover, in the late 1990s, scientists discovered that life can occur and thrive in conditions previously thought to be completely inhospitable to biological systems—such as in near-boiling hydrothermal vents on the ocean floor, or in poison methane ice.

Creationist argument: Small-scale evolutionary change may occur for some animals, but large-scale evolution is not possible because lifeforms cannot progress beyond their own "kind."

Answer: Several problems here:

(1) Despite loud and angry insistence that creationism is science-based rather than Bible-based, the above objection feigns no pretense to a scientific argument. The belief that lifeforms cannot evolve beyond their "kind" is based directly and solely upon the Book of Genesis, which uses the term "kind" in the Story of Creation.

The scientifically recognized method of taxonomical classification is the familiar Linnean system: kingdom, phylum, class, order, family, genus and species. Each step of the Linnean ladder represents a meaningful, clearly defined differentiation among anatomical structures. The notion of "kind" (sic) is a biblical doctrine and represents no legitimate scientific distinction among lifeforms.

(2) The above "creationist argument" is also a textbook illustration of logical error. The conclusion (that large-scale evolution cannot occur) is built into the "supporting" premise (that lifeforms cannot progress beyond their "kind"). Such a premise assumes the conclusion that it supposedly proves, and therefore proves nothing at all.

(3) Creationists use the term "kind" in a wildly inconsistent way. For example, most creationists think of birds as a "kind." Fish are viewed as another "kind." So by this definition, a bird or fish may evolve adaptive traits, under the restriction that a bird remains a bird and a fish remains a fish.

If birds and fish are examples of "kinds," however, then the term is quite inclusive and corresponds roughly to the Linnean grouping of *class*: all birds are grouped within the class *Aves*, while fish are divided into two superclasses, *Agnatha* and *Gnathostomata*. The problem this poses for creationists is that their definition of "kind" permits more evolution than would be necessary for *Homo erectus* to evolve into *Homo sapiens*, since *Homo erectus* and *Homo sapiens* are already the same genus (*Homo*).

How do creationists escape this predicament? By abruptly changing their definition of "kind" so that, in the case of *Homo sapiens*, the term "kind" is specific down to the level of species.

(4) The only scientific principle truly restricting the degree of evolutionary change is time. Suppose, for example, that during a period of 100 years, scientists clearly observe that a modern lifeform, such as the peppered moth, has evolved X degree. In 1000 years, the degree of evolution, on average, would be *10X*. In one million years, a *10,000X* change would be possible. And in one billion years, a *10,000,000X* change could occur. (The genetic codes of human beings and chimpanzees differ by less than 1 percent.)

The actual degree of evolution depends partially upon the duration and intensity of environmental pressure brought against the lifeform. Generally speaking, if micro-evolution occurs on a micro-timescale, then macro-evolution can occur on a macro-timescale. If there is a scientific mechanism limiting evolutionary progress, then what is it? How does this mechanism operate? What tests can be performed to detect its presence and operation? What evidence supports such a belief in these limits for evolution? To these questions, the creationists respond with Scripture, not science.

(5) The fossil record unequivocally attests macro-evolutionary transition. The *lobe-finned fish*, which lived in water but had lungs and leg-like fins, was an intermediate between fish and amphibians. *Amphibians* themselves provided a macro-evolutionary transition from aquatic to land-dwelling reptilian life. *Cynodonts* bridged the gap between reptiles and mammals, possessing combined traits of both.

On a separate branch of the evolutionary tree, *Archaeopteryx*, part reptile and part bird, is the perfect example of macro-evolution in action. *Archaeopteryx* was first unearthed in Bavaria in 1860. When paleontologists later realized what they had discovered, creationists became so distraught that they accused the paleontologists of gluing bird feathers on a reptile fossil. After several additional fossils of *Archaeopteryx* were recovered, creationists refrained from embarrassing themselves again.

(6) The Linnean system of classification has the effect of masking intermediate fossils. Regardless of its intermediate anatomical structure, a newly discovered species is assigned to only one kingdom, one phylum, one class, one order, one family, one genus and one species. Within the Linnean system, there is no special provision for transitional fossils or intermediate forms.

Librarians sometimes face a similar dilemma when cataloguing a new book. Suppose the library purchases a book called *The Historical Impact of Scientific Discovery*. Does this book belong in the history section or the science section? The answer is unclear. Since the book must be cataloged as either "history" or "science" and shelved

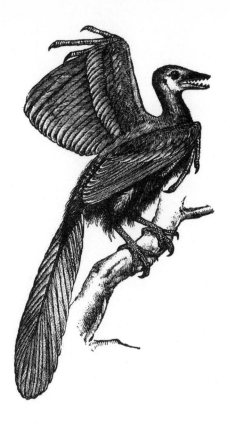

Archaeopteryx, which displayed both reptilian and avian anatomy, is one of many fossil discoveries attesting macro-evolutionary transition.

in only one section of the library, the half-and-half nature of its subject matter is obscured. Likewise for the intermediate lifeforms classified by the Linnean system.

Creationist argument: Even if a random mutation produced a slightly-more-adaptive trait, the new characteristic could not be propagated throughout the species without two identical mutants—one male and one female. The odds are millions-to-one against the simultaneous appearance and mating of *two* identical mutations.

Answer: The necessity of both a male and female mutation has become a celebrated and often-repeated argument within creationist folklore. Many of the newer creationist books omit this argument (for good reason). But my mail indicates that the Fundamentalist community is still convinced of evolution's need for two identical mutations, whose simultaneous appearance defies all credibility.

In reality—as every freshman biology student learns—only one parent usually need possess a particular gene in order to pass the characteristic to the offspring. The exception is a mutation that affects a recessive allele (i.e., one member of a pair or series of genes that occupy a specific position on a specific chromosome). In such an exceptional case, the creationist argument would be valid: two identical mutants would be necessary to propagate the altered genetic instructions—and such a scenario would indeed be practically impossible.

Most of the time, however, one dominant allele may be passed to the offspring, whether or not the other parent possesses the same mutant allele. Creationists are attempting to change the exception into the rule, and the rule into the "impossible" exception.

Creationist argument: The second law of thermodynamics—or entropy—proves that disorder within the universe is increasing. Evolution teaches that lifeforms have become more organized, not less. Evolution, therefore, contradicts the second law of thermodynamics.

Answer: Creationists like to attach a deeply philosophical meaning to the principle of thermodynamics, which simply means "heat movement." Quite characteristically, creationists have distorted and misapplied this scientific principle. The second law actually states that "disorder *in a closed system* tends to increase." By "closed system" scientists mean a system receiving no energy from an outside source. The universe as a whole is considered a "closed system" since the total amount of energy within the universe remains constant. The universe as a whole thus reveals an ever-increasing disorder.

Within the universe, however, local regions may receive an energy input, and are therefore considered "open systems." Our own planet is an open system because Earth receives energy from an outside source: the sun. Without the sun's energy, life on Earth would be impossible.

If we think of the Earth and sun together as a closed system—receiving no external input of energy—then the Earth–sun combination will always suffer an increase in disorder. Yet, amid the increasing disorder, pockets of greater complexity and organization arise. On the sun, for instance, the nuclear fusion reactions that produce the sun's heat and light also transform solar hydrogen into helium and other, more complex elements. An upward progression or "evolution of elements" occurs within the sun's core. Overall, however, the sun is becoming more disorderly, its mass being converted "downward" (for the most part) into heat and other radiant energy.

Because Earth is an open system, receiving the sun's radiant energy, disorder on Earth may decrease in localized spheres. Over millions of years, lifeforms may increase in complexity, as long as a constant energy source is maintained. For biological systems, the necessary energy supply consists not only of the sun's heat and light, but also of abundant sources of food and water.

The second law of thermodynamics does not, in any sense, contradict evolutionary theory. I find it ironic that creationists argue *for* a Creator by citing the second law of thermodynamics, which describes the universe as drifting further and further into chaos. It seems to me that a universe of ever-increasing chaos argues *against* a miracle-working Sustainer of the cosmos.

(I once heard a local minister preach to his flock that the first law of thermodynamics—i.e., the conservation of energy—contradicts the second law—i.e., entropy, or the "running down" of the universe. "Therefore," said the preacher, "scientists are actually confused about these issues and shouldn't be trusted."

To clarify: The first law states that, in a closed system, total energy remains constant. The second law states that, in a closed system, usable energy decreases. The difference between the total energy and the usable energy is found in the generation of heat, which is the "lowest" and least-usable form of energy. Unfortunately, heat is an almost unavoidable byproduct of any mechanical device or physical interaction. In other words, contrary to this pastor's uninformed assertions, Entropy decreases the usable energy by increasing heat energy, thus equalizing the total energy within the system. So there is no inconsistency whatever between the first and second laws of thermodynamics. I might add that it is exceptionally arrogant on the part of creationists to believe that they themselves casually noticed a fundamental "contradiction" in the laws of physics that physicists like Albert Einstein and Stephen Hawking somehow forgot to notice.)

Creationist argument: The geologic column was formed not by millions of years of sedimentary deposits, but by the sudden worldwide deluge recorded in the Book of Genesis.

Answer: We noted previously that if God had simultaneously created all lifeforms, then we should see a simultaneous appearance of these lifeforms in the geologic column. Instead, we find that primitive, single-celled life appears first, followed later by simple multicellular creatures. Next we observe fish, followed millions of years later by amphibians. Higher on the column, reptiles begin to appear—and, later, small mammals. Primates are found only in the uppermost layers, while fossils of *Homo sapiens* appear only at the very top.

The Theory of Evolution is completely consistent with the progression of life observed in the geologic column. But for the creationist, the geologic column is very difficult to explain. Why are the fossils arranged from bottom to top in an order of gradually increasing complexity?

Creationists know why. It's because Noah's flood killed—then meticulously sorted—the fossilized lifeforms we find today in the geologic column. When God caused forty days of torrential rainfall, the most primitive organisms supposedly sank to the bottom of the ocean, where they were preserved in the geologic column. More complicated, multicellular life sank slower and was fossilized in higher layers. Reptiles living on land tried to outrun the rising flood waters. But mammals ran faster, beating reptiles to upper layers of mountain tops. Man, being the most intelligent, knew to sit on the very peaks of mountains to escape the deluge as long as possible.

And what about animals living on flat plains, where there were no mountains to climb? How did their fossils become systematically arranged into layers of ever-increasing complexity?

Creationists again boast the answer: Different "kinds" of animals possessed differing abilities to float. The same "kinds" of animals shared similar properties of buoyancy, and therefore drowned at similar depths of flood water—reptiles with reptiles, birds with birds, mammals with mammals, etc.[1]

A few comments:

(1) It is lunacy to suggest that a flood can sort and organize fossils, or anything else. I would ask the creationists to cite *one* example of a modern flood that left behind such systematic morphology. All people who have actually experienced a flood understand that the waters leave in their wake absolute disarray, rather than absolute order.

(2) Even more bizarre is the claim that complex lifeforms float better than primitive ones. Human beings are among the *least* buoyant of all species. Using creationist "logic," humans should be near the bottom of the geologic column instead of the top. There is, in actuality, no relationship at all between a lifeform's complexity and its buoyancy.

(3) How did Noah's flood kill and fossilize fish, then place them on the bottom of the column beneath reptiles and mammals? Did fish drown in the flood before reptiles and mammals?

(4) Can we realistically believe that, at the onset of the Genesis flood, not one human being on Earth was trapped in

a low-lying valley? Not one human was at sea level and swept into the ocean? Not one human died beneath the level of the most elevated dinosaur on Earth? Shouldn't we find at least a few human fossils in lower layers of the geologic column? Why are there absolutely no exceptions to this rule?

(5) If Noah's flood rapidly created the geologic column and quickly fossilized most of Earth's animals, then why do radiometric dating techniques return older ages for the most primitive fossils and younger ages for the most complex?

Creationists sometimes respond that the Genesis flood somehow "reset Earth's radioactive time clock." If so, then why do the oldest lunar and Martian rocks also test at 4.5 billion years (the same age as Earth)? Did Noah's flood "reset the radioactive time clocks" on the moon and Mars too?

(6) At the time the Old Testament was written—around 500 B.C.—primitive man did not realize that plants and vegetation were also forms of life. The Old Testament God therefore neglected to make provisions aboard the Ark for preserving plant life, which, like the Animal Kingdom, would have been totally and forever eradicated under thousands of feet of seawater.

(7) The story of Noah's Ark was adapted by the Hebrews from an earlier Babylonian myth called the *Epic of Gilgamesh*. In many respects, the Babylonian flood story—which is older than the biblical tale—is virtually identical to the biblical clone, but describes different gods and ark-building characters.

Greek mythology also has a flood story. When Zeus decided to flood the Earth to punish an evil human race, Prometheus instructed Deucalion and his wife, Pyrrha, to build a wooden ark. After the flood waters receded, they were the only surviving creatures on Earth. As Robert Ingersoll has noted, "There is nothing new or original in Christianity. Its maxims, miracles and mistakes, its doctrines, sacraments and ceremonies, were all borrowed."

Creationist argument: Scientists recently discovered that all human beings descended from a woman named Eve. This finding confirms the Genesis account of Creation.

Answer: In recent years, scientists have developed exciting new techniques for tracing our evolutionary ancestry. One such innovation attempts to study the mutation rate and history of human mitochondrial DNA. Unlike an individual's "regular" DNA, which represents the union of both parents' genetic structures, mitochondrial DNA is passed from mother to child unaltered by the father's genes. My daughter's mitochondrial DNA is identical to her mother's.

Through additional research, geneticists hope to aid paleontologists in determining precisely when and where *Homo erectus* first evolved into *Homo sapiens*. Very preliminary results indicate an African origin of our mitochondrial DNA approximately 200,000 years ago. Many paleontologists, however, challenge these tentative findings, arguing that humans appeared earlier.

Theoretically, if we could retrace the history and mutational alterations of our mitochondrial DNA, then we could pinpoint the first group of women who possessed *Homo sapiens'* modern DNA structure. Such a discovery would allow scientists to understand more precisely the chronology and geography of human evolution. To denote their search for human origins, geneticists have dubbed their efforts the "Eve Hypothesis." Because of this title, however, some creationists have misinterpreted the research as being confirmation of the Genesis story of Adam and Eve.

Here, my primary criticism is directed not against creationists, but against some members of the scientific community itself. With a name like "Eve Hypothesis," I find it easy to forgive those who misunderstand the nature of the genetics research. Some scientists—though a small minority—seem to enjoy using religious terminology in their writings. They title their books *The Moment of Creation* or *Reading the Mind of God*. Others speak of "seeing God face to face." The initial impression conveyed is that these scientists are devout creationists. Such a conclusion, though understandable, is nonetheless completely erroneous.

James Trefil, who wrote *The Moment of Creation* and *Reading the Mind of God* is very much anti-creationism. When astronomer George Smoot spoke of "seeing God face-to-face," he was referring to his discovery of small asymmetries in cosmic microwave background radiation—hardly a literal face-to-face chat with Jehovah. I enthusiastically defend the right of these scientists to articulate their views metaphorically. But I believe that, unless science writers intend to convey a belief in the supernatural, they should omit such metaphorical expressions from their writings. Perhaps these scientists and their academic colleagues easily differentiate the metaphorical from the literal. But many other intelligent people are undeniably misled by the empty use of these religious expressions. These scientists then complain loudly that their writings are "misinterpreted" by creationists.

I realize that, to some, my position may appear extremist. Some readers may think that I'm just as rigid and literal-minded as the creationists—though on the opposite end of the philosophical spectrum. Nonetheless I believe that clarity should be the highest goal of science writing. Moreover, I believe that if the subject about which a scientist is writing is non-supernatural, then it's best to avoid language that is indistinguishable from a Billy Graham sermon. What is the purpose of using theological language in a science book? To sell more books? To appeal to a general public uninterested in purely secular science? It seems that some science writers are willing to "sell their souls."

Often, however, science writers are not to blame for their misleading book titles. Nor are writers usually responsible for jacket blurbs which routinely grovel that "the author is sympathetic to all religious viewpoints." The publishing industry is (and should be) a money-making endeavor—and editors change book titles and write jacket blurbs to appeal to as wide an audience as possible. Books that are openly atheistic do not always become runaway bestsellers—trust me.

6

Can Genesis Be Reconciled with Modern Science?

"The study of theology, as it stands in Christian churches, is the study of nothing; it is founded on nothing; it rests on nothing; it proceeds by no authorities; it has no data; it can demonstrate nothing."

—THOMAS PAINE (1737–1809), American Revolutionary hero,
in *The Age of Reason*

"A knowledge of the true age of the earth and of the fossil record makes it impossible for any balanced intellect to believe in the literal truth of every part of the Bible in the way that fundamentalists do. And if some of the Bible is manifestly wrong, why should any of the rest of it be accepted automatically?"

—FRANCIS CRICK (1916–2004), Nobel Prize–winning British biophysicist
and co-discoverer of DNA's structure, in *What Mad Pursuit*

Here's a riddle: When my daughter, Sophia, was born, I was 36 years old. When I was born, my father, Harry, was 35 years old. When my father was born, his father, Shelby, was 28 years old. If my daughter is 5 years old in the year 2000, then in what year was my grandfather, Shelby, born?

As riddles go, this one is straightforward. The answer is determined simply by adding the ages (36+35+28+5), then subtracting the sum (104) from a fixed date: 2000-104=1896. So my grandfather, Shelby, was born in 1896.

Your interest in the Mills family tree is probably nonexistent. But I felt that my "riddle" was more palatable and illustrative than quoting endless passages of Scripture. For it is through identical reckoning that creationists calculate the number of years since Creation, and thus the age of Planet Earth.

According to Genesis, God made Adam and Eve on the sixth day of Creation Week. The Genesis genealogies then detail the exact ages at which Adam and his male descendants "begat" their own male offspring. The Old Testament chronology traces the generations from Adam to Noah, from Noah to Abraham and from Abraham to David. The New Testament books of Matthew and Luke then continue the genealogy from David to Jesus, again specifying the age at which each male descendant "begat" the next generation. Since we have a fixed "historical" time period for Jesus' birth, creationists thereby calculate that the heavens and Earth were created by God in the year 4004 B.C.[1] Earth, therefore, is only 6000 years old by the biblical chronology.

Despite widely divergent viewpoints, creationists and evolutionary biologists agree on a crucial fact: Six-thousand years is insufficient time for evolution to have produced the complex life-forms we observe on Earth today. *Homo sapiens* could evolve only if given hundreds of millions of years to accumulate selective advantages. A 6000-year-old Earth means therefore that Genesis and the Theory of Evolution are forever irreconcilable.

Creationists frequently point to this timescale conflict as proof that evolution is a fraud. They echo the sentiments of St. Thomas Aquinas, who believed that any discord between science and Scripture was due to errors of science, rather than errors of Scripture. Henry Morris, whose revered books founded "scientific" creationism, writes that "It is impossible to devise a legitimate means of harmonizing the Bible with evolution."

The findings of modern astronomy further spotlight the irrevocable divorce between Genesis and the scientific method. Using a powerful array of ground- and space-based telescopes, astronomers can detect galaxies billions of light-years from Earth.

Because light requires one year of time to travel one light-year of distance, our detection of these galaxies proves incontrovertibly that they existed billions of years ago. Otherwise the electromagnetic radiation emitted by these galaxies could not yet have traversed the billion-light-year distance to Earth.

What do creationists say about these distant galaxies? Most creationist books ignore the subject completely, pretending, as in the case of evolution, that modern science is a fraud. One book, however, tackles the issue directly. A widely used and highly popular textbook, *The Creation-Evolution Controversy*, by creationist writer R. L. Wysong, asserts without explanation that "the time required (for light) to reach us from the most distant stars is only 15 years."[2]

Imagine those naive dupes at the Harvard-Smithsonian Center for Astrophysics—they gullibly swallow the myth that light requires a full year to travel one-light-year's distance. Pity those hapless dullards at NASA's Jet Propulsion Laboratory—they're suckers for the same nonsense. Oh how misguided they all were—Hubble, Einstein, Feynman, Hawking, Asimov, Sagan. How fortunate we are today that creationist R. L. Wysong, a veterinarian, has finally straightened us out. Apparently, Wysong believes that light can travel faster than the speed of light (sic)—and so Creation of the heavens and Earth occurred 6000 years ago after all.

Yet another irreconcilable conflict between science and the Genesis genealogies involves the story of Noah's Ark. By a literal interpretation of the Bible, the worldwide deluge occurred in the year 2348 B.C. Supposedly, the only humans to survive the flood were members of Noah's own family, who rode in the Ark with Noah and the animals.

Difficult for creationists to explain, however, is the fact that the Tigris-Euphrates Valley Civ-

> "The study of anthropology confirmed my atheism, which was the faith of my fathers anyway. Religions were exhibited and studied as the Rube Goldberg inventions I'd always thought they were."
>
> —KURT VONNEGUT, JR., "Self-Interview"

ilization (in the Middle East), the Nile Valley Civilization (in Egypt) and the Aegean Civilization (in Greece) maintained uninterrupted written historical records extending before, throughout and following the year 2348 B.C. Their written chains of history were unbroken by the flood. Peoples of these vast civilizations failed to notice their own "destruction."

Creationists occasionally admit that the heavens and the Earth appear to be billions of years old. But this "appearance of age" is a "deceptive illusion." Writes Henry Clarence Thiessen in *Lectures in Systematic Theology*, "The fact that Adam was created full-grown seems obvious from Genesis, Chapter 2. Therefore, in at least the creation of Adam, we have the appearance of age. Is it not also conceivable that the whole creation of God had the appearance of age, perhaps even including the fossils?"

Several responses to Thiessen:

1. The entire "appearance of age" contrivance is another sorry example of creationists' illogically incorporating their argument's conclusion into the "supporting" premise. To "prove" their conclusion that the Genesis genealogies are correct—and that Earth is actually young—creationists assume as factual the Genesis account of Adam's being created with the "appearance of age." In other words, we can "prove" Genesis reliable if we first *assume* that Genesis is reliable. Such "logic" is analogous to claiming proof of Rudolph's red nose by citing Dasher's eyewitness testimony. What creationists are really saying is that they know the Bible is true because it's the Bible.

2. For what conceivable reason would God salt the geologic column with fossils of animals that never existed? To create the "appearance of age"? Why?

3. If our planet is only 6000 years old, how could Earth's plate-tectonic activity separate North America from Europe, and South America from Africa, with spreading rates of only 4 inches per year? The separation of these continents took at least 200 million years.

4. Why do river and ocean sedimentary deposits consist of hundreds of thousands of annual layers, all of which lie above much older rock?

Creationists truly suffer a schizophrenic mindset on the issue of radiometric dating techniques, which point to a 4.5-billion-year-old Earth. First, creationists scoff at these dating methods, claiming that they are highly unreliable. Then, in the next breath, creationists say that they *expected* radiometric dating to reveal an ancient Earth, since Earth was created by God with the "appearance of age."

Creationists assert that radiometric dating is based upon the "fallacy" of *uniformitarianism*. Uniformitarianism holds that the laws of physics operate today as they have in past centuries and in ancient times. Earlier in this book, we noted that the constancy of physical law is cited by creationists as evidence of God's existence. Regarding the physical laws describing radioactive decay, however, creationists sing a different tune. Here, creationists assume that the laws of Nature were completely different only a few thousand years ago—so that any geologist who assumes a constant rate of radioactive decay will conclude "erroneously" that Earth is much older than 6000 years.

What evidence is offered by creationists to substantiate a recent reversal of the rates of radioactive decay? None. Their only "evidence" is that the Book of Genesis disagrees with the radiometric test results. So while masquerading as scientists, creationists choose Scripture over science every time.

Creationists commonly argue that external forces may have affected radioactive decay rates and that uniformitarianism is therefore a blind assumption. But such an argument reveals the creationists' embarrassing unfamiliarity with atomic structure. For all chemical reactions to which the radioactive elements may have been exposed would involve only the electron shells—never the nucleus. And it is precisely for this reason that atomic nuclei are so thoroughly isolated from any external influences. An element's rate of nuclear decay is independent of the element's chemical reactions and interactions.

As part of basic research, various science laboratories have attempted to deliberately alter the decay rates of several radioactive elements.[3] Using all possible means—fair and foul—to induce a decay-rate variance, the greatest variance ever observed has been roughly two percent. Compare this two percent discrepancy with the hundred-million-percent discrepancy between these radiometric tests and Earth's age as calculated by Genesis.

If uniformitarianism is an "assumption," then it is an assumption based upon sound theory and voluminous empirical data. Creationism, by contrast, is an assumption contradicted by all empirical data.

If Earth's history began with Creation Week, and if Genesis provides an accurate historical record, then Earth had no prehistoric eras, no prehistoric peoples and no prehistoric animals. Dinosaurs walked the Earth only a few thousand years ago, side-by-side with modern man. The Flintstones had it right all along!

But what about archaeological discoveries of primitive peoples living hundreds of thousands of years ago? What about the innumerable findings of primitive Stone Age tools and artifacts? Creationist R. L. Wysong once again provides the answer: "Primitive civilizations are simply wreckages of more highly developed societies forced through various circumstances to lead a much simpler, less-developed life."[4] Creation "science" thus proposes not only the "appearance of age" for a young Earth, but also the "appearance of squalor" for highly developed civilizations. Perhaps people of the "Stone Age" were forced into their primitive condition by a collapse of their stock portfolios in the crash of 1929.

If we believe in a 6000-year-old Earth, then we must believe that God conspired with Nature to perpetrate the grandest and most elaborate fraud imaginable. Light from distant stars is a fraud: it didn't really take billions of years to reach Earth. The geologic column is a fraud: it quickly washed together during Noah's flood. River beds and ocean floors—showing hundreds of thousands of annual sedimentary layers—are a fraud, placed there to "test our faith." Earth's plate-tectonic activity (or continental drift) is a fraud for reasons never clearly specified by creationists. The whole of Nature—in the sky, on land and in the sea—is one big joke. Nothing is as it appears. The heavens and the Earth are playing devilish tricks on us, cleverly camouflaging their youth with the "appearance of age." The laws of Nature are likewise a joke, since they recently rewrote themselves to fool radiometric dating techniques. It is therefore the ultimate hypocrisy for creationism to simultaneously assert (1) that Nature attests God's existence, and (2) that Nature is a deceptive contrivance, not to be accepted at face value.

▲▼▲

Today, some creationists are abandoning their long-held belief in a 6000-year-old Earth. Why this abrupt reversal of opinion? Were startling new chapters suddenly discovered in the Book of Genesis? Did Moses appear in a miraculous vision, revising his previous chronology, and teaching the geological history of an ancient Earth? No. The change of heart among some creationists is due to the fact that modern scientific research has shown the Genesis chronology to be nothing short of ridiculous.

Earlier in this book (see Chapter 4), we noted that creationism is divided into two conflicting camps. The biblical literalists (or Fundamentalists), whom we have been discussing, believe that Earth is only a few thousand years old, and that evolution is essentially a myth. The literalists concede that small-scale evolutionary adaptations may occur, but deny that animals may evolve beyond their "kind."

More-liberal-minded creationists, however, strive mightily to disassociate themselves from the conservative Fundamentalists. These non-literalists often refuse to call themselves "creationists," even though they believe in God as the Almighty Creator of the heavens and the Earth. This non-literalist group believes in an ancient Earth and in macro (large-scale) evolution. They believe that Genesis and modern science may be successfully reconciled. The primary difference between the literalists and the non-literalists is this: The literalists distort science to make it harmonize with Genesis. The non-literalists distort Genesis to make it harmonize with science.

The possibility of a reconciliation between science and religion is rapidly gaining popularity, not only among those who call themselves "creationists" but also among the general public. Millions yearn to believe that science and the Bible are ultimately compatible, perhaps even complementary. Religious individuals like to think of themselves as science-minded. And science-minded individuals like to think of themselves as maintaining some kind of religious belief. But is agreement genuinely possible between science and the Book of Genesis?

No. Genesis and the scientific method are mutually exclusive. They cannot be reconciled. How, then, do we explain the wildly popular belief that the Bible and science are, in the end, harmonious?

Generally speaking, religious-minded individuals know little about science. And science-minded individuals know even less about the Bible. With each camp sadly uninformed about the other, reconciliation seems possible and desirable to both sides. In reality, agreement is possible only by (1) perverting science, as the Fundamentalists do, or by (2) perverting the Book of Genesis, as the non-literalists do.

> "There is nothing more negative than the result of the critical study of the life of Jesus. The Jesus of Nazareth who came forward publicly as the Messiah, who preached the Kingdom of God, who founded the Kingdom of Heaven upon earth, and died to give his work its final consecration, never had any existence."
>
> —ALBERT SCHWEITZER (1875–1965), French physician, philosopher and humanitarian, in *The Quest of the Historical Jesus*

Non-literalists

The British philosopher Bertrand Russell once remarked that "the Bible is known for many things, but clarity is not among them." Even the most devout Fundamentalist has to agree that some passages of Scripture are difficult to comprehend and do require skilled interpretation. The Old Testament prophets, for example, and the Book of Revelation in the New Testament use obscure language that can be interpreted to mean just about anything.

Many churchgoers believe that these cryptic Bible prophecies correctly predicted historical events that actually transpired in the 20th century. Because of the extreme ambiguity of many scriptural passages, however, it is easy to prejudicially incorporate recent historical events into one's interpretations of these vague prophecies. Whatever happens in the world, someone always finds a Bible verse—or an astrologer or a psychic—that supposedly predicted the event beforehand. The Bible is highly accurate at predicting the past. But foretelling the future brings us back to the maddening and hopeless question of how to interpret Scripture.

Since interpreting Scripture is simply one person's opinion against another's, why do I harshly call a non-literal interpretation of Genesis a "perversion" rather than a "reinterpretation" of Scripture? And who am I, a dedicated atheist, to defend a Fundamentalist, literal-minded reading of Genesis?[5]

The perversion of Genesis is to be found in the "explanations" articulated by non-literalists to resolve conflicts between science and Scripture. For example:

1. The non-literalists believe that Earth is much older than 6000 years. To rationalize their belief in an ancient Earth, non-literalists claim that the Genesis genealogies contain "errors of omission." In other words, the genealogies are only partial lists, overlooking many intermediate generations between Adam and Jesus. When Scripture says, for example, that "Salah lived thirty years, and begat Eber," that really means that Salah lived thirty years and begat

Eber's grandfather or great, great, great, grandfather. When the "missing" generations are added to the chronology, the date of Creation drifts further into the past.

To me, such a position is absolutely mind-boggling. How can we believe (A) that Genesis is the Inspired, Perfect, Holy, Infallible Word of God, while simultaneously believing (B) that the Genesis genealogies should be disregarded because they contain "errors of omission"? Was God in a forgetful mood when He "inspired" Genesis? Creationist Henry Clarence Thiessen, suggesting that the Genesis genealogies may be overlooked, writes that "a study of the various [other] biblical genealogies indicates that they are incomplete and contain omissions."[6]

Thiessen is almost certainly referring here to the fouled-up genealogical records in Matthew, Chapter 1, and Luke, Chapter 3. Both of these genealogies claim to record the ancestral lineage from David to Jesus, yet the two lists present contradictory data.

A skeptic might also ponder the question of why a child supposedly "born of a Virgin" should be provided with two genealogies listing *Joseph's* genetic heritage. Speculation among Christian apologists that "one of the genealogies may belong to Mary" is of no value in avoiding a clear-cut Bible contradiction, since both Gospel writers specifically declared their genealogies to represent Joseph's lineage.

So the non-literalist argument goes like this: We believe that the Genesis genealogies may be unreliable since other biblical genealogies are also unreliable.

Personally, I agree that all the biblical genealogies are unreliable. But it is a mockery for the non-literalists to maintain that their "errors-of-omission" argument does not challenge the Bible's integrity and infallibility. I am reminded here of the 1960s anti-war slogan that "the United States is destroying Vietnam in the name of saving it." The non-literalists are defiling the time-honored "infallible" interpretation of the genealogies for the "higher" purpose of saving Genesis from scientific error on Earth's antiquity.

Genealogy according to Matthew:

1. Christ
2. Joseph
3. Jacob
4. Matthan
5. Eleazar
6. Eliud
7. Achim
8. Sadoc
9. Azor
10. Eliakim
11. Abiud
12. Zorobabel
13. Salathiel
14. Jechonias
15. Josias
16. Amon
17. Manasses
18. Ezekias
19. Achaz
20. Joatham
21. Ozias
22. Joram
23. Josaphat
24. Asa
25. Abia
26. Roboam
27. Solomon
28. David

Genealogy according to Luke:

1. Christ
2. Joseph
3. Heli
4. Matthat
5. Levi
6. Melchi
7. Janna
8. Joseph
9. Mattathias
10. Amos
11. Naum
12. Esli
13. Nagge
14. Maath
15. Mattathias
16. Semei
17. Joseph
18. Juda
19. Joanna
20. Rhesa
21. Zorobabel
22. Salathiel
23. Neri
24. Melchi
25. Addi
26. Cosam
27. Elmodam
28. Er
29. Jose
30. Eliezer
31. Jorim
32. Matthat
33. Levi
34. Simeon
35. Juda
36. Joseph
37. Jonan
38. Eliakim
39. Melea
40. Menan
41. Mattatha
42. Nathan
43. David

In order to reconcile the Genesis genealogies with a 4.5-billion-year-old Earth, we must believe that the "errors of omission" number in the tens of millions. For what purpose would God include such fragmented and misleading genealogies in His infallible Word? Was He attempting to create an "appearance of youth" for an ancient Earth, while His Fundamentalist worshipers were busy concocting an "appearance of age"?

2. Another means by which non-literalists attempt to pervert Genesis is by claiming that the genealogies were not meant to be interpreted literally—i.e., that the genealogies are in fact metaphors. But how could a dry and colorless list of names and numbers be a metaphor? A metaphor for what?

Let's review a mercifully brief sampling of the Genesis chronology from Genesis, Chapter 11: *Peleg lived thirty years, and begat Reu. And Reu lived two and thirty years, and begat Serug. And Serug lived thirty years, and begat Nahor. And Nahor lived nine and twenty years, and begat Terah.*

Honestly now, did the author of the above genealogy intend a literal or a metaphorical interpretation of his data? If we are to interpret these names and numbers metaphorically, then I suppose that the telephone book—which is also a list of names and numbers—is also a collection of deeply profound metaphors. And anyone who can't appreciate this "fact" is a narrow-minded literalist incapable of elevated, metaphorical abstraction.

When viewed in isolation, the Genesis genealogies themselves posit no miraculous events or supernatural Beings. If we cannot interpret these mundane genealogies literally, then we cannot interpret *anything* in the Bible literally. These same creationists, however, demand that we interpret literally the existence of God, Jesus, the Holy Ghost, the Devil, Angels, Heaven and Hell. All miraculous events portrayed in the Bible are likewise to be interpreted in a strictly literal sense: Jesus literally turned water into wine—literally cast out demons—literally walked on the Sea of Galilee—literally placed a magic curse on a fig tree—literally rose from the dead. Apparently, it's only the Genesis genealogies that we are supposed to interpret metaphorically.

The only reason why some creationists now propose a metaphorical interpretation of Genesis is that science has shown that a literal interpretation is absurd: Earth is not a mere 6000 years old. Let us remember that a young Earth was always posited by religious leaders throughout the entire history of Christianity. No medieval priest ever asserted that Genesis described a 4.5-billion-year-old Earth. No ancient church document ever claimed that Adam and Eve lived hundreds of millions of years ago. And no pre-Renaissance missionary ever preached a sermon about "omissions" or "time gaps" in the Genesis genealogies. If creationists now wish to abandon their historical position and acquiesce to an ancient Earth, then I applaud their progress. But it is a farce to maintain that Genesis never really demanded a young Earth since the genealogies were always intended as metaphors.

3. Perhaps the easiest and most popular way for "science-minded" individuals to deal with the Genesis genealogies is simply to ignore them. Of the 94 percent of Americans who profess a belief in God, I suspect that fewer than 1 percent have actually read the genealogies or have devoted any serious thought to the accuracy of the Genesis time frame.

When did you last hear these genealogies mentioned during a Sunday school lesson? Who preached the last sermon you attended on the Genesis genealogies? The subject is avoided deliberately, because many religious adherents take comfort in the masquerade that science and the Bible harmonize completely. No religious leader wants to raise doubt among his flock by overtly pointing out the Bible's scientific errors. These individuals who try to ignore or sidestep the issue of Earth's age I label "The Great Pretenders,"[7] for they attempt to resolve the conflict between science and Scripture by pretending that no conflict exists.

The Great Pretenders also completely ignore many other biblical absurdities, such as:

Impossibly old men

"And all the days that Adam lived were 930 years: and he died."—Genesis 5:5

"And all the days of Methuselah were 969 years: and he died."—Genesis 5:27

"And all the days of Noah were 950 years: and he died."—Genesis 9:29

The existence of unicorns

"Will the unicorn be willing to serve thee, or abide by thy crib? Canst thou bind the unicorn with his band in the furrow? or will he harrow the valleys after thee?"—Job 39:9-10.

"Save me from the lion's mouth: for thou hast heard me from the horns of the unicorns."—Psalm 22:21.

Unicorns are likewise presented as truly existent in Numbers 23:22; Numbers 24:8; Psalm 29:6; Psalm 92:10; Deuteronomy 33:17 and Isaiah 34:7.

The existence of witches

"Thou shalt not suffer a witch to live."—Exodus 22:18.

Witches and wizards are also mentioned in 1 Samuel 15:23; 2 Kings 21:6 and Leviticus 19:31. These verses, among others, were cited by Christians for centuries to justify the burning of "witches." Hundreds of thousands of innocent women—including female children as young as two years of age—were routinely tortured to death by devout believers obeying these biblical injunctions to take the life of any "witch."[8]

The existence of dragons

"...it shall be an habitation of dragons, and a court for owls."—Isaiah 34:13.

"...the young lion and the dragon shalt thou trample under feet."—Psalm 91:13.

The mythical dragon is described as a reality in over a dozen additional Bible verses, including Psalm 74:13; Deuteronomy 32:33 and Micah 1:8.

The Bible contains innumerable other references to fanciful creatures, such as the Cockatrice—a serpent hatched from the egg of a cock whose mere glance could kill its enemies (Isaiah 11:8); Satyrs—creatures that were half man and half goat or horse (Isaiah 13:21); Fiery serpents (Deuteronomy 8:15) and Flying serpents (Isaiah 30:6).

Just once, I'd like to hear a sermon preached on the following verses:

"And owls shall dwell there, and satyrs shall dance there. And the wild beasts of the islands shall cry in their desolate houses, and dragons in their pleasant palaces."—Isaiah 13:21-22.

"Out of the serpent's root shall come forth a cockatrice, and his fruit shall be a fiery flying serpent."—Isaiah 14:29.

At this point, creationists of the non-literalist variety will respond that "dragon" doesn't really mean "dragon," that "cockatrice" couldn't possibly mean "cockatrice," that "satyr" absolutely doesn't mean "satyr," that "fiery serpent" wasn't intended to denote a real "fiery serpent," that "witch" doesn't actually mean "witch" and that "unicorn" most certainly doesn't mean "unicorn." The Great Pretenders simply dismiss all Bible absurdities as metaphors and pretend that nothing in Scripture really conflicts with science.

I also find it revealing that, in the newer, modern-language translations of the Bible, these ridiculous passages of Scripture have been dishonestly excised, rewritten or edited beyond recognition from their original translation in the King James. So not only are the Great Pretenders forsaking long-honored and long-held Christian beliefs, but the Bible itself, under their supervision, appears to be experiencing a quiet, behind-the-scenes, Hollywood makeover as well.

4. This brings us to the grand finale—the most "elevated" and "profound" argument used by non-literalists to defend the Bible's scientific credibility: *The Day-Age theory*. The Day-Age theory asserts that the seven days of Creation Week do not refer to literal

24-hour days. Rather, Genesis uses the word "day" as a metaphor to denote vast geological eras.

The Day-Age theory is usually postulated by liberal theologians and college professors who, for the most part, are genuinely science-minded individuals. Proponents of the Day-Age theory reject the literal "truth" and Divine inspiration of Scripture, yet want to avoid the dreaded "A" label. To openly declare oneself an atheist is, in our society, morally offensive to most people and is therefore socially stigmatizing. Citing the Day-Age theory, these Great Pretenders make believe that Genesis actually describes an ancient Earth. The purpose of this pompous intellectual charade is to allow the Great Pretenders to "have it both ways"—imagining themselves to be both religious and scientific at the same time.

In seeming anticipation and preemptive rebuttal of the Day-Age theory, however, the Book of Genesis itself provides a clear and specific definition of "day" as used in the account of Creation Week:

"And the evening and the morning were the first day."— Genesis 1:5

In case we missed the point, Genesis reiterates in verse 8 that "the evening and the morning were the second day." Again in verse 13, "the evening and the morning were the third day." And so forth until the seven days of Creation Week are concluded.

It is interesting why Genesis describes a day as evening followed by morning, rather than morning followed by evening as we do today. The Hebrews adopted many customs and myths from their Babylonian captors. Among the plagiarized myths were *Creation Story* (i.e., the Babylonian "Adam and Eve") and the *Epic of Gilgamesh* (i.e., the Babylonian "Noah"). Among the adopted customs was the tradition that each day began, not at sunrise, but at sunset, and lasted until sunset the following day. Thus the Hebrews emulated the Babylonian custom that "the evening and the morning" were a day—a literal 24-hour day.

I suppose that non-literalists could argue that, in the Creation Story, "evening" doesn't literally mean "evening," and "morning" doesn't literally mean "morning." But if the Bible is all metaphorical, how then does it differ from *Aesop's Fables* or *Grimm's Fairy Tales*? If the Bible's literal truths are scant, how, then, does Scripture differ from a typical supermarket tabloid, which, like the Bible, is a collection of supernatural claims, half-truths and unscientific nonsense?

Why was the Day-Age theory proposed only *after* scientists discovered independently the ancient history of our planet? Why was no Day-Age theory articulated during the early years of Christianity or during the Middle Ages? Isn't it disingenuous to now claim that Genesis always portrayed an ancient Earth? If the Bible's alleged depiction of an ancient Earth can be correctly interpreted only after modern science arrives at the same conclusion, isn't the Bible useless as a scientific guide? Should scientists now undertake a detailed study of the Bible to learn the mass-density of black holes in space, or perhaps to reveal the energy source powering distant quasars? For when, after years of painstaking work, scientists resolve these cosmic puzzles, creationists will doubtlessly cite metaphors of Scripture to prove that the scientific answers were to be found in the Bible all along.

▲▼▲

A few pages back, we asked the question: "Can Genesis be reconciled with modern science?" What possible answers, now, may we summarize?

The overwhelming majority of American people envision themselves as both scientific in attitude and religious in nature. Such a dual and contradictory self-perception is derived from one of two psychological ploys: (1) for those who interpret the Bible literally, the findings of science are wholly dismissed or absurdly distorted; (2) for those who recognize the empirical discoveries of modern science, the Bible is conveniently ignored or painfully reinterpreted in a manner contrary to Christianity's historical interpretation. This latter group is extremely reluctant to overtly renounce all religious belief because of social ostracism and because of the alleged inextricable link between religion and moral virtue. A person without religious belief is unfairly perceived in our culture as bankrupt in character.

Recalling the principle of Ockham's Razor—i.e., that the simplest explanation is usually the most accurate—we must conclude that the Bible is simply *wrong* about Earth's age and about human origins. Any other conclusion requires either: (1) the postulation of tortuous *ad hoc* "reasoning" (to allegedly discredit the findings of modern science), or (2) the postulation of wildly far-fetched rationalizations (to allegedly reestablish the Bible's scientific credibility through last-minute reinterpretation).

Perhaps it is time for citizens of the scientific age to grow up, to swallow hard and to forgo the religious superstitions of their childhood. It's time, moreover, for Americans to forgo the bigoted notion that ethical behavior flows only from religious belief. Such religious bigotry—ubiquitous but indiscernible to the God-fearing majority—is no less vulgar than asserting that only Caucasians are ethical, or that only males possess the strength of character to be president of the United States. In the end, much religious belief is sustained by tarring the nonbeliever as a literal demon.

▲▼▲

If the Bible is unequivocally wrong about a 6000-year-old Earth, why then would the Hebrew authors of Scripture assert that our planet is so young?

When the authors of Scripture attempted to reconstruct Earth's history and origins, their only source of knowledge was a chain of written history dating back to the Sumerian civilization. The Sumerians were the first to invent writing—cuneiform—approximately 4000 B.C. or shortly thereafter. Before 4000 B.C., all written history ceases. Instead of recognizing, as we do today, that writing was invented around 4000 B.C., the Hebrews apparently concluded that Earth and mankind were "invented" at that time, since written history fell abruptly silent before that period.

The Hebrew and Babylonian civilizations—out of which the Old Testament arose—were literate cultures, advanced for their time. But the authors of Scripture lived millennia before the Era of Enlightenment and, through no fault of their own, knew nothing of geology, paleontology or biology. Even such scientific geniuses as Johannes Kepler, Copernicus, Galileo and Isaac Newton—who lived 2000 years after the Old Testament was written—knew nothing of Earth's ancient history, nor even of the past existence of dinosaurs, which were not discovered and understood until the early 1800s. The Bible, therefore, could not, and did not, transcend the unscientific barriers imposed by the unenlightened era in which it was written. The Bible, in other words, was all-too-human in origin.

▲▼▲

Throughout this chapter, I sought to address specific issues related to the conflict between science and religion. In closing, let me outline a few general observations about the philosophical differences separating religion from science:

1. Any religion worthy of the name must, by definition, include some form of belief in the supernatural (e.g., gods, devils, holy ghosts, angels, heaven, hell). Science, however, addresses only naturally occurring phenomena and thus, by definition, excludes consideration of the supernatural.

2. Religion derives its belief system from "Divine Revelation" and from "inner conviction." Science, by contrast, derives its laws from real-world experimentation and through mathematical and logical reasoning.

3. The religious adherent believes that "all things are possible to them that love God." If asked whether Jesus could throw a rock faster than the speed of light, the religious believer would unhesitatingly say yes. Science, however, establishes

laws restricting Nature's behavior. Science says, for example, that Jesus could not throw a rock faster than light.

4. Because religious doctrines are supposedly ordained of God, the religious adherent cannot easily question the teachings of his chosen church, even when those teachings are provably false. The scientist, on the other hand, is most rewarded when he proves the conventional wisdom wrong and revolutionizes our understanding of the universe.

5. The religious individual strives to behave "morally" in order to please God and to gain heavenly reward. The science-minded individual derives his ethical system from the real-world consequences of his actions upon others and upon himself.

6. The religious individual tends to hold his beliefs rigidly, fanatically and with a closed mind—never seriously questioning the accuracy of his Church's teachings. The scientist, however, is eagerly and open-mindedly searching for new theories and for evidence to topple old theories.

7

■ "Miracles" of Christian Perception

> "Scientific research is based on the idea that everything
> that takes place is determined by laws of nature, and therefore
> this holds for the action of people. For this reason, a research scientist
> will hardly be inclined to believe that events could be influenced by a
> prayer, i.e., by a wish addressed to a Supernatural Being."
>
> —ALBERT EINSTEIN (1879–1955), in his biography
> *Albert Einstein: The Human Side*

> "Miracles have no claim whatever to the character of historical facts
> and are wholly invalid as evidence of any revelation."
>
> —JOHN STUART MILL (1806–1873), British philosopher, economist,
> logician and political scientist, in *Theism*

If you have read, even casually, the six preceding chapters of this book, then you have become somewhat of an expert on the arguments for, and against, the Bible's reliability and Divine inspiration. You are therefore better informed than most Christians on these issues of science and theology. You are also more knowledgeable than 90 percent of the professional clergy in America, who know a lot about preaching the Gospel, but little about proving the Gospel.

The unadorned fact is that most religious believers are not particularly interested in technical discussions about evolution or cosmology because their religious faith is not rooted in such esoteric minutiae. For the average Christian, his faith is adequately confirmed by what he perceives in his daily life—by "miracles" of Christian perception.

Foremost among these daily "miracles" is the "comforting presence of the Holy Ghost." Christians claim that external or scientific proof of God's existence is for them unnecessary, because the Holy Ghost bears witness in their hearts that He is real and that the Bible is God's Word. Christians pity the "fools" and "lost souls" who reject religious dogma because these skeptics fail to appreciate and to experience for themselves the self-evident proof that God provides through His "Inner Comforter."

Christians claim that the Holy Ghost may instill either serenity or disquiet within an individual's emotional constitution. If a Christian believes that he is pleasing the Lord and striving to obey God's commandments, then the Holy Ghost brings peace to his heart and strength to his soul. If, instead, a person believes that he is straying outside God's will and is thus displeasing God, then the Holy Ghost "convicts him of his sins" and troubles his conscience in an effort to motivate repentance. So whether soothed or distressed by their religious beliefs, Christian Fundamentalists view their own emotions as miraculous confirmation of God's immediate presence.

In reality, emotions derived from religious belief prove only that Christians do hold certain beliefs—intense beliefs to which they generate intense emotional responses. The more deeply held the beliefs, the more deeply felt are the resulting emotions. Religion-inspired emotions do not prove, however, that the religious beliefs themselves are true. Take, for example, a friend of mine who received a telephone call one evening from the State Lottery Commission. She learned that her entry had been selected at random from the drawing barrel and that she had won a spot on the televised final guaranteeing $2,500, with potential winnings of up to $50,000! Needless to say, my friend was elated, telephoning everyone in the neighborhood about her unexpected good fortune. Her emotions were intense because her beliefs were intense: she was going to be on TV and might even win a small fortune!

Sadly, though, my friend's feelings of euphoria proved nothing about good fortune because, as she soon learned, the phone call from the Lottery Commission had been a tasteless hoax, perpetrated by a bored teenager. My friend had not been selected for the TV finals; she had won nothing. Her initial feelings of euphoria, therefore, proved only that she believed she had won. Even though intense and overwhelming, her internal emotions proved literally nothing about external reality. If my friend had concluded that her emotions proved that she was a lottery winner, then she would have been wrong.

Christians fall victim to this identical error of logic when they perceive their own emotions to be proof of God's existence. Emotions derived from religious belief prove merely that individuals do hold their beliefs religiously. However dramatic, comforting or disturbing they may be, our religion-inspired emotions do not prove that the doctrines of the religion are true, any more than my friend's euphoria proved that she was a lottery winner.

Nonetheless, most Christians egoistically imagine that their own inner feelings are somehow more authentic and more God-inspired than the feelings of people who hold different religious beliefs. Meanwhile, adherents of these other religions similarly maintain that their inner feelings prove *their* religious beliefs to be true. And who is right? A skeptic once observed that "In Holy War, God is always on the side of the biggest battalion."

Selective Observation

Religious followers generally find it irksome to confess that their belief in God is rooted principally in raw emotion and blind faith. Finding God through the rumblings of your own gut doesn't sound too scientific, even to the Fundamentalists. Publicly at least, believers often maintain the facade that their faith is confirmed by external proof—i.e., evidence apart from their Holy Ghost–instilled emotions. Many believers, these days, consider themselves too sophisticated even to use the term "Holy Ghost," preferring instead "Holy Spirit," which to them sounds more dignified and less subject to ridicule from those who cynically question the existence of ghosts.[1]

> "The fact that an opinion has been widely held is no evidence that it is not utterly absurd; indeed, in view of the silliness of the majority of mankind, a widespread belief is more likely to be foolish than sensible."
>
> —LORD BERTRAND RUSSELL (1872–1970), British Nobel Laureate, mathematician, philosopher and peace activist, in "Christian Ethics" from *Marriage and Morals*

Aside from feeling God's presence, the most common "miracle of Christian perception" is having one's prayers answered by God, or otherwise witnessing God's direct intervention into the natural course of human events. For example, church congregations often pray for the swift recovery of a sick or hospitalized individual. If this bedfast individual later recuperates, the church boastfully attributes his recovery to their miracle-working God. If, instead, the afflicted person dies, this sad outcome is literally never counted as evidence against God's existence or against God's ability to answer prayer. The disappointment is stoically accepted as "God's will" or as a purely natural event irrelevant to theological debate. "It was simply his time to go."

In other words, believers create the illusion of answered prayer by systematically employing the fallacy known as "Selective Observation," a perceptual error also referred to as "counting the hits and ignoring the misses." To illustrate, let's suppose that for two decades, the tobacco industry sponsors fifty different studies to determine whether smoking is actually harmful to your health. Forty-seven of these studies, let's assume, reveal a link between smoking and lung cancer. The remaining three studies, however, find no such correlation. The tobacco industry then issues a press release boasting that three valid scientific studies have determined that smoking does not cause lung cancer as was previously believed. Such a press release might be perfectly accurate in its characterization of the three studies cited. But by hand-picking the results that support their position, and by deliberately weeding out and suppressing contrary evidence, the tobacco industry is guilty of "counting the hits and ignoring the misses." The important point to remember here is that any conclusion drawn from these prejudicially chosen premises is wholly meaningless, such as the conclusion that smoking is harmless to your health or the conviction that God has healed a sick person. If there are plenty of contrary case histories, then we cannot legitimately propose causal links only where it suits our purpose.

Even from my own life, I can cite similar examples of biased or selective observation. In 1993 my father suffered a heart attack, went into a coma, and spent two months in the intensive care unit. No one, including me, thought he would survive. His liver, lungs and kidneys all stopped functioning, and he was kept alive—barely—through artificial life support. Dad then startled everyone by making a sudden and complete recovery. Many people told me that they had been praying for Dad and that God had miraculously healed him. Whatever the reason, I was delighted that Dad came home alive and well.

The very next month, my energetic, always-optimistic mother checked into the hospital for a relatively minor, long-postponed knee reparation. Shortly after the routine procedure, Mom unexpectedly dropped dead in her hospital room—cause a mystery. Nobody said to me then that Mom's unforeseen death proved that God was a myth. Yet everyone had said to me, only weeks before, that Dad's unforeseen recovery proved that God was a reality. Why? Because God is presumed to be "good" and is therefore given credit for statistically unlikely positive occurrences, such as Dad's recovery. But statistically unlikely negative events, such as Mom's death, are brushed

> "I believe that religion, generally speaking, has been a curse to mankind."
>
> —H. L. MENCKEN
> (1880–1956), editor and critic, in
> New York Times Magazine
> (September 11, 1955)

aside as bad luck or as incompetence on the part of the hospital staff. Again, if the premises of your theological argument are chosen in a biased or *ad hoc* manner, then the conclusions you draw are meaningless.

Moreover, in order to protect themselves from malpractice lawsuits, doctors frequently lowball the stated odds of a patient's recovery from a serious operation or illness. The patient (and his next of kin) are then less inclined to blame the doctor if tragedy does strike. After all, "the odds were against him all along." If, on the other hand, the patient recuperates successfully, he will appear to have "beaten the odds." The doctor will then be a hero for having presided over a "medical miracle." I personally know of several individuals alive today who were given a "1 percent chance of survival."

One factor common to *all* "medical miracles" is ambiguity. Just how sick really was this person in the first place? Would he have recovered even without prayer? The answers to these questions are always nebulous. Why are God's "miracles" never clearcut? Why couldn't a man who had had no legs whatever for twenty years suddenly wake up with a brand-new pair? Is this feat impossible for God to achieve? If God has the power to miraculously cure others (though invariably in a vague and uncertain way), why doesn't God ever help amputees?

During John Glenn's second trip into space—aboard the Space Shuttle—he looked down at the Earth and said that the beauty he witnessed proved God's existence. "There must truly be a Creator," said Glenn, as he gazed out the window at the blue, cloud-covered planet below. At that time, many Christians sent email to me quoting Glenn's words affirming God's governance of Nature. "Isn't John Glenn an intelligent man of science?" asked one Christian. "I hope you see now that everyone who believes in God is not some kind of wimpish moron."

The writer of that email was indisputably correct: John Glenn is certainly no coward or halfwit. And, clearly, there are millions of other highly intelligent, competent, talented, courageous and

> "Christianity is such a silly religion."
>
> —GORE VIDAL, writer, in *Time* magazine (September 28, 1992)

admirable people who, like Glenn, believe in God. Let's make no mistake about that. And, for the most part, the evidence cited by these believers is real, rather than imagined. The Earth *is* remarkably beautiful from space. Nature does show a degree of underlying order.

But I also recall vividly that, at the very moment Glenn uttered his oft-repeated words about a Creator, the Shuttle was flying over Central America, where Hurricane Mitch had just destroyed the infrastructures of five entire nations. Thousands of people had just been killed and hundreds of thousands left homeless. Government officials calculated that it would take 30 years to rebuild. But none of my Christian email correspondents said a thing to me about the carnage and catastrophic damage wrought by the storm, which was raging only 200 miles beneath Glenn and the Shuttle. I hesitate to emphasize the negative. But, here again, Glenn's "vision of God" was based on selective observation. If Glenn's family had just been wiped out by the storm, I doubt that he would have voiced such an idyllic view of Nature. So whenever Christians point out to me that many intelligent people believe in God, I agree wholeheartedly. But I, in turn, point out that the empirical observations made by these intelligent individuals, though usually accurate, are frequently selectively employed.

The fact is that Nature displays *some* degree of beauty and organization. But all too often, Nature also mindlessly slaughters scores of perfectly innocent men, women and children through natural disasters: hurricanes, tornadoes, earthquakes, floods, drought, lightning, fires, starvation and epidemic disease. Nature is obviously a mixture of order and disorder, the appealing and the loathsome, the purposeful and the arbitrary. Such an undeniably mixed bag would lead an objective observer to conclude that Nature is governed neither by benevolent gods nor by evil demons. Nature simply exists and, irrespective of our desires or best interests, operates through natural law, rather than through mystical or purposeful legerdemain.

For every person "miraculously" healed against the odds, there is another who, against the odds, died a premature and meaningless death. For every magnificent sunset to behold, there is another child stricken with leukemia. For every breathtaking night sky filled with radiant stars, an unexpected heart attack turns a happy wife into a grieving widow. The universe in which we live is located equidistant between absolute order and absolute chaos—a neutral position which we should expect from a universe impervious to our wishes.[2]

In criticizing the fallacy of selective observation, I find myself in the peculiar position of criticizing individuals who consistently emphasize the positive. As a character trait, it is highly desirable if we focus only on the positive aspects of our planet and the universe in which we live. Nobody likes negative people, always pointing out what's wrong with everything. I like to think that I myself am ordinarily quite optimistic in attitude. Nonetheless, the scientific method demands that we include all relevant observations—not just the agreeable ones—when constructing our logical arguments for, and against, God's existence. Moreover, the scientific method obligates us to discern whether positive occurrences are truly miraculous or whether less extravagant explanations may adequately suffice.

A true miracle is, by definition, impossible through natural means—or at least highly improbable. The chances are always greater therefore that the *report* of the miracle is mistaken in its account of what actually occurred or why it occurred.

For example, if I read a tabloid headline claiming that John Kennedy has risen from the dead, then I must assess which probability is greater: (1) that John Kennedy truly rose from the grave, or (2) that the story of his resurrection is inaccurate. Virtually everyone would conclude immediately that the latter alternative is by far the more probable: that the story is false.

> "If revealed religions have revealed anything it is that they are usually wrong."
>
> —FRANCIS CRICK (1916–2004), Nobel Prize–winning British biophysicist and co-discoverer of DNA's structure

Suppose that I were standing near Kennedy's grave at Arlington National Cemetery, and the ground suddenly opened up revealing a coffin. I see the casket opening; and a man who looks exactly like John Kennedy sits up and walks away. Even under these bizarre circumstances, it is still more probable that: (a) I am misperceiving what is occurring, or (b) that someone is playing an ingenious trick, or (c) that I am witnessing the filming of a movie, or (d) that I am dreaming, or (e) that the man I saw was not actually John Kennedy, or (f) that someone has slipped me a hallucinogenic drug, or (g) that I have fallen victim to psychosis or (h) that I am completely fabricating this story. Any of these explanations is infinitely more plausible than the assertion that John Kennedy genuinely rose from the dead. These explanations are more plausible even when I claim to be an eyewitness to the event. Whenever miraculous tales are secondhand or, like Scripture, are handed down from generation to generation, the veracity of the original stories is forever untestable and is thus unworthy of serious consideration. A naturalistic explanation—however far-fetched it seems—is invariably more likely to be accurate than a supernatural explanation.

Not only do we create "miracles" through our selective and inconsistent employment of biased premises, but our very definition of "miracle" is itself evidence of our irrational prejudices. For we reserve our use of the term "miracle" to describe only those events that we personally consider positive. If, for instance, you alone were seriously injured by a one-in-a-million freak accident, then you would be less inclined to label your experience as "miraculous" than if you walked away unscathed from a 70mph head-on collision. If we like the outcome, it's much easier to see the event as a miracle, even though our personal desires are, objectively speaking, irrelevant in determining whether the causal factors were natural or supernatural. We are therefore highly biased in favor of seeing miracles.

Moreover, the "miraculous" event, even though positive, will lose its holy luster if the event is perceived to conflict with "God's will" or with the Ten Commandments. When I was a teenager, for example, I frequently rode my bicycle around the neighborhood. One evening, I rode past the home of a girl with whom I went to high school. All of the boys at school, including me, thought that this girl was exceptionally attractive. As I pedaled past, I glanced over for a split second at the girl's house. And at that precise instant, she walked by her bedroom window topless, wearing only her panties!

As you might imagine, I, as a teenage boy, regarded this event as more historically significant than World War II and the Moon Landing put together. I couldn't believe my incredible good luck! "What were the odds," I kept asking myself, "that I would glance in her window at the exact moment that she scurried past topless?" My titillating peek defied all laws of probability. As I pedaled back home, I said aloud "There *must* be a God. There *must* be a God." When I boasted to the boys at school about my delightful voyeuristic experience, few of them believed me. It all sounded so unlikely and just "too good to be true."

I'm willing to bet that, under absolutely no circumstances, would the Vatican ever declare my cheap, teenage thrill to be an officially recognized miracle of the Catholic Church. No religious pilgrims will ever retrace my bicycle journey in hope of being blessed by the same miraculous vision that I beheld years earlier. Even though my prurient glimpse, like a miracle, was highly unlikely statistically and, like a miracle, was quite positive (in my opinion), no religious leader would consider the event miraculous because God is allegedly opposed to ogling our neighbors' breasts. In other words, our perception of what is, and what is not, a Divine "miracle" is prejudicially determined by what we *already* believe about God's nature. Witnessing "miracles" therefore does not evoke belief in God. Rather, belief in God evokes the witnessing of "miracles."

Miracles and the Media

As the 21st century begins, it seems that the individuals most inclined to see miracles are not necessarily religious adherents, but members of the news media. Almost every day, television network news and local newspapers run stories about people who "miraculously" survived a gruesome accident, illness or natural disaster. Regardless of how many innocent people were killed senselessly, the calamity is invariably twisted into a tale of Divine benevolence. I have dubbed this media tendency *The Rule of Inverse Entropy*, because natural disasters that *least* attest an "orderly universe" are portrayed as the *greatest* evidence of God's existence. The more tragic the event—and the higher the body count—the more inclined are the media to feature "Miracle Survivors" on the six o'clock news.

Let's say that a powerful tornado rips through a mobile home park in Iowa. If no one is killed by the storm, then the news headline will be "All Residents Miraculously Survive Tornado." Witnesses will say that "God wrapped His protective arms around our Christian community." But since everyone survived the twister, townspeople may reason that "the storm wasn't all that bad."

If a few residents are killed, the tornado is then appropriately viewed as having been quite ominous. The majority who survived the ordeal will believe thereafter that only through supernatural intervention could their lives have been spared throughout the deadly storm. Some will claim to have seen "angels of mercy" shielding their homes and families from destruction.

If, by contrast, the tornado kills most of the residents of the mobile home park, then the news media focus intently on the few "Miracle Survivors" and rhetorically ask "Why were these few spared when so many others died?" The implication, of course, is that God (for reasons unknown) chose to save these few, while the majority perished. If, in particular, there is only one survivor of the storm—or of an airplane crash—then the news media reverentially characterize this lone individual as the veritable personification of the miraculous. His or her photo will be published worldwide, along with a tear-jerking story of "God's Deliverance."

So regardless of how many—or how few—die in the incident, God has always performed a miracle. The more deadly the disaster, the more credit God is given for sparing the survivors. When, however, everyone dies in a catastrophe, such as a jumbo jet crash, the newspaper headline never reads "Jehovah Out to Lunch during Doomed Flight." The accident is realistically seen as having occurred for natural or manmade reasons.

Because of our tendency toward selective observation, the dead multitudes are never counted as evidence of disorder, whereas the few survivors are seen as evidence of an orderly, miracle-working God. We "count the hits, but ignore the misses."

It never seems to occur to anyone that a God powerful enough to miraculously deliver the survivors could just as easily have forestalled the disaster altogether and spared the innocent victims. Actually, many people do think of this obvious point, but never say so out loud because such a statement is considered blasphemous.

Little credit is ever given to courageous rescue workers or to highly trained doctors performing emergency surgery on disaster victims. It was God—the *Christian* God, of course—Who saved the survivors. Zeus and Allah are continually being shortchanged in the American media. Surely Allah and Zeus perform their share of miraculous rescues and healings from time to time. Yet the local Christian God always steals the headlines!

> "If you talk to God, you are praying; if God talks to you, you have schizophrenia."
> —THOMAS SZASZ, M.D., psychiatrist, in *The Second Sin*

Whenever disaster strikes—be it a tornado, hurricane, earthquake or airline accident—scientists often face extreme difficulty in tracking down and retracing the chain of causation leading to the event. Despite their sophisticated equipment for making predictions, meteorologists and seismologists are sometimes completely baffled when killer storms or earthquakes strike without warning. Even when commercial airliners are equipped with flight-data recorders—specifically designed to reveal the cause of any accident—skilled investigators often struggle for months or years to ascertain the details of why the plane actually crashed. Occasionally, the cause is never isolated.

If scientists face such an uphill battle in determining why a disaster occurred, then we should not be surprised that investigators usually find it impossible to specify individually why Disaster Victims A, B and C died, while Victims D, E and F survived. The physics involved in such a determination are so unimaginably complex that no supercomputer in operation today could perform the necessary calculations. Moreover, how could scientists possibly record the billions of pieces of relevant data upon which to perform these calculations? Few disasters occur within a controlled, laboratory setting.

In plain English, we usually don't know why specific individuals live or die in disasters. We know that Christians are no more likely to survive than non-Christians, and the virtuous are just as likely to perish as the corrupt. In a very general sense, we may speculate that the survivors suffered less of a physical impact during the crash or the storm than did the deceased, but this explanation is not particularly satisfying. There remain significant gaps in our cause-effect understanding of the event.

Thus, we end this section of the book where we began several chapters ago (Chapter 3)—with a "God of the Gaps." For whenever human knowledge is incomplete, God is hastily recruited to fill the vacuum. We crave a deeper and more philosophical reason for someone's death than merely that "a tree fell on her head" or that "he had a car wreck." These appear to be such flippant and shallow excuses to account for such heart-wrenching losses. A piece of the puzzle seems to be missing.

Likewise, when our circumstances are unexpectedly favorable, we seek a more substantive explanation than simply that "we were lucky" or that "we were at the right place at the right time." That's just too much of a coincidence to accept. We search for a "higher purpose." But what *is* that "higher purpose"? The answer is ever elusive. So we invent, within our minds, a God of the Gaps to fill the void in our cause-effect understanding of a universe indifferent to human preference.

8

The Myth of Hell

"I cannot imagine a God who rewards and punishes the
objects of his creation, whose purposes are modeled after our own—a
God, in short, who is but a reflection of human frailty. Neither can I
believe that the individual survives
the death of his body, although feeble souls harbor
such thoughts through fear or ridiculous egotisms."

—ALBERT EINSTEIN (1879–1955), in the *New York Times* (April 19, 1955)

"There is no hell. There is only France."

—FRANK ZAPPA (1940–1993), musician, in
You Can't Do That On Stage Anymore

The alleged existence of God has always been a fascinating topic
of debate among theologians and secularists. Churchmen say that
only a supernatural Power could have brought the universe into
being. These religious-minded individuals accept no scientific theory that relies solely upon a naturalistic explanation of universal
origins. Creationists say that man himself is too complex an
organism to have evolved from non-living, inert matter. And
where, creationists ask, did this inert matter come from?

Supernaturalism quickly comes under attack, however, from
scientists who propose that man resulted from an evolutionary
process. Presenting their position, secularists say that no evidence

supports the existence of gods, devils, leprechauns, fairies, angels, elves or anything else we label "supernatural." Scientists remind us that recent fossil discoveries and new DNA technology provide overwhelming evidence that man did indeed evolve from a lower form of life. Finally, religious skeptics posit that senseless tragedies such as hurricanes, earthquakes, floods, starvation, drought, birth defects and disease demonstrate that our world was not created and governed by an omnipotent, loving god.

The purpose of this chapter, however, is not to debate the existence of God. We shall assume, for the purpose of discussion, that a god does exist. The goal of this chapter, rather, is to forcefully rebut the alleged existence of Hell, which millions believe that God created to punish "sin." The question at hand, then, is not "Does God exist?" The question posed and, I believe, answered in this chapter is "Would God create a hell?"

Common sense tells us that God would create Hell only if He had a *reason* to inflict this punishment. In other words, God would not have decided arbitrarily that He would enjoy torturing humans (and fallen angels) and have created a hell on that basis, for this scenario would imply that God behaved sadistically and brought this lake of fire into existence to satisfy his desires to perceive suffering and to hear screams of pain.

We have no proof that God could not behave sadistically. But this idea appears to make little sense. It makes more sense to believe that a god intelligent enough to create the universe and the life therein would not have a deranged mind—and certainly would not be so cruel as to enjoy the suffering of His Creation. It seems logical to conclude, then, that a Deity would punish individuals in Hell only if He had a reason for this action.

So concerning punishment in Hell, implemented by God, we have the following possibilities:

(1) God had a reason to create Hell and therefore did so.

(2) God had no reason to create Hell, but did so anyway—He just enjoys torturing others.

(3) God had no reason to create Hell and therefore did not.

We shall now attempt to differentiate punishment implemented without reason from punishment implemented for good cause. We shall first discuss various punishments with which we in American society are familiar, along with the reasons for these social penalties. We discuss these social penalties not because they have direct relevance to the biblical doctrine of Hell, but rather to lay an analogical foundation upon which to construct our differentiation of the rational from the ridiculous.

What reasons, then, motivate punishment? Why are law-breakers sent to prison? Why are unruly students expelled from school?

Generally speaking, there are three main reasons why an individual may suffer punishment:

(1) To establish a precedent that will benefit society, by serving as a deterrent to future offenses;

(2) To separate the offender from those individuals whose rights he would violate;

(3) To correct the offender for his and others' benefit.

Let's now flesh out, briefly, each of these reasons for punishment:

Deterrence

All of us strive to live as happily as possible. We work to obtain those tangibles and intangibles that we consider desirable and to rid ourselves of unnecessary burdens. Virtually everyone goes about this practice in such a way as not to interfere with the personal rights of other individuals.

Unfortunately, however, some people do not exhibit such consideration for their neighbors. A very small minority of people strive for happiness in ways that seriously violate the rights of others in society. For example, someone may steal money from another individual. Because such unethical behavior is condemned by the majority, laws exist for the protection of the "general welfare." One law states that stealing money shall bring forth a specific punishment. The existence of jails and prisons will hopefully deter those individuals who contemplate violating the rights of others. Society will benefit in that this deterrent potentially reduces the crime rate.

Those of us over forty can remember in elementary school when the teacher pulled the paddle from her desk and said that the class brat would surely "get it" the next time he opened his mouth. Instantly, the class brat was transformed into a quiet young man absorbed into his schoolwork. The class brat's fear of a paddling usually forestalled further shenanigans. Punishing the minority who misbehaved produced an orderly class, wherein all could receive an education. To deter potential law- or rule-breakers, then, in order to make conditions better for the majority, is one reason for the use of punishment.

Separation

In a society, there invariably remains a minority of people who, if allowed to roam free, would waste little time before resuming a lifestyle detrimental to other individuals. Charles Manson, for example, by ordering his followers to commit wholesale murder, has unarguably violated the rights of his fellow citizens. Authorities consider Manson an extremely dangerous threat to society in that releasing this famous butcher would almost certainly result in the murder of additional individuals.

Because the majority of individuals in society have a strong desire not to be murdered, Manson has been "exiled." Although he could not possibly kill the majority of society, any member within that society might fall victim to his angry knife if police released Manson from custody.

Punishment—to accomplish separation—is also used in the public schools. Mischievous classroom behavior, destruction of school property, or physically threatening or abusing others may lead to a student's being

> "One of the proofs of the immortality of the soul is that myriads have believed in it. They have also believed the world was flat."
>
> —MARK TWAIN (1835–1910), in *Notebook*

suspended or expelled. The school, desiring to carry on the educational process, punishes troublemakers in this manner to eliminate their opportunity to hinder other students or to vandalize school property. Separation, then, to prevent future infringement upon the rights of others, constitutes an additional reason for punishment.

Rehabilitation

Individuals found guilty of a criminal offense frequently find themselves behind bars. Society hopes that these offenders—who were not deterred from crime by the threat of punishment—will be deterred in the future by their unpleasant incarceration.

Moreover, many prisons attempt to rehabilitate offenders by teaching them a skill or trade. Although most penal institutions lack the necessary facilities, a few offer classes to the inmates in such fields as electronics, plumbing and carpentry. Some correctional institutions even make psychotherapy available. Society hopes that the offenders' learning different modes of thought and behavior will result in their refraining from criminal activity upon their future release; hence society will benefit. To correct or rehabilitate offenders is therefore a reason for punishment.

These comprise the three possible reasons why an individual may be punished. We must recognize, however, that deterrence, separation and rehabilitation are reasons for punishment because (and only because) they produce beneficial results. Thus, the punishment of an individual—or the promulgation of the possibility thereof (i.e., deterrence)—that produces a better social environment than the *absence* of punishment would produce has a reason for implementation.

We must now differentiate punishment implemented for good cause from punishment enacted solely for vengeance or sadistic pleasure. Let's read a brief illustrative story:

Mrs. Jones felt startled one afternoon by a violent knocking on her front door. She rose hurriedly to greet her unknown visitor.

"What can I do for you?" said Mrs. Jones to the neighbor standing on her doorstep. She wondered what her neighbor wanted.

"Forget the pleasantries," said the neighbor. "Your son, Johnny, picked up a rock a minute ago and threw it deliberately through my living room window. I saw him with my own eyes!"

Mrs. Jones apologized profusely for her son's destructive behavior and promised to pay for a new window. Mrs. Jones also told her neighbor that Johnny will be punished when he returns home.

Now, here's a question for you: What reason would motivate Johnny's punishment? Which of the following two statements presents that reason?

(1) Johnny will be punished because he deliberately broke the neighbor's window.

(2) Johnny will be punished to hopefully deter him from repeating destructive behavior in the future.

Number 2, which presents the beneficial end of the punishment, presents the reason: Johnny will be deterred from repeating destructive behavior. Number 1 merely states the fact that Johnny broke the window. Number 1 does not, however, present a reason (i.e., purpose or motivation) for the punishment.

To state that a broken window is the "reason" for Johnny's punishment is to state that we can go backward in time and prevent the window from being broken, or that we can somehow repair the window by punishing Johnny. But will punishing Johnny accomplish these goals? Obviously not.

While it is clearly possible to change the direction of future events—in that punishment may deter Johnny from repeating destructive actions—punishing Johnny cannot and will not change the fact that he broke a window in the past. The important point to remember here is that "teaching Johnny a lesson" is indeed a justifiable reason for punishment. But hot-headed revenge—directed only at unalterable past events—is not, in itself, a justifiable reason for punishment, because nothing beneficial is thereby achieved.

▲▼▲

The Christian Church—whether Protestant or Catholic—preaches that God had reason to punish "sinful souls" and "fallen angels" and, consequently, created Hell for that purpose. We shall now explore the logic, credibility and morality of this teaching.

Deterrence

Because the beneficial end of creating a deterrent is to prevent undesirable, antisocial acts, and because these acts have to be undesirable *to* someone (or to some group) in order for deterrence to have value, we can divide this section into two possibilities: (1) Hell, created as a deterrent to antisocial sin,[1] for the benefit of humanity; (2) Hell, created as a deterrent to sin, for the benefit of God.

The first question at hand, then, reads as follows: Did God create Hell to benefit humanity by using the threat of punishment therein as a deterrent to sin?

To investigate the hypothetical creation of Hell—to allegedly benefit humanity—we must attain a good understanding of what the Christian Church preaches about humanity: The Church proclaims that the majority of human beings on Earth will suffer punishment after death in Hell's lake of fire. When asked for evidence to support their doctrine, Church leaders refer primarily to Matthew 7:13,14—

"Enter ye in at the strait gate: for wide is the gate, and broad is the way, that leadeth to destruction, and many there be which go in thereat:

"Because strait is the gate and narrow is the way, which leadeth into life, and few there be that find it."[2]

> "Although the time of death is approaching me, I am not afraid of dying and going to Hell or (what would be considerably worse) going to the popularized version of Heaven. I expect death to be nothingness and, for removing me from all possible fears of death, I am thankful to atheism."
>
> —ISAAC ASIMOV (1920–1992), scientist and writer, in "On Religiosity," *Free Inquiry*

The Christian Church wholeheartedly believes this "Divine" biblical prophecy, which announces that the majority of humanity will follow the wrong road in life and will, as a result, end up in Hell instead of Heaven. We cannot possibly, then, accept the hypothesis that Hell's creation could have sought to benefit humanity, for a God—in His infinite wisdom—would have known in advance that the majority of humanity would fall victim to the gruesome torture chamber supposedly created for humanity's own benefit. If we assume that a prevailing fear of Hell would benefit humanity by operating as a deterrent to crime or "sin," then we face the question: Would the good attained from the deterrent outweigh the price of going to Hell forever? The answer: an obvious no.

As an analogy, let's suppose that someone invites you to dinner at the finest restaurant in town. He promises to pick you up in his limousine, wine you and dine you at his expense, and return you home. But in exchange for his generosity, this man insists upon satisfying his pyromaniacal desires to burn down your home. Your choice: (A) accept the dinner invitation and, as a consequence, see your home incinerated; or (B) decline the invitation in order to save your home from destruction.

Literally everyone would decline the dinner invitation to avoid suffering a tremendous loss (i.e., your home). If, however, you selectively viewed only the fact that this individual offered you a lavish dinner, then you could say that an acceptance of his invitation would be beneficial. But viewing the entire situation, you would have to conclude that accepting the invitation would not be beneficial overall because the loss (i.e., your home) would far overshadow the gain (i.e., a free meal).

Humanity, as in our analogy, would of course prefer (B) forfeiting the deterrence of antisocial sin, over (A) receiving the deterrence of antisocial sin and receiving the accompanying, subsequent torture in Hell's fiery dungeon. Should the torture in Hell feel even modestly uncomfortable, it would, because of its duration throughout eternity, negate even the greatest of good that it would allegedly bring (as a deterrent to antisocial sin) in the comparatively short period of time that it could serve humanity in this capacity. In simple terms, the good of having a hell would be overshadowed by the bad. Hell's creation would therefore be a net loss for humanity.

There is additional evidence that Hell's creation was not to benefit humanity by means of deterring antisocial sin. First, hell-fearing people often abstain from many enjoyable activities condemned by their church but condoned by their society. Unfortunately, these religiously tormented individuals have been frightened into foregoing many pleasurable activities that would infringe upon the rights of no one. Such self-imposed masochism is not beneficial.

Second, even when a religious-minded individual does "risk" one of these "unholy" acts, such as premarital sex, he frequently believes that he will be roasted eternally for his "sin." He therefore suffers needless and "unbeneficial" guilt and anxiety.

Third, God, because of His omniscience, would have known in advance that humanity would establish its own penal system as a deterrent to behavior which does infringe upon the rights of others.

Fourth, God would also have recognized that many individuals would not believe in Hell at all, and thus would in no way be deterred from sin by the threat of eternal damnation.

So to the question: *"Did God create Hell to benefit humanity, by using the threat of punishment therein as a deterrent to sin?"* we must answer: No.

At this point, another question comes to mind: Did God create Hell to benefit humanity, not necessarily by deterring crime or sin, but by motivating humanity to repent and be saved by Jesus?

In addressing this question, we must recall that the essential purpose and result of an individual's repentance is to escape Hell and go to Heaven. Because no one could burn in Hell if it had never been created in the first place, and because more of humanity will supposedly fall victim *to* Hell's inferno than will repent because of Hell's existence, we must conclude that Hell's purpose was not to benefit humanity. Therefore, we must answer no to the question.

If the creation of Hell would not benefit humans, could its creation have sought to benefit God, through causing humans, out of fear, to abstain from activities that He found objectionable? In other words, was God literally trying to scare the hell out of people to pressure them into worshiping Him?

> "Sunday school: A prison in which children do penance for the evil conscience of their parents."
>
> —H. L. MENCKEN (1880–1956), editor and critic, in *A Mencken Chrestomathy*

Accepting this hypothesis as an accurate portrayal of God's nature would, in my view, constitute a highly blasphemous assertion—this scenario would imply that God behaved far more fiendishly than Stalin or Hitler at the height of their World War II atrocities, for Stalin and Hitler had certain goals which they wanted to achieve also. In order to get what they wanted, Stalin and Hitler likewise thought that it was necessary to torture and kill millions of people. As the men in charge of their nations, Stalin and Hitler likewise held in their power the choice of either torturing and killing human beings or simply leaving them alone. Stalin and Hitler likewise chose to take cruel and barbaric action because their desires to behave humanely were likewise overshadowed and subordinated to their own selfish agendas.

Just as Stalin and Hitler had the choice to kill, or not to kill, citizens of their own and neighboring countries, God, if existent, would have the choice to transport, or not to transport, literally billions of individuals to Hell. History justifiably regards Stalin and Hitler as evil and sadistic madmen because of their inhumane tyranny against nations and peoples who allegedly stood in the way of their goals. If we conclude, then, that God would create Hell to deter human behavior which He disliked—knowing beforehand that the majority of humanity would, as a result, suffer eternal torture—then we would be forced to label this god as evil and sadistic also, because He likewise would have inhumanely tortured individuals in order to accomplish His goals.

Needless to say, devout churchgoers are morally outraged by this unflattering characterization of their "loving God." They invariably retort that God gave each person a "free will"[3] to decide his own eternal destiny by accepting or rejecting Jesus as Savior.

Church leaders invalidate their own argument, however, by simultaneously asserting that God is omniscient: He possesses total knowledge of the past, present and future. Thus, the fact—that the majority of humanity would "forsake Jesus" (and would therefore suffer an eternal roasting)—was recognized by God before He chose to create Hell, before He chose to create man, before He chose to give man an eternal soul, before He chose to make the eternal destinies of human souls contingent upon "accepting Jesus," and before He chose to create a devil to deceive man into forsaking Jesus. Stated otherwise: if God is truly omniscient, as Christians believe, then He would have foreseen that His "Master Plan" would be disastrous for humanity. Yet, according to biblical doctrine, He crafted His plan of contingent salvation, so that billions of individuals, whom He brought into existence, would be consigned to an eternal chamber of torture. *He*, therefore, would bear direct responsibility for any suffering brought upon humanity.

> "The most heinous and the most cruel crimes of which history has record have been committed under the cover of religion or equally noble motives."
>
> —MOHANDAS GANDHI (1869–1948), in *The Degeneration of Belief*

The Christian Church maintains that "Jesus is God," the loving and benevolent Savior, Who died on the cross to save mankind from eternal torment. But who, may I ask, is threatening to impose this eternal torment? The answer is the very same God. So Jesus, in effect, became a victim of His own judgment when dying on the cross as a substitutionary sacrifice—a blood ritual which Jesus offered to Himself so that He could forgive "sin." The entire biblical plan of salvation is therefore a bogus tautology (i.e., a needless redundancy). A truly benevolent and omnipotent God could simply let bygones be bygones and forgive "sinners" even though they adopted mistaken religious beliefs. If this universal and unconditional forgiveness is impossible for God to bestow, then He is not omnipotent; He is controlled and tossed about by circumstances superseding His authority. If He *could* forgive all "sinners" unconditionally, but refused, then He is not benevolent.

Suppose, by analogy, that a stranger pulls a gun on you and says, "Your money or your life." You refuse to surrender your money, and the robber kills you. Do you believe that a jury would acquit the gunman because he had offered you a "free choice"?

Would this gunman deserve praise and worship if, after putting a gun to your head, he decided to spare your life? No, because he was merely removing the threat that he himself had imposed upon you unasked and unwanted. Yet the biblical God is viewed as "merciful" because He "saves" a minority of human beings from His own hideous tortures, imposed upon humanity unasked and unwanted.

"But," Christians respond, "without the shedding of blood, there can be no forgiveness of sin. And God asks only that we accept the blood sacrifice that Jesus offered for us on the cross."

And who, may I ask, established this rule that "without the shedding of blood, there can be no forgiveness of sin"? The answer, again, is "God." If truly omnipotent, God could have proclaimed that "without the drinking of apple cider, there can be no forgiveness of sin," or "without the expulsion of farts, there can be no forgiveness of sin." God, if omnipotent, could do anything He wanted, including forgiving all "sinners" unconditionally. The fact that God supposedly demands blood before He offers forgiveness is indicative of the bestial mindset of the primitive cultures extant when the Bible was written. The biblical God was created in man's own vengeful, bloodletting image.

If my family or friends "do me wrong," I soon forgive them and hold no long-term grudge. And I'm willing to bet that you're

> "It seems to me that the idea of a personal God is an anthropological concept which I cannot take seriously. I also cannot imagine some will or goal outside the human sphere . . . Science has been charged with undermining morality, but the charge is unjust. A man's ethical behavior should be based effectually on sympathy, education, and social ties and needs; no religious basis is necessary. Man would indeed be in a poor way if he had to be restrained by fear of punishment and hope of reward after death."
>
> —ALBERT EINSTEIN (1879–1955), in "Religion and Science," *New York Times Magazine* (November 9, 1930)

equally forgiving. There is no rational purpose in fuming and fussing in childish anger or—even more childishly—seeking savage and pointless revenge. Moreover, I certainly do not demand that "blood be shed" to compensate for my friends' or family's "improper" conduct. Such "blood payment" is usually demanded only by Mafia bosses, rather than Beings of "infinite mercy."

Even we lowly humans find it ethically repugnant to penalize individuals for their religious beliefs, regardless of how mistaken we consider their beliefs to be. It is against the law, for example, to refuse employment or housing to a person simply because his or her religious beliefs differ from our own version of "the truth." Surely a god of "infinite love and mercy" would be more merciful and more forgiving, rather than less merciful and less forgiving, than mere humans. Yet according to Church teaching, God Himself is the Supreme Bigot, in that He allegedly plans to gruesomely and eternally torture people if they hold divergent religious beliefs.

Finally, Christians argue that God is forced to torture sinners because He is so holy. Leaving aside the question of how an omnipotent god can be "forced" to do anything, and leaving aside the contradictory nature of "holy torture," the entire notion that "God is holy" is itself philosophically empty. Labeling God as "holy" has no more meaning than labeling the Pope as a good Catholic, for each controls the definition of the concept he fulfills.

The Pope, to a large extent, has the power to establish Catholic doctrine and to set forth official Catholic teaching. To label the Pope himself as a "good Catholic" is therefore practically meaningless—though the phrase may carry some substance in that a Pope may fulfill historical or traditional definitions of "good Catholic" as established by his predecessors. However, to label God Himself as "holy" is absolutely meaningless, since God presumably has absolute control over the definition of "holy." The statement that "God is holy" is thus another example of tautological error. Yet Christians unhesitatingly cite this logical error as "justification" for God's plan to torture billions of human beings. God and Hitler therefore share the abominable belief that it is morally permissible to torture human beings if they belong to the "wrong" religion.

Let us now restate the original question at hand: *"Could Hell's creation have sought to benefit God by deterring human activities which He disliked?"*

There appear to be two possible answers to this question:

(1) Yes, if we conclude also that this Stalinistic-Hitlerian god (a) prefers fulfilling his own whims—i.e., to frighten others into a life of "purity"—over behaving humanely, (b) does not give an omnipotent damn that His creation of Hell directly caused the eternal torture of humans whom He Himself also created, (c) behaves hypocritically when warning others to "forgive and forget," while He Himself engages in contingent forgiveness only, and (d) acts, therefore, like a true horse's ass.

(2) No, if we conclude that God would not deliberately inflict cruel and purposeless torture.

Separation

Did God create Hell to separate the "lost souls" from the "saved"? A cornerstone belief of the Christian faith is that no "sinful soul" may pass through Heaven's pearly gates. Christians believe, moreover, that individuals who reject Jesus as Savior are "sinners" in God's sight. Christians "logically" conclude, therefore, that individuals who reject Jesus cannot be admitted to Heaven, and must instead go to Hell. The Church tells us that God doesn't *want* to sentence "souls" to damnation in Hell, but, because of His perfect "holiness," He is "forced" to keep sinners out of His sinless Paradise.

If we pretend that a god does exist and that He presides over a heavenly city into which sin cannot enter, then we must recognize that two rational, non-hellish alternatives could separate the "lost souls" from the "saved."

(1) God, after a "sinner's" death, could return the "sinner's" soul" to a state of nonexistence, as it was before his birth.

(2) God, after a "sinner's" death, could transport the "sinner's" soul" to a location away from Heaven, but a location wherein he would not undergo pointless torture.

Even though an omnipotent God is "forced" to block from entering Heaven those "souls" who "forsook Jesus," either of the above alternatives would achieve this goal. Sadistic and barbaric torture is not required to separate the "lost souls" from the "saved."

Let's say, by analogy, that you are sitting at home, talking with some friends about the gift you bought your five-year-old son for his upcoming birthday. In the midst of your conversation, your son walks into the room. Since you obviously don't want your son to hear the topic of discussion, you courteously ask your daughter, who is older, to play with her brother elsewhere. Perhaps your daughter and son could go to another part of the house to watch television, or maybe next door to visit a friend. It would be an overreaction indeed for your daughter, in attempting to separate her brother from the conversation, to take him behind the house and throw him into the barrel in which the trash is burning. The Church's "separation" argument is no better—logically or ethically—than this ghastly parallel.

So to the question: *"Did God create Hell to separate the 'lost souls' from the 'saved?'"* we must reply no, because this goal could have been achieved through more humane alternatives.

Rehabilitation

Did God create Hell to rehabilitate those individuals who, during their lives, failed to obey biblical commandments? The idea that Hell's purpose is to rehabilitate "sinners" may be dismissed immediately because the Church tells us that Hell's tortures continue forever. No one is ever paroled. Even if we assume humorously that Hell does transform "sinners" into "saints," this torture chamber would still serve no beneficial purpose, since the rehabilitated sinners would never return to society to benefit from their correction. Nor, obviously, would society itself benefit—nor would any other conceivable natural or supernatural entity benefit—from the eternal, hard-boiled roasting of human beings.

In Summary

We have proposed that punishment has a reason for implementation only when it produces some kind of real or potential benefit for someone or for some larger group. Otherwise, the use of punishment degenerates into primitive and pointless revenge, whose sole and sadistic purpose is to inflict human suffering. Moreover, we have speculated what reason, if any, might have motivated God to create a hell. We have discovered no such reason.

In fairness, however, we should emphasize that the Christian Church never claimed that Hell was created for rehabilitation of "souls." And although Christian theologians do occasionally ponder whether "deterrence of sin" and "segregation of souls" were partial motivations for God to create Hell, these (flawed) arguments are never offered as the sole or primary reason for Hell's existence.

What, then, is the reason offered by the Church for punishment in Hell? Historically, the Christian Church, whether Catholic or Protestant, has consistently maintained that human beings are punished in Hell "because they lived in sin and rejected Jesus as their Savior."

Did you notice the words "lived" and "rejected"? They refer, as you can clearly see, to the past tense. In other words, this fiery punishment is directed, even according to the Church, exclusively at the offenders' past, and is not intended to have future beneficial effects. Punishment in Hell is therefore an end in itself, admittedly implemented for no beneficial purpose.

To put it simply, when Christianity's defenders say that God punishes "sinners" in Hell "because they lived in sin and rejected Jesus," these defenders of the faith are saying nothing. Their arguments do not present a good reason for Hell's existence. Nor do they present a bad reason. Christian defenders have presented no reason or purpose whatsoever for God's torturing human beings. The unavoidable conclusion is that the "reason" for Hell's torture is simply to torture—as a purposeless, vengeful end in itself. To claim that God is "forced" unwillingly to torture humanity is to deny God's omnipotence and ultimate authority. To claim that God *wants* to torture humanity is to deny God's benevolence. In either case, there is an irreconcilable doctrinal conflict.

As a last-straw argument, religious leaders claim that we humans are foolish to question God's Master Plan. "The fool hath said in his heart, 'There is no God.'" The Bible is the perfect and infallible Word of God and, although we may not comprehend all of God's mysteries, we know that God always behaves fairly and consistently. Just as a child may not understand why he is being disciplined by a loving parent, we too may be ignorant of God's ultimate purposes. If God created Hell to punish humans and fallen angels, then He definitely had a good reason to do so.

> "Belief, thus, in the supernatural, great as are the services which it rendered in the early stages of human development, cannot be considered to be any longer required, either for enabling us to know what is right and wrong in social morality, or for supplying us with motives to do right and to abstain from wrong."
>
> —JOHN STUART MILL (1806–1873), British philosopher, economist, logician and political scientist, in *Utility of Religion*

The obvious fallacy in this "logic" is that it blindly assumes the conclusion that it sets out to prove. If you begin your argument by assuming (1) that God exists, (2) that He is the God of the Christian Bible (rather than the God of Islam or a Greek god), (3) that He always behaves fairly, (4) that He is omnipotent and omniscient, (5) that He created the universe, Earth, mankind, Heaven and Hell, and (6) that all of His actions are purposeful, then of course your subsequent, "logically deduced" conclusions will identically parrot these premises, which you have already accepted uncritically by blind faith. Such "logic" is identical to "proving" Batman's existence by citing the eyewitness testimony of Robin, the Boy Wonder. One's conclusions are meaningless if the "supporting" premises are themselves articles of faith or figments of the imagination.

Finally, the Church totally overlooks the crucial question of proportionality of punishment: Does the punishment fit the crime? The U.S. Constitution specifically prohibits cruel and unusual punishment, regardless of how grotesque the criminal offense committed by the perpetrator. This means that even serial murderers and child molesters cannot be tortured or physically abused while incarcerated. For God, however, no amount of torture seems sufficient to satisfy His lust for vengeance. "Sinners" will be fiendishly roasted forever—not merely a thousand years, or a million years, or a billion years, but eternally.

Think about that. Let's suppose that, during a person's particularly mischievous lifetime, he commits a sum total of 100,000 sins, each of which God avenges singularly through fiery torture. If a "sinner" were sentenced to one year of uninterrupted torture for each sin he committed—an unimaginably sadistic judgment—then his punishment would be over in 100,000 years. But, according to Christian doctrine, the torture continues longer than 100,000 years, so the penalty must be more than one year of uninterrupted torture per offense. If God tortured a "sinner" 100 years for each "sin" he committed, then the punishment would be over in 10,000,000 years, but Hell continues longer. A mere 100 years of torture per sin is therefore insufficient punishment. Even a million years of torture per offense would be a light sentence compared to everlasting torture.

So if you'd prefer to watch football on Sunday instead of going to church, then you will be tortured more than a million years for this single offense. If you scream out "shit" when you drop a heavy suitcase on your ankle, then you will be tortured more than a million years for this one "sin." If you stare too long at that girl in the bikini—or that rock musician—then you will be tortured more than a million years for this single ungodly act. If you were reared by Muslim parents and adopted their religion instead of Christianity, then you will be tortured more than a million years for your theological error.

Although God, if existent, would obviously transcend and supersede U.S. Constitutional authority, Hell's torture would be considered cruel and unusual punishment by any sane analysis. Jefferson, Madison and the other framers of our Constitution therefore showed far more compassion and mercy than the "loving Heavenly Father" of the Christian Bible. Would you, as a loving father or mother, torture and burn your children at the stake for misbehaving?

Christians may argue that "unsaved" individuals are not "children of God." But is it morally permissible, then, to torture children unrelated to you? I hope and trust that your answer is no.

What, then, is our conclusion?

HELL EXISTS

This conclusion means that God would rather torture humanity than to forgive humanity unconditionally. This conclusion carries the charge that God created Hell for no reason other than to inflict suffering. In this case, as Thomas Paine noted, the Bible could more accurately be called *The Word of a Demon* than *The Word of God*. If we proceed under the assumption that God does exist, then I firmly believe that He would be insulted by the blasphemous assertion that He created a hell.

HELL DOES NOT EXIST

This conclusion means that God chose not to inflict sadistic and pointless torture upon the souls He created. This conclusion carries the charge that man, not God, created Hell. In my estimation, this conclusion is the more probable. As Robert Ingersoll stated, the myth of hell represents "all the meanness, all the revenge, all the selfishness, all the cruelty, all the hatred, all the infamy of which the heart of man is capable." God was indeed created in man's own image.

9

Christian Fundamentalists and the "Danger" of Internet Porn

"I do not believe in immortality of the individual,
and I consider ethics to be an exclusively human concern
with no superhuman authority behind it."

—ALBERT EINSTEIN (1879–1955), in his biography *Albert Einstein: The Human Side*

"Organized religion is a sham and a crutch
for weak-minded people who need strength in numbers.
It tells people to go out and stick their noses
in other people's business."

—JESSE VENTURA, former pro wrestler and former governor of Minnesota,
in *Playboy* (November 1999)

Perhaps I'm unsophisticated or culturally deprived, but I'm not the least bit interested in the history of French ballet. I know absolutely nothing about the subject, and I don't want to know anything about it. A list of my favorite 10,000 subjects would contain no reference at all to the history of French ballet. In fact, I'd much rather lie down and take a nap than read about the history of French ballet. I respect and appreciate those artists and scholars who find the topic fascinating. But as for me, forget it. I'm just not interested.

What I am interested in, among other things, is computers. I bought my first computer in the early 1980s, when the machines were first introduced for home use. My first computer, purchased at Radio Shack, had all of 4K memory—not 4 *megs* mind you—I mean 4K (4096 bytes). I marveled at this enormous RAM and was awestruck by the machine's incredible CPU speed, which was slightly less than 1MHz. In its most powerful graphics mode, my first computer could simultaneously display four different colors!

The internet back then was almost exclusively the province of a few elite universities and research centers. No one had ever heard of Netscape, Windows Internet Explorer or Bill Gates. The World Wide Web was a decade into the future. The internet then was a text-only medium, requiring the manual entry of painfully intricate address codes to navigate the system. My first modem occasionally achieved a blazing 300 baud, though most of the time I had to settle for 150. Since those days—which don't seem that long ago—computers and the internet have changed unimaginably, becoming exponentially more powerful and (perhaps) a little easier to use.

During the 1980s and 1990s, I logged onto the internet thousands of times, connecting to tens of thousands of sites around the globe. In all those years of net surfing, however, I never—not even once—connected to a site referencing the history of French ballet. I'm confident that many such references exist on the internet. But I have never bothered to search for them because I don't give a damn about the subject. Even if I knew exactly where to look, I would *not* look.

▲▼▲

During the 1980s, I never heard a single negative comment voiced about the internet. Sure, internet users themselves were constantly complaining that the system was slow and difficult to navigate. But no one ever suggested that the internet was a bad thing or an evil force. Starting in the early 1990s, however, Fundamentalist Christians—and sensation-seeking news media—began portraying the internet as a mortal danger to humanity.

For a few years, we heard frightening stories about terrorists' allegedly using the internet to pilfer plans for building a nuclear bomb. The internet, it seemed, was literally going to destroy the planet. Never mind that the same nuclear technology was also available in any college textbook. Because the internet was the messenger, all these conspiracy stories seemed far more ominous, and more likely to result in Armageddon. The internet was little understood by the average citizen, who feared what he didn't understand.

The next horror story circulated about the internet was that millions of murderers, kidnappers and pedophiles were lying in wait behind their computer terminals, ready to attack any member of your family who went online. Supposedly, these violent predators were all computer geniuses who could decipher your home address simply by viewing your email address. Using this cryptic information, these internet stalkers could break into your home and slit your throat as you lie sleeping. Ironically, those voicing such fears of internet stalking voiced no objection whatever to publishing a city phone directory, which provides full names and home addresses of practically everyone in town.[1]

But fear of internet-inspired nuclear bombs and internet-savvy criminals has currently taken a back seat to the gravest threat of all: the horrifying possibility that someone—perhaps even an "underage" teenage male—may use the internet to view photographs of nude women!

Motivated by campaign contributions from Christian conservatives, the U.S. Congress in 1995 passed the Communications Decency Act (CDA). The CDA sought to "protect minors" from the "threat" of internet pornography. Moreover, software publishers and internet service providers began offering tools to block out selected internet sites deemed "harmful to minors." Programs such as Net Nanny, Cyber Patrol, Cybersitter, Internet Filter and Surfwatch sold hundreds of thousands of copies to parents concerned about their children's unsupervised computer usage. Thousands of sexually oriented websites began using Adult Check, an age-verification system to deny entrance to minors. Donna Rice Hughes, who thought nothing of sleeping with any married man "destined for the White House," became spokeswoman for Enough Is Enough, a group of born-again Christians striving to "protect our children from the dangers of viewing internet pornography."

> "The pioneers and missionaries of religion have been the real cause of more trouble and war than all other classes of mankind."
> —EDGAR ALLAN POE
> (1809–1849), writer

▲▼▲

Is there truly a problem of children's accessing pornography on the internet? And if there is, shouldn't we, as adults, strive mightily to prevent impressionable children from viewing sexually oriented material intended solely for adults?

The answers to these questions are: (1) There is no problem; and (2) We should not strive to "child-proof" the internet.

When I assert that we should not child-proof the internet, I am not attempting to raise a First Amendment or Constitutionally rooted objection to government censorship. Although I enthusiastically applauded the U.S. Supreme Court's declaration that the CDA was unconstitutional, I wish to argue on completely different grounds why I believe that internet censorship is both unnecessary and quite counterproductive in shielding our children from imaginary "harm."

▲▼▲

The crucial, relevant—and invariably overlooked—fact about children and pornography is that children have no libido. In other words, children have as much attraction to sexually oriented websites as I have to French ballet websites: None. For this reason, any thunderous public effort to shield children from viewing internet porn is likely to be iatrogenic. "Iatrogenic" is an obscure term denoting a disease caused entirely by the attending physician and his prescribed "remedy."

To the tiny extent that adult websites attract children, the attraction is not one of lust, but of curiosity—curiosity generated by our endless discussion and public hand-wringing over the issue. Morally crusading adults awaken in children an attraction to websites that, naturally, children do not possess. Experts on child psychology—including both Sigmund Freud and Jean Piaget—demonstrated decades ago that all children experience a prolonged period of sexual latency, during which they have no lustful inclinations whatever. This period of sexual latency ends with the onset of puberty in the early-to-mid teens.

That children have no sexual urges or erotic fantasies is almost impossible for adults, particularly male adults, to comprehend or accept. The average adult male is pretty much obsessed with sexual imagery. So he tends to project his own psychological framework and habits onto others, including children. It is difficult for adults to really believe that children spend literally no time engaging in erotic fantasy. Precisely because sexual imagery does not occur naturally during the childhood latency period, most—not all, but most—children's accounts of sexual abuse by adults are probably true. Unless spoon-fed these fantasies by an incompetent psychotherapist or social worker, sexual imagery and desire are totally absent within children until puberty begins. A desire to download sexually stimulating computer images is likewise wholly absent within pre-adolescent children. Let's firmly keep in mind that websites, regardless of their content, must be actively selected by the computer user. The only things that appear on your monitor uninvited are advertisements and error messages.

I mentioned earlier that, during my two decades of internet use, I never accessed a single website referencing the history of French ballet, even though such sites certainly exist. No law of Congress prohibited my viewing such material. No "blocking" software or Adult Check screened me out. And no political or religious group tried to deter me from entering those sites. My own intrinsic lack of interest was by far the best "safeguard" against my exposure to the ballet.

Suppose, however, that Congress passed a law called the French Ballet Decency Act. I think that my curiosity would suddenly awaken. Suppose also that software companies and internet service providers were working feverishly to guarantee that I never learned the secrets of the ballet. And imagine that the commentators and religious activists were endlessly preaching about the "dangers" of my accessing French ballet websites. I think that I would probably lie awake at night wondering what all the commotion was about. The next time that I logged onto the internet, what sites do you think I would search for? Again, any alleged "problem" of children's accessing internet pornography is entirely iatrogenic, caused by the guardian physicians of morality.

We can easily think of numerous examples in which the moralistic "cure" caused the "disease." One of my favorite television programs of all time was *Married with Children*, whose every episode was admittedly filled with sexual innuendo and unabashed lusting, though never for the characters' own spouses. When FOX Television first aired *Married with Children* in 1987, its ratings were abysmal. Nobody watched the show, and FOX planned to cancel the program.

Then a woman, whose name, alas, I do not know, began to publicly voice her outrage at the show's raunchiness. She wrote letters. She tried to persuade the show's sponsors to discontinue their advertising. She organized protests. The result was that public attention began to focus on *Married with Children*. The show's ratings went up instantly and dramatically. And the program continued to run for ten seasons! If I only possessed the name of this saintly woman, I would certainly send her a thank-you card for her indispensable contribution to keeping my favorite program on the air.

Another example: I live in a rather small town in the heart of Appalachia. In 1997 the local Ku Klux Klan announced that it was planning a demonstration in a local park. Such a demonstration, far from any residential or populated area, would have involved five or six semi-literate racists garbed in their white costumes. No one in town would have paid the slightest attention to these kooks, let alone be influenced by their message of hatred.

Local politicians, however, were determined to thwart plans for the Klan rally. First, local officials tried to challenge the constitutionality of such a gathering. When that failed, they sought to organize a massive counter-demonstration across the park from the Klan rally. The result was that, for months, each day's newspaper carried banner headlines detailing the battle over the proposed Klan rally. And, sadly, Klan membership grew as never before. Millions of dollars could not have purchased the newspaper and television coverage given freely to the Klan, courtesy of local politicians. The point here is that you shouldn't direct the public's attention toward an issue that you want the public to ignore.

▲▼▲

Even if one concedes that children do not lust for erotic materials—and that anti-porn campaigns only provoke children to investigate—the question still remains: What about post-pubescent teenagers? Don't they actively seek out internet pornography of their own accord?

The answer here depends entirely upon the gender of the teenager. Females, whether teenage or adult, are rarely aroused by visual pornography. Men may fantasize that millions of women surf the net in search of penis portraits, but such a belief reflects basic unfamiliarity with female psychology. Visual pornography is almost exclusively a male pastime.

So if we leave aside the supposed "problem" of women and children's lusting over internet porn, then the remaining demographic group is the post-pubescent teenage male. This group includes males from approximately 13 to 17 years of age, having experienced puberty and sexual maturity, but who are still legally "underage." Are these males "jeopardized" by girly pictures on the net?

When viewed in historical perspective, it is difficult to believe that teenage males are genuinely harmed by sexual images. Let us recall that throughout 99 percent of human history, males began copulating as soon as they reached sexual maturity in their early to mid teens. All other animal species likewise engage in sexual activity as soon as they are physically capable. In earlier times, teenagers commonly married, reared children, held jobs, operated businesses and occasionally ruled nations. *The World Book Encyclopedia* says, "Most teenagers mature psychologically at the rate set by their society." The reason why we, today, gasp in horror at the thought of early teenage copulation is that the Industrial Revolution necessitated formal education throughout the teen years. Today we correctly view as foolhardy any teenage couple dropping out of high school to marry or to have children. The Industrial Revolution demanded that marriage and children be postponed until formal education ended at age 18.

During the last quarter century, economic and technological advancement have required education beyond mere high school. Thus the median age of marriage rose well above 18. And, again, we viewed as foolish any couple marrying or having children before finishing college at age 22. As advanced degrees become more and more necessary in tomorrow's economy, the median marital age will likely continue to rise.

So economic reality, more than anything else, has crafted our perception that teenage males are "harmed" by sexual preoccupation. Today's male faces a frustrating gap of approximately ten years between the onset of his sexual maturity and the median marital age. Genetically and hormonally, however, today's teenage male is unchanged from the day when early teenage copulation was the accepted norm. During this extended gap between puberty and marriage, all teenage males masturbate frequently, and the overwhelming majority of them view pornography as well.

Again I pose the question: If, throughout the entirety of human history, teenage males were not "jeopardized" by full penile-vaginal intercourse with their teenage partners, how then are today's teenage males "endangered" by mere photographs of women?

No credible sociological or psychological study of this question has discerned any harmful effects whatever of a teenage male's viewing photos of nude women or of adult copulation. When all the religious and moralistic blathering is dismissed, opponents of internet porn have failed utterly to document any empirical "harm" to teenage males, who simply use porn as a masturbatory stimulant. In the end, arguments against net porn are identical to arguments voiced against masturbation itself: it grieves the Holy Ghost; it corrupts the soul; it transmutes males into monstrous criminals.

▲▼▲

Religious conservatives often quote a report issued by the Meese Commission to "substantiate" their contention that pornography leads to crime[2]—especially violent crime against women. So let's open-mindedly examine the Meese Commission, its charter and background, and the report it issued in 1986:

During the election campaign of 1980, Ronald Reagan courted and won the support of America's Fundamentalist Christian community. Historically, this voting bloc had supported Democratic candidates in presidential elections. But by 1980, Fundamentalists were fed up with "sinful" Jimmy Carter, who had supported the "satanic" Equal Rights Amendment to the U.S. Constitution. The rejection of Carter by the Fundamentalists was particularly ironic because Jimmy Carter was indisputably a devoutly religious man, who openly professed to having been "born again." Reagan's religious views, by contrast, were transparently scripted by pollsters and speech writers.

Once Reagan won the election and assumed the throne, his Fundamentalist worshipers expected the new President to wholeheartedly push their extremist agenda (i.e., end all abortions, return mandatory prayer to public schools, require high school biology courses to include Creation "science"). Whenever the Reagan Administration occasionally showed signs of slight moderation or pragmatism on social issues, the Fundamentalists openly chastised the President for "forgetting his electoral base."

So to throw a bone to this gaggle of religious malcontents, Reagan instructed Edwin Meese in 1986 to form a commission to attest the evils of pornography, a longstanding thorn in the flesh of Protestant Fundamentalists.

Edwin Meese was Reagan's ruthless, scandal-ridden, political hatchet man, who was given the job of U.S. Attorney General as a blatant political payoff. Meese was deeply entangled in the Iran-Contra scandal, the Wedtech scandal and half a dozen other sleazy affairs. But, now, Meese was to sit in moral judgment on "depraved" publications such as *Playboy* and *Penthouse*.

Meese carefully selected his cohorts for the Inquisition. Foremost among them was radio and television evangelist James Dobson, whose *Focus on the Family* broadcast was legendary for its stridently conservative, anti-porn sentiment. Other members of the Commission, though not household names like Dobson, were similarly predisposed to reflect the Meesian viewpoint. So the Commission launched its quest to discover the real truth about pornography in the United States.

Since the stated goal of the Commission was to link pornography to crime, many observers expected the members to carefully examine crime statistics and to consult with outside experts on the psychology and background of criminal offenders. The Commission, however, had other ideas. Instead of trying to discern the underlying causes of crime, Commission members decided that, before anything else, they wanted to see a little pornography for themselves. So

> "Missionaries are perfect nuisances and leave every place worse than they found it."
> —CHARLES DICKENS
> (1812–1870)

a literal truckload of material was delivered for the Commission's close inspection.

The members began by looking at twenty-five hardcore pornographic films. (One might speculate that the viewing of twenty-five such "movies" would have provided the Commission with a graphically clear impression of the subject matter. But no.) The Meese Commission decided that they needed to study *more* porno films. So they examined more—and more—and more—and more. The Commission also ordered a massive shipment of pornographic magazines, examining each one thoroughly and meticulously. By the time the Inquisition was finished, the Commission had reviewed no fewer than 2370 hardcore films, 2323 magazines and 725 books—proving that, for right-wing conservatives at least, pornography appeared to be addictive.

The Commission then published a 300-page summary of the pornography it had examined. Among the summarized movie dialogue was: "I want to taste your cum. I want you to cum in my mouth. I want to feel your hot cum squirt in my mouth." The Commission's summary contained innumerable such references and was itself one of the most pornographic documents ever compiled, setting a new milestone for government publications. (It was not until Ken Starr's sexual inquisition a decade later that Republicans trumped themselves, producing even more titillating government publications about Presidential cigars in Monica Lewinsky's vagina.)

The conclusion reached by Commission members was that they alone should be allowed to view such erotic material, whereas everyone else should be restricted by law from access. The stated rationale for such a conclusion was that "pornography causes crime." Yet the Meese Commission presented no evidence whatever to substantiate their dubious conclusion, which had been scripted and preordained from day one. The Commission's goal, however, had been achieved: the Fundamentalist "electoral base" had been pacified—temporarily, at least.

Hypocritically, members of the Meese Commission never expressed fear that they themselves might become criminals after viewing such huge volumes of pornography. They did not consider themselves poorer husbands or fathers. Nor did they consider themselves greater threats to neighborhood safety. In their defense, however, I should point out that no Commission member resorted thereafter to a life of crime—the lone exception being Meese himself. Conservatives who declare "Guns don't kill. People kill" are the same conservatives who instantly blame pornography, rather than individual choice, for every crime imaginable. Were it consistent, true conservatism would demand *less* government restriction of pornography and the internet.

▲▼▲

I don't mean to suggest that all members of the Reagan Administration were as biased and closed-minded as Edwin Meese. Reagan's Surgeon General, Dr. C. Everett Koop, was in ways the quintessence of scientific objectivity. Despite his vehemently anti-abortion views, for example, Dr. Koop refused to sign a statement prepared by Fundamentalists declaring that abortion caused women permanent psychological injury. Koop said that, despite his personal distaste for abortion, no evidence supported the assertion of prolonged psychological harm.

Koop was likewise personally opposed to pornography. But when questioned directly about the true harm of pornography, Koop responded that "only two reliable generalizations could be made about the impact of exposure to 'degrading' sexual material on its viewers: it caused them to think that a variety of sexual practices were more common than they had previously believed, and it caused them to more accurately estimate the prevalence of varied sexual practices." In other words, pornography appeared to cause no harm and was, in fact, moderately educational. This was the conclusion of an extremely conservative Surgeon General, whose courageous adherence to the scientific method precluded his echoing the party line.

Individuals of religious persuasion have every right to trumpet their objections to pornography and masturbation. But their objections, we should realize, are rooted in religion rather than science. Be very skeptical of any religious spokesperson who claims that her objections to internet pornography have nothing to do with her religious beliefs. When this crusader claims that she is trying to protect children from the dangers of the internet, what she really means is that she is trying to save teenage "souls" from Hell. Since the crusader cannot convincingly present a Scripture-based argument to a secular audience, she must concoct some fictitious "danger" that supposedly exists wholly independent of her religious convictions—i.e., photos of nude women increase the crime rate.

The best way, I have found, to "smoke out" the true motivations of anti-porn crusaders is to point out that many European nations have much lower crime rates than the United States, yet have far more liberal laws regarding pornography. Moreover, in countries such as Saudi Arabia, Iran and China, where pornography is punishable by death, violent crime against women is disgustingly common. So if crime rates are indeed "directly linked" to the volume of pornography, then we should unhesitatingly truck *more* porn into the U.S. to reduce crime as in Europe.[3] In reality, however, the true motivation of anti-porn crusaders has nothing to do with "crime rates." These Christian Fundamentalists simply want to impose their religious viewpoint on everyone else, like it or not, by force of federal and state legislation.

There are many psychological parallels between Christian Fundamentalists and the Muslim Fundamentalists who brought Ayatollah Khomeini to power in Iran in 1979. Both Fundamentalist groups want their religious beliefs enshrined as the secular Law of the Land. Both groups are absolutely intolerant of democracy or opposing viewpoints since only *their* opinions are "ordained of God." Neither group of Fundamentalists would ever permit freedom of choice, allowing each person to choose for himself whether or not to view pornography. Instead, the "scourge" of pornography must be eradicated from the face of the earth, and all smut peddlers consigned to eternal damnation. If untempered by secular culture and by the historical and legal safeguards of our Constitution, many religious zealots would today be burning "witches" as did their spiritual forefathers.

A little known yet well-documented preparatory step in the burning of a witch was the close-up inspection of her vagina by the priests and ruling male authorities. With full erections, the men inserted their fingers into the "witch's" vagina, spreading it apart in search of hidden satanic amulets. One of the reasons why witch burning continued for many centuries was that the "inspectors" enjoyed the procedure so much. It is a shame that the Meese Commission was forced by circumstance to live in the 20th century. I have no doubt that, centuries ago, the Meese Commission would have joyously searched for witches and hidden amulets with unprecedented thoroughness.

10

Was America Really Founded upon Christian Principles?

"I have found Christian dogma unintelligible. Early in life I absented myself from Christian assemblies."
—BENJAMIN FRANKLIN (1706–1790)

"Anyone who knows history will recognize that the domination of education or of government by any one particular religious faith is never a happy arrangement for the people."
—ELEANOR ROOSEVELT (1884–1962),
in a letter to Cardinal Spellman (July 23, 1949)

"We have the most religious freedom of any country in the world, including the freedom not to believe."
—BILL CLINTON, 1996 presidential debate in San Diego

Bible-thumping evangelists and right-wing politicians preach endlessly these days of "America's being founded on Christian principles." They tell us that America's Founding Fathers were all devout, born-again Christians who wanted God included in every facet of American society, and the Bible used as the moral foundation for American law and government.

But are these neoconservatives presenting us with an accurate historical record, or a revisionist history concocted to promote their own political agenda? In other words: Was America really founded upon Christian principles?

To the extent that our Founding Fathers had any religious affiliation at all, it was a tepid embracing of the philosophy of Deism, a popular system of thought in the 18th century. Deism is the belief that a supernatural Power originally created the universe but does not currently manage its day-to-day operation or intervene personally into human affairs. Thomas Jefferson, Benjamin Franklin and Thomas Paine, among many others, held Deist, rather than Christian, religious beliefs.

If one dismisses all preconceived historical inaccuracies and Christian propaganda, then an extraordinary and very revealing fact emerges: The two documents upon which our country was actually founded—i.e., the Declaration of Independence and the Constitution of the United States—contain not a single word about Christianity, Christian principles, the Bible or Jesus Christ. Neither is there any mention at all of the Ten Commandments, Heaven, Hell or being saved. Not a word! The phrase "they are endowed by their Creator with certain unalienable Rights" was a reference to the Deist Creator, rather than the God of Christianity.

The Christian clergy of the Revolutionary period tried again and again to have references to Christianity inserted directly into the U.S. Constitution, but they were refused every time by the Founders. It is no coincidence therefore that there is no reference at all to Christianity or to the Bible in the two documents which founded the United States of America. It is historically incorrect, thus, to claim that America was "founded upon Christianity."

During the Presidential campaign of 1800, Jefferson was labeled "a howling atheist" by his political opponents. Thomas Paine—author of the Revolution-inspiring pamphlet *Common Sense* and craftsman of the immortal phrase "These are the times that try men's souls"—wrote an entire book, *The Age of Reason* (still in print), which directly attacked and rejected the Bible as being the Word of God.

Two "Christian principles" may indeed have influenced the Founding Fathers as they wrote the Declaration and Constitution. One "Christian principle" all too fresh in mind was the Puritan practice of executing "witches." Jefferson wrote in *Autobiography* that "Millions of innocent men, women and children, since the introduction of Christianity, have been burnt, tortured, fined or imprisoned."

> "The day will come when the mystical generation of Jesus, by the Supreme Being as his father, in the womb of a virgin, will be classed with the fable of the generation of Minerva in the brain of Jupiter."
>
> —THOMAS JEFFERSON (1743–1826), in a letter to John Adams (April 11, 1823)

The second "Christian" influence over the Founding Fathers was King George III's absolute mandate that his subjects worship in a manner approved by the Church of England. Witch burning and mandatory church affiliation, among other factors, led the Founding Fathers to establish a "Wall of Separation between Church and State," allowing, at each citizen's discretion, freedom of religion or freedom from religion.

In 1797 the United States ratified the Treaty of Tripoli, which was negotiated by George Washington himself and signed by his successor, John Adams. The treaty declared that "the government of the United States is not, in any sense, founded on the Christian religion." Congress unanimously approved the text of this treaty.

So whom should we believe? Pulpit-pounding TV evangelists who claim America was founded upon Christianity? Or should we perhaps give the benefit of the doubt to George Washington, John Adams and a unanimous Congress at the time our nation began? Let's carefully reread their legal affirmation: "The government of the United States is not, in any sense, founded on the Christian religion." (The original text of the Treaty of Tripoli is available for your personal examination at almost any public library or on the internet.)

The national motto was not changed to "In God We Trust" until 1956, 180 years after the founding of our nation. Likewise, the phrase "under God" was not added to the Pledge of Allegiance until 1954.

Modern-day conservative propaganda about the "Christian birth of our nation" is therefore just as erroneous and self-serving as Christian pronouncements about the birth of our universe. In both cases, "men of God" completely ignore the actual evidence at hand and conjure up a fictitious tale. They then spread the myth, along with fabricated evidence, and repeat the myth so frequently that it is soon accepted uncritically by the citizenry.

Fortunately, the United States has historically chosen its leaders democratically. To be elected, a political candidate must give lip service to the prevailing religious view of the moment, regardless of his own true opinions. We may therefore easily dig up Scripture-laced quotations from almost any political figure in American history, pandering for votes from Christian believers. So it is only through looking behind the scenes—at private correspondence or statements uttered after leaving office—that an accurate historical picture may be drawn.

11

▨ "Intelligent Design": Christianity's Newest Cult

"All thinking men are atheists."
—ERNEST HEMINGWAY (1899–1961), in *A Farewell to Arms*

"I have seldom met an intelligent person whose views
were not narrowed and distorted by religion."
—JAMES BUCHANAN (1791–1868)

"That's all religion is—some principle you believe in . . . man has
accomplished far more miracles than the God he invented."
—ROD STEIGER (1925–2002), actor, in *Playboy* (1969)

The Rise of Intelligent Design

Since I published *Atheist Universe* in 2004, a powerful new Christian cult has risen to the forefront of theological debate and influence in America. This movement—advocating a philosophy called "Intelligent Design"—has preached its gospel for many years, but is now rapidly gaining popularity among Fundamentalists and Evangelicals. The movement's growing popularity directly corresponds to the general rise of the political and religious right in the United States, and, I'm sorry to say, to the dramatic decline of science literacy among the American public. Following the reelection of George W. Bush in late 2004, the Intelligent Design (or ID) movement was reinvigorated and began aggressively exercising its new political muscle, striving to bulldoze ID textbooks into public school classrooms.

The same public credulity that gave fertile ground to the ID movement also led the American electorate to gullibly swallow the religious slick-talk—or, in the case of George W. Bush, the disjointed babble—of any Bible-toting politician claiming to be "born again." Politically, it no longer mattered whether a candidate's policies led to peace and prosperity or to war and bankruptcy. Middle-class and low-income voters enthusiastically supported candidates who openly endorsed policies favoring only the wealthiest Americans. All that mattered was who, among the candidates, most loved Jesus and His Father, the Intelligent Designer of the cosmos.

I call the Intelligent Design crusade a "cult" because, as I shall demonstrate, ID espouses beliefs that bear little resemblance to Christianity's historical teachings. Neither does ID harmonize with any literal—or even metaphorical—interpretation of the Book of Genesis regarding the origin of the universe and mankind. The purpose of this chapter update is therefore twofold: (1) to rebut the "new" arguments allegedly proving Intelligent Design of the universe; and (2) to demonstrate that, even if accepted uncritically and at face value, the tenets of the ID movement conflict irreconcilably and flagrantly with traditional Bible-based Christianity—a heresy that few Fundamentalists and Evangelicals seem to recognize or appreciate.

> "The luckiest thing that ever happened to me was that my father didn't believe in God, and so he had no hang-ups about souls. I see ourselves as products of evolution, which itself is a great mystery."
>
> —JAMES WATSON, Nobel Prize–winning biologist and co-discoverer of DNA's structure, in *Discover* magazine (July 2003)

Historical Background

One may argue that the philosophy of Intelligent Design is as old as religion itself, since religion, almost by definition, must incorporate some belief in an Intelligent Designer of the cosmos. But the origin of the current ID campaign is more recent. So let's briefly review when and how this new sect came into being, and what, precisely, it teaches:

In 1859, British naturalist Charles Darwin published his historic volume, *The Origin of Species*, which presented his collected evidence for evolution by natural selection. Although Darwin's original volume made no reference to the evolution of human beings, the implication was evident to the Christian community. Few of the religious faithful realized that Darwin had initially intended to become a Christian minister, having studied theology at Cambridge University. But in 1871, Darwin published another work, *The Descent of Man*, which unequivocally asserted the evolution of human beings as well. Since that time, Charles Darwin has been despised, misrepresented and unethically vilified by the world's Christian clergy. Although Darwin was a highly honored man and is entombed at Westminster Abbey, the very mention of his name leaves a rancid taste in the mouths of religious Fundamentalists.

An early and historic showdown between evolution and Christianity occurred in 1925 in Dayton, Tennessee. John Scopes, a high school biology teacher, was charged with the crime of teaching evolution—a "crime" that he openly confessed to having committed. But the "Scopes Monkey Trial" continued nonetheless as a vehicle to publicly promote the views of the two opposing camps. Representing Scopes—and defending evolutionary theory—was the prominent trial attorney Clarence Darrow. Arguing for the prosecution—and

> "I don't believe in God because I don't believe in Mother Goose."
>
> —CLARENCE DARROW (1857–1938), trial lawyer, from a speech in Toronto, Canada (1930)

defending Bible-based creationism—was William Jennings Bryan, former U.S. Secretary of State and three-time Democratic Presidential candidate. Although Scopes was eventually convicted of teaching evolution and fined 100 dollars, the trial proved to be a public-relations disaster for creationism. During the eloquent interchange at the trial, creationism was clearly shown to be a religious dogma rather than a scientific fact. Evolution was publicly vindicated as the scientific foundation of biological study. Bryan and the creationists were humiliated at the trial and Bryan literally dropped dead in Dayton within a week of the trial's conclusion.

Public perception of evolution's triumph, however, did not mirror practical reality. Although the Scopes trial revealed the scientific folly of Bible-based creationism, the real-world consequence of the trial was that textbook publishers became afraid thereafter to include any reference to evolution in their science books, fearing a hostile backlash or boycott from Fundamentalists. So from 1925 until the late 1950s, American schoolchildren were taught little or nothing about evolutionary science. American students therefore fell academically behind students in other developed countries, where science education was emphasized.

In 1957, however, America was shaken when the Soviet Union successfully launched a satellite into space, an unprecedented scientific achievement. *Sputnik I* orbited above our heads, worrying Americans that Soviet scientific superiority would lead to nuclear bombs being dropped on our cities from space. America quickly revamped its science education programs in an effort to catch up to the Soviets. The U.S. federal budget allocation for math and science education was doubled, and antiquated science textbooks were revised.

By the early 1960s, evidence supporting evolution had accumulated to such a voluminous degree that no science textbook could possibly omit reference to Darwin's theory. New and updated science textbooks—including evolutionary science— were purchased by the government for all public school students in the United States. Evolutionary science then became part of America's public school curriculum.

Needless to say, the teaching of evolution in public schools was met with rabid opposition from the conservative Christian community. To them, evolution in the schools conjured up images of Sodom and Gomorrah, and the religious right was certain that America would suffer the same fate unless some dramatic effort were undertaken to save our nation's soul from the Darwinian heresy.

This perceived spiritual crisis—i.e., the immediate necessity of stopping evolution before it corrupted our children in the public schools—gave birth to the movement called Scientific Creationism, whose name was soon thereafter changed to Creation science. Founded principally by Henry Morris, a Virginia hydraulic engineer, Creation science sought to explain Earth's geology, including the fossil record, within the framework of a literal interpretation of the Book of Genesis.

Morris and his followers authored dozens of books claiming to prove that God directly created the heavens and the Earth only 6000 years ago, as Genesis demanded in its genealogical records. The six days of Creation Week, along with the story of Adam and Eve, were likewise argued by Creation science to be literal facts, rather than religious metaphor or mythology. In his most famous book, *The Genesis Flood*, Morris asserted that the Old Testament story of Noah's Ark was true as well and that science could confirm the actual occurrence of this worldwide deluge. The Creation science movement overtly strove to replace or supplement the teaching of evolution in public schools with Scripture-based tales of human origins. Morris and company attempted to strong-arm local schoolboards into buying and using their Creation science textbooks.

Although religious Fundamentalists openly thanked God for these Creation science textbooks, dispassionate observers in the scientific establishment recognized these texts as Bible-based rather than science-based. Morris and his legions did enjoy limited, momentary success in placing their textbooks into a few public schools. But the Creation science campaign was, overall, a failure and an embarrassment to educated religious believers. The world's entire professional scientific body officially opposed and methodically fought against the teaching of Creation science, correctly labeling it a blatant pseudoscience. Evolution continued to be taught in public schools. And Creation science eventually lost the battle entirely.

The Fundamentalists, however, were not about to resign themselves to the teaching of evolution in public schools. After a period of rethinking and regrouping—and a brief timeout to impeach Bill Clinton for lying about a blow job—the religious right once again marshaled its power as George W. Bush became Commander-in-Chief. The "new and improved" Creation science would now be repackaged, remarketed and renamed "Intelligent Design."

A New Cult Emerges

Essentially, ID teaches that our universe and the life within it are too complex to have arisen without the guiding force of an Intelligent Designer. Although Creation science likewise believed that God was necessary to explain Nature's complexity, ID distinguishes itself from Creation science in one surprising and controversial way:

> "So far as I can remember, there is not one word in the Gospels in praise of intelligence."
>
> —LORD BERTRAND RUSSELL (1872–1970), British Nobel Laureate, mathematician, philosopher and peace activist

Creation science taught that the Bible was literally true—both Old and New Testaments—whereas ID does not accept the literal truth of the entire Bible.

Leaders of the current ID movement do seem to wholeheartedly embrace the New Testament, believing that Jesus literally walked on water, literally filled pigs with demons, literally cast a magic spell on a fig tree, literally rose from the dead, etc. But the voluminous writings of the preachers of ID leave no doubt that they do not believe the Old Testament in the same literal sense, if at all. ID openly accepts contemporary Big Bang cosmology, which, when discussed honestly, bears no similarity whatever to the six-day Creation Story of Adam and Eve in the Book of Genesis. By traditional Christian canon, therefore, the ID movement is a cult, because ID rejects historically accepted Bible teachings and inter-pretations. Instead, ID preaches modernistic revisionism, contrary to the doctrines of conventional, Bible-based Christianity.

For 2000 years, Christians of all persuasions—both Catholic and Protestant—believed in the Genesis account of Creation. Even Jews and many non-Christians affirmed the teachings of Genesis 1:1—"In the beginning, God created the heavens and the Earth." Historically, this verse was universally accepted to mean that God literally created the heavens (i.e., the planets, moons, stars and galaxies) and the Earth at the beginning of time. The truth and meaning of this doctrine were unambiguous and undis-puted for twenty centuries.

Today, however, the ID movement forthrightly rejects this Bible teaching. To its credit, ID has recognized the scientific reality that the universe, or "the heavens," existed 8 to 10 billion years *prior* to the formation of the Earth. The heavens and the Earth were *not* created together "in the beginning" after all. There was a multibillion-year gap separating their two origins. While I cer-tainly applaud ID for moving into the 21st century on the study of astronomy, we must point out, for consistency's sake, that ID's newly adopted cosmology conflicts starkly and dramatically with Christianity's historical teachings and with the unequivocal state-ment of Genesis 1:1—i.e., the heavens and the Earth were created together "in the beginning." Rather than glossing over this crucial timeframe discrepancy as ID leaders would prefer us to do, we must highlight and emphasize this disparity as a fundamental and irreconcilable conflict between current ID doctrine and the Book of Genesis.

If, as science tells us, the cosmos is roughly 14 billion years old and Earth is 5 billion years old, then Earth is only about one-third the age of the universe as a whole (generally speaking). By analogy, a football game is 60 minutes of playing time. Two-thirds of that time—or the game's first 40 minutes—would represent the time the cosmos existed before Earth formed. Would it be fair to claim that a touchdown scored during the game's fortieth minute—or five minutes before the start of the fourth quarter—was scored "in the beginning" of the game? I don't think that any reasonable person could truthfully answer yes to this question. Neither can anyone honestly assert that the 14-billion-year-old heavens and a 5-billion-year-old Earth were both created together "in the beginning," as Genesis 1:1 declares.

> "I'm not somebody who goes to church on a regular basis. The specific elements of Christianity are not something I'm a huge believer in."
> —BILL GATES

The point here is twofold: (1) Genesis 1:1 is in error, and (2) by recognizing this error and rejecting even the opening verses of the Bible, the ID cult has forsaken traditional, Bible-based Christianity.

ID Hypocrisy

While disdainfully blaming "liberals" and "liberal theology" for every imaginable evil, ID leaders hypocritically embrace the core tenet of liberal theology—i.e., the belief that Genesis is not to be taken literally. ID's preachers of course claim that they believe Genesis as written, but, like the liberal theologians they deride, they engage in tormented, Herculean, bend-over-backward, ankle-behind-the-ear philosophical gymnastics to "reinterpret" the Book of Genesis in harmony with modern science. As George Bernard Shaw observed, "No man ever believes that the Bible means what it says: He is always convinced that it says what *he* means."

For twenty centuries, Christianity taught that God created the heavens, the Earth and all of Earth's lifeforms during the six literal days of Creation Week. Anyone who doubted this truth was labeled a heretic and genuinely risked being tortured or executed by the Church for heresy. Christian scholars argued that, within the Book of Genesis itself, God Himself provided a clear and specific definition of "day" as used in the Creation account:

> *"And the evening and the morning were the first day."*
> —Genesis 1:5

> *"And the evening and the morning were the second day."*
> —Genesis 1:8

> *"And the evening and the morning were the third day."*
> —Genesis 1:13

Moses, the supposed author of the opening five books of the Bible, directly linked the six literal days of Creation Week to the length of a man's workweek:

> *"Six days you shall labor and do all your work, but the seventh day is a Sabbath to the Lord your God. For in six days the Lord made the heavens and the Earth . . . and rested on the seventh day."*
> —Exodus 20:9,11

Are we to believe that man's workweek was six *eons* long—rather than six literal days long—before God permitted man a day of rest for the Sabbath? A non-literal interpretation of these passages is thoroughly dishonest and wholly disingenuous. Scholars additionally pointed out that in the original Hebrew text of Genesis, the word "day" is *yom*, which, when used with an ordinal—e.g., first day, second day, third day—refers invariably to a literal 24-hour period throughout the entire Bible.

So there was never any doubt voiced—or even contemplated—that "day" didn't mean "day" in the Book of Genesis. Even Henry Morris and other Creation science champions reaffirmed completely their belief that Genesis was literally true.

Not so for the ID followers. They reject Genesis as being literally true but can't seem to bring themselves to say that Genesis is literally false. They are torn schizophrenically between their emotional dependence on the local religion and their embarrassment at having to accept the serpent in the Garden along with their Savior on the cross. The ID cultists want to be counted among the religious faithful, but long to be perceived as science-minded as well.

ID's evangelists are embarrassed by the content of their own Bible. Despite innumerable biblical references to "the devil," ID's preachers never use the term publicly because they are ashamed of it. Despite chapter after morbid chapter in the Bible describing a literal, fiery hell for non-Christians, ID never mentions the lake of fire because hell and the devil conflict with ID's highest goal— to appear rational and urbane. When asked directly whether they believe that all non-Christians will burn eternally in hell, ID leaders avoid the issue by claiming that "it is not for them to judge." They are, of course, among the most judgmental human beings on Earth. ID's refusal to discuss the fiery damnation of non-Christians is evidence not of the movement's nonjudgmental character, but of their embarrassment and attempts to ignore and hide the Bible's actual teachings.

ID has likewise outgrown the "Holy Ghost," forsaking any public utterance of this sacred Christian term, and only occasionally referring instead to the now-updated "Holy Spirit." ID supporters would probably feel more comfortable and less conflicted by starting a completely new religion, tossing out all the absurd mythical baggage from Christianity. But they are stuck—psychologically, emotionally and financially—with the Holy Book of the ruling majority. They must therefore "reinterpret," rather than rewrite, their Holy Scriptures.

One striking difference between the previous Creation science movement and the new ID bandwagon is that whenever conflict appeared to exist between science and Scripture, Creation science, despite its name, would abandon or distort science in favor of Scripture. ID, however, habitually abandons or distorts Scripture in favor of science—definitely a positive step in my atheistic opinion, but a habit that leaves ID's message convoluted and heretical to traditional Christianity.

If ID's defenders have suddenly changed their interpretation of the Book of Genesis, their change of heart did not result from a sudden change in the text of Genesis. They flip-flopped instead because the ID movement is blown by the wind of current secular thought, and values intellectual respectability over devotion to the Bible. In this very crucial respect, then, ID has already conceded its subservience to secular science.

To me, what is among the most astounding examples of ID's abandonment of Scripture is Gerald Schroeder's book *The Science of God*. Schroeder actually argues that the Book of Genesis makes reference to Einstein's theory of relativity! Allegedly, Einstein's time-dilation explains why the Creation "days" are actually long eons of time. Elsewhere in the book, Schroeder declares that quantum mechanics can be used to explain other apparent contradictions between Genesis and the findings of modern science. To call such reinterpretations of Scripture "a stretch" is to be excessively generous.

Moreover, as is well known among physicists, relativity and quantum mechanics are mutually exclusive when extrapolated beyond their regional spheres. So if the Bible is supposedly anchored both on relativity and quantum mechanics, then parts of the Bible will have to be scrapped when a unified theory of physics is finally achieved. Such future forsaking of Scripture, however, should pose no problem whatever for the ID cult, which already has rejected much of the Bible in favor of current secular trends.

> "If god wanted people to believe in him, why'd he invent logic then?"
>
> —DAVID FEHERTY, PGA tour golfer, CBS Sports commentator, Feherty website: www.protourgolfers.com/announcers/feherty

In many ways, ID leaders haven't yet *decided* what to believe or teach. They love to cite the Cambrian Explosion as purportedly disproving evolution. The Cambrian Explosion refers to a period of Earth's geologic history, approximately 570 million years ago, when many new lifeforms first appeared in the geologic column. Is the Cambrian Explosion supposed to represent Creation Week as portrayed in the Book of Genesis? ID leaders never tell us the answer, even though they themselves teasingly raised the possibility.

ID acknowledges the existence of simple Precambrian life-forms and grudgingly confesses that Cambrian rock layers contain the remains of neither reptiles nor mammals. Both of these facts contradict a simultaneous Creation of all life by God at the Cambrian Explosion. Simple life existed *prior to* Cambrian times, whereas modern lifeforms did not appear until millions of years *after* the Cambrian Explosion. But since most ID books make no attempt whatever to harmonize their philosophies with the Bible, we are left to draw our own conclusions. ID defenders want this geologic chronology to be vague and unimportant in your mind because the specifics are not on ID's side. Apparently, God first created simple life in Precambrian times. Then God really got ambitious and created many new lifeforms at the Cambrian Explosion. Only later, however, did God create the higher forms of life such as reptiles and mammals. Finally—and fairly recently on the geologic timescale—God created man. In other words, ID essentially proposes—to the degree that it proposes any chronology at all—that God's progressive method of Creation precisely mimicked evolution by natural selection!

ID's Logical Downfall

If evolution by natural selection adequately explains the complexity of life on our planet, then why do Intelligent Design enthusiasts reject this scientific explanation?

Many of the preceding chapters of this book address and rebut the challenges posed to evolutionary theory by Christian Fundamentalists. Since the ID movement consists almost exclusively of Fundamentalists, their objections to evolution are identical to those of the Creation science campaign discussed in earlier chapters.

The one additional ingredient that ID stirs into the cauldron of creationist pseudoscience is summarized in two simple words: backward reasoning. Through the use—or misuse—of *ex post facto* (i.e., after the fact) reasoning, ID theory can make any event, circumstance, consequence, operation, causal antecedent, object or lifeform appear to be miraculously complex and, thus, evidence of an Intelligent Designer. This logical fallacy is at the absolute heart of ID philosophy. So I want to pause briefly here to provide a good, clear illustration of exactly what I mean by "backward reasoning" and to share with you how I myself recently fell victim to this logical error.

A few months ago, I was flipping through a magazine late at night. Almost asleep, I happened upon an intriguing fact within the text of an article on geography. I read that "almost every major city in the entire United States has a river running directly beside it."

This was a startling revelation to me. The chances seemed infinitesimally small, I thought, that all of these cities should be coincidentally blessed with both a necessary supply of drinking water and a valuable means of transportation. Was Divine Benevolence perhaps involved in the incredibly fortunate placement of all these rivers?

After a moment of fatigued bewilderment, I realized that my reasoning was totally backward. The rivers weren't placed in their locations because the cities needed them. Rather, the cities were settled and grew up around the rivers, which were essential to the survival of the inhabitants. Any dispute over this question could be quickly resolved by noting the order of events—*first* came the rivers, *then* came the cities. But when erroneously perceived in a backward fashion, as I had done, the convenient placement of the rivers seemed almost miraculous in design.

Let's look at a more complex illustration of backward logic. Outside your home, let's imagine, you discover a large hole in the ground. This hole, let's say, is of a particularly irregular shape. It's not perfectly cylindrical nor rectangular. There are many twists, turns and asymmetric angles and curves to this hole. After much study and careful analysis, you realize that a scientific description of this hole would require no fewer than 10,000 data points on a three-dimensional graph. You painstakingly plot them all using CAD (Computer Aided Design) software and eventually create a perfect reproduction of the hole on your computer monitor. There's no doubt that the computer-generated graphic of your hole in the ground was done through intelligent design.

After weeks of work on your 10,000 data points, an unexpected thunderstorm completely fills your hole with water, which freezes solid overnight. After meticulously surveying this new block of ice sitting in the hole, you conclude that a Divine miracle has occurred. Why? Because your irregularly shaped hole is observed to be precisely the same shape as the ice now filling it. How did the hole know beforehand what shape it needed to be? This absolutely perfect matching of all 10,000 data points (between the hole and the ice) defies indisputably the laws of probability and chance. How could the hole have been fine-tuned with such precision without the aid of an Intelligent Designer? You calculate that, even if each one of your data points had only two possible values—0 and 1—the odds would be hundreds of trillions to one against the hole's being exactly the shape necessary to hold the irregular block of ice. You conclude that the only plausible explanation is that the hole was Intelligently Designed by a supernatural Creator.

Does this story sound ridiculous to you—or even insulting to your intelligence? Does the logical flaw seem so obvious that any kindergarten student could immediately recognize the error? Again, the chronology and logic are backward in the example. The hole existed first, and the water and ice that came later and filled the hole had to conform their shape to the surroundings. The hole did not transform itself ahead of time into the shape of the future ice-block.

We may scrawl fancy mathematical equations over dozens of pages in a high-brow analysis of the ice-block's shape and the hole's shape, but no miracle has occurred. It is only when our logic is backward that an Intelligent Designer seems necessary to explain the perfect matching of their shapes.

If you do indeed find this entire scenario a bit juvenile, then your rational faculties should not hesitate to dismiss immediately the core doctrines of ID theory, since their "proofs" of an Intelligent Designer, as we shall see, are based upon an identical error of backward reckoning.

ID's most-repeated argument for God's existence is called *The Anthropic Principle*—so named because mankind (anthro) is supposedly the reason why the universe exists and displays the characteristics that it does. In other words, the universe—even before Earth and mankind existed within it—transfigured itself, through God's Intelligent Design, into a form accommodating the needs of the humans who would follow billions of years later. Life on Earth did not develop and evolve to fit the environment as it was. No. The entire cosmos was personally tailored beforehand by Jesus' Father to match human specifications.

It seems almost superfluous to rebut this ID argument other than to ask: Which came first: the universe or mankind? If mankind came first and the universe followed later—displaying the characteristics necessary for human survival—then we might wonder about this incredibly fortunate coincidence and search for a possible Intelligent Designer of the universe. If, however, the universe came first, and life developed afterward, then obviously life was forced, like it or not, to adapt to the environment in which it found itself. Evolution by natural selection provides a completely satisfying and comprehensive explanation to the fine-tuning between a lifeform's needs and the environment in which it lives. It is only when our logic is backward that an Intelligent Designer seems required.

ID churchmen have an unassailable right to preach that God created the universe for man's benefit. Their freedom of religious expression is not at issue. Neither is the question whether humanity and other lifeforms are suited to their environments. Often they are indeed suited, though extinction has globally eradicated most of the species that ever existed on Earth due to *mismatches* with their environments. The salient issue, rather, is whether: (a) the universe adapted itself ahead of time to suit humanity; or (b) life on Earth adapted to fit the environment as it was. I submit to you that ID's Anthropic Principle is no more scientific or logical than asserting the hole's preemptive conformity to the ice-block, or the rivers' positioning themselves for the benefit of future cities. The Anthropic Principle is a supremely egotistical manifestation of human self-centeredness, self-delusion and self-importance gone into orbit. ID's man-centered universe is hauntingly reminiscent of Christianity's medieval belief in an Earth-centered universe.

Obviously, ID's Anthropic Principle assumes beforehand a Creator's Intelligent Design of the cosmos—a claim that ID is supposedly "proving" through its argumentation. ID's circular argument therefore proves nothing whatever and reverts to being blind-faith religion rather than science.

More ID Bloopers

When assessing the arguments of the Intelligent Design movement, a fact that we should continually reiterate is that no new evidence for a Creator is being postulated. ID is merely the deceptive repackaging and remarketing of old, discredited arguments. The previous Creation science effort suffered a painful crucifixion and was laid in a tomb. ID is the attempted resurrection of Creation science in a new body and form. Here are some additional examples of reincarnated bloopers, logical blunders, and wacky assertions proffered by ID evangelists:

THE DOGMA OF "IRREDUCIBLE COMPLEXITY"

A common argument pervading ID books is that even cellular life is extraordinarily complex. We are told that the DNA sequence of the simplest lifeform contains more information than an entire set of encyclopedias. So only an Intelligent Designer could have created this "irreducibly complex" structure—i.e., a structure whose every part is essential to its operation and survival.

The error of this argument is that, once again using backward logic, ID cites a *modern* example of life—the result of four billion years of cellular evolution—then asks how such a complicated structure could randomly pop into existence. Needless to say, such complexity *couldn't* randomly pop into existence, and no origin-of-life researcher ever made such an outlandish proposal. ID arguments appealing to the DNA sequence are empty strawmen. The first cells *had no* DNA. They reproduced their simple forms merely by division—i.e., by falling apart.

The intricate double-helix structure of DNA was finally unraveled in 1953 by the brilliant work of Francis Crick and James Watson. For their historic discovery, Crick and Watson were awarded the 1962 Nobel Prize in physiology. Because ID is incessantly pointing to the structure of DNA as evidence of Intelligent Design (even though the first cells contained no DNA), let's hear what Crick and Watson themselves have to say about this matter:

> *"If revealed religions have revealed anything it is that they are usually wrong."*
>
> *"A knowledge of the true age of the Earth and of the fossil record makes it impossible for any balanced intellect to believe in the literal truth of every part of the Bible in the way that fundamentalists do. And if some of the Bible is manifestly wrong, why should any of the rest of it be accepted automatically?"*
>
> —Francis Crick,
> "How I Got Inclined towards Atheism"
> from his autobiography *What Mad Pursuit*

> *"Today, the theory of evolution is an accepted fact for everyone but a fundamentalist minority, whose objections are based not on reasoning but on doctrinaire adherence to religious principles."*

"The luckiest thing that ever happened to me was that my father didn't believe in God, and so he had no hang-ups about souls. I see ourselves as products of evolution, which itself is a great mystery."

—James Watson,
"Discover Dialogue: Reversing Bad Truths"
in *Discover* (July 2003)

Does it sound to you like Crick and Watson agree or disagree with ID theory on DNA? To whom should we give more credibility on the subject of DNA: the two scientists who won a Nobel Prize for its discovery, or ID pulpit-pounders?

ID frequently misuses the vaguely defined term "irreducible complexity." ID proponent Michael Behe has convinced his readers that evolution has no means of explaining complex systems. But natural selection is, in reality, extraordinarily efficient in its production of multifaceted lifeforms. The creed of "irreducible complexity" is yet another attempt to propose a single-step, supernatural "explanation" of life—an "explanation" that assumes pre-existing Divine complexity, and therefore explains nothing at all. Natural selection, by contrast, does indeed provide a workable, realistic, testable, mechanistic explanation as to how complexity may arise from simplicity.

Showing that a system is "irreducibly complex" does not indicate that a gradual, natural development of the system did not occur. Nature is replete with diverse biological systems spanning the entire gamut from the very simple to the highly intricate—with every intermediate level of complexity still available today for our direct visual observation. ID's demand for an all-or-nothing appearance of complexity within a something-from-nothing universe reflects an extremist mindset incapable of subtle perceptions of gradation. The notion of irreducible complexity likewise assumes erroneously that all parts of a system must always have functioned expressly as they do today and that other uses and adaptive advantages were impossible during the lifeforms evolutionary development—all bogus assumptions.

Finally, ID needs a cold slap in the face to a disagreeable reality: very few naturally occurring systems or lifeforms are actually irreducibly complex. Portions of the human genetic sequence, for example, are redundant, while body parts such as our appendix and wisdom teeth are actually detrimental to our well-being. Cancer, a naturally occurring disorder of the cells, kills millions of innocent victims every year worldwide. Employing the fallacy of selective observation, ID cites complexity as evidence of God only when the results of complexity are desirable, such as a healthy, functioning human body. If, however, the results of complexity are adverse, such as a complex killer virus or an intricately constructed parasite or multifarious incurable disease, ID ascribes the complexity solely to natural causes.

ID'S MISUSE OF STATISTICS

The ID crusade is notorious for its persistent and deliberate misuse of statistics. A question continually posed to atheists by ID defenders is: "What are the odds that the universe would, at random, be perfectly fine-tuned to support human life?"

We have already seen that the universe was not "fine-tuned" to support human life. Rather, human life—and life in general— were fine-tuned to the universe through natural selection. ID then continues its argument with a related, follow-up question: "What are the odds, then, that the universe would display the exact characteristics that it does?"

When a statistical analysis of this question starts at the conclusion of events, and assumes that this final result was inevitable from the start—as ID invariably does through its backward reasoning—then the odds are indeed miniscule that the cosmos would display the specific properties that it now displays. But by such a convoluted analysis, the odds against *any* specific properties existing and operating within the cosmos are miniscule.

What are the odds, by analogy, against your having the specific Social Security number that you do? If you're like me, then you have a nine-digit number, allowing the possibility of one billion combinations of digits. Considering that the federal government could have randomly generated any nine-digit number that it wished for your card, the chances were literally one-in-a-billion that you would

> "If fifty million people say a foolish thing, it's still a foolish thing."
>
> —LORD BERTRAND RUSSELL (1872–1970), British Nobel Laureate, mathematician, philosopher and peace activist

receive your current number. Do you therefore possess a miraculous Social Security number? No. Why not? Because there was no predetermined necessity of your having a specific number.

This necessity of predetermining or prophesying an exact outcome is why state lotteries are almost impossible for individuals to win. You must perfectly predict the winning numbers from millions of possible combinations. Although the lucky winners probably do believe that their jackpot was Divinely ordained, most dispassionate observers would discount God's hand-selecting the winning ping-pong balls. So even where a prediction is essential, such as a state lottery, and even when our predicted numbers win the jackpot, there is no scientific reason to postulate a Creator's intervention. When there is no predicted outcome—such as the particular physical state of the universe—laws of probability become altogether meaningless and irrelevant when misapplied *ex post facto*.

There was no preordained or predetermined reason why the universe had to be the way it is today. To believe there was indeed such a predetermined reason (the Anthropic Principle) is to incorporate ID's conclusions of Design into the "supporting" premise of ID's argument—thus invalidating the entire logical syllogism. Theoretically, "life as we know it" could have been "life as we don't know it" or "life as we can't possibly imagine it" or "life at another place and time" or "something other than life" or "no life at all." It is only when our reasoning is backward—i.e., when we believe after the fact that things had to emerge as they are today— that a mystical aura muddies our thinking and contaminates our mathematical analyses of events. ID's logical mistake is to assume what it sets out to prove. ID assumes that mankind's appearance was inevitable. Why? Because the Bible says so. Yet we are told over and over that the theory of Intelligent Design rests solely upon science.

So is it just a fortunate accident, then, that the universe supports human life? No, it is no accident at all. Life was tailored through natural selection to the environment in which it found itself. Contrary to the distortions of ID's preachers and the Creation science evangelists who preceded them, evolution is not governed by "blind chance" and "fortunate accident." (See Chapter 5.)

"DARWINISM" AND THE ICONS OF EVOLUTION

In a very consistent and calculated effort, ID apologists almost invariably refer to evolution as "Darwinism," rather than evolution. ID irrationally believes that if tiny errors can be found within Charles Darwin's 150-year-old body of work, then "Darwinism" will be discredited and, presumably, Intelligent Design will be vindicated.

For example, Darwin drew a variety of sketches during his years of research, speculating how the tree of life may have evolved and how various lifeforms may be related to one another. Incredibly, fossil discoveries during these subsequent 150 years have revealed much of Darwin's intuition to have been beautifully on target. Quite unsurprisingly, however, some elements of Darwin's speculative drawings have been shown to be partially inaccurate or incomplete. The tree of life branched and evolved in different directions from those Darwin originally conjectured.

ID's supporters become giddy with glee and dance a jig in the Holy Ghost when they point out small errors in these 150-year-old sketches. If the ID movement can link evolution directly and solely to Charles Darwin—by renaming it "Darwinism"—then ID imagines that evolutionary theory has been falsified. We could of course play the same childish game by pointing out that Thomas Aquinas—13th-century architect of ID's "First Cause" argument—

believed that the eyes of a menstruating woman affected a mirror. Would this centuries-old trivia invalidate ID's current arguments regarding the existence of a Creator? No.

While Charles Darwin was indeed the historical personality given credit for first describing evolution by natural selection, the voluminous evidence available today to document evolution has little to do with Darwin's original work. Literally tens of thousands of fossils have been unearthed in the years since Darwin's death, and these fossils—rather than Darwin's drawings or other work—provide the proof of biological evolution.

Another reason why ID's supporters refer to evolution as "Darwinism" is that they are embarrassed to state that they reject evolution completely. Rejecting "Darwinism," however, somehow seems more palatable and less humiliating to those striving to camouflage themselves as scientists.

Besides Darwin's drawings, ID resurrects from the past numerous other antiquated and irrelevant arguments. Jonathan Wells, an Intelligent Design sage, wrote a book titled *Icons of Evolution*, which criticized Darwin's original drawings, as well as other historical memorabilia. Following publication of his book, many of the experts Wells cited in the text as supporters of his arguments publicly rebutted and lambasted him for completely distorting and misquoting their statements and the evidence itself.

Another "Icon of Evolution" Wells attempts to discredit is the transitional fossil known as *Archaeopteryx*. Despite the obvious and indisputable fact that *Archaeopteryx* displayed both avian and reptilian characteristics, Wells simply labels it "a bird," believing that he can define out of existence this powerful evidence of macro-evolution. Not only do ID writers such as Wells gloss over and pervert such evidence for evolution, but many of their belittled and criticized "Icons of Evolution" are icons only to the ID congregation itself. The true scientific community hasn't cited Wells' "Icons" as the primary evidence for evolution in fifty years.

ID FALSEHOODS ABOUT BIG BANG COSMOLOGY

Despite its pretentious facade of sincerity, there is a surplus of deliberate distortion of fact within ID. At present, Lee Strobel is probably the most famous author and hero of the ID faction. His books have sold millions of copies. He is a wildly popular speaker at Republican church gatherings, and he is himself a Fundamentalist pastor. The following words are highlighted on the cover of Strobel's mega-selling book *The Case for a Creator*:

> *"Cosmologists agree that the universe arose suddenly out of absolute nothingness. But how? And how did it unfold with such painstaking precision?"*

This jacket blurb is the worst conceivable misrepresentation of fact. Strobel's promotional teaser does indeed accurately describe the content of his book. But that is unfortunately the problem. Chapter after chapter, Strobel ridicules the folly of a (supposedly secular) something-from-nothing origin of the universe—an argument that is an artificially propped up strawman, erected by Strobel solely to be knocked down. Cosmologists emphatically do *not* assert "that the universe arose suddenly out of absolute nothingness." Strobel's mischaracterization is not only a total distortion of current cosmological thought, but it is typical of the ID movement's use of the logical error known as "suppressed quantification."

In the error of suppressed quantification, the number of "experts" endorsing your position is deliberately withheld to create the illusion of popular support. Strobel says "cosmologists agree"—meaning, two or more cosmologists. Perhaps, in the entire world, there may be two isolated cosmologists who agree "that the universe arose suddenly out of absolute nothingness." But this is not an opinion held by any respected authority of whom I am aware.

Stephen Hawking, the world's preeminent cosmologist, says that the universe had neither a starting point nor a supernatural beginning. Hawking clearly states in *A Brief History of Time*:

"So long as the universe had a beginning, we could sup-pose it had a creator. But if the universe is really com-pletely self-contained, having no boundary or edge, it would have neither beginning nor end: it would simply be. What place, then, for a creator?" (page 141).

This is likewise the view of every respected cosmologist on Earth. But the proponents of ID cannot live with this state of affairs, since it flatly contradicts their dire need for a something-from-nothing beginning to the universe. Like most of the general public, ID thoroughly misinterprets Big Bang cosmology as pro-posing a magical, something-from-nothing appearance of mass-energy immediately prior to universal expansion. Again, this is a bogus interpretation and misuse of science. Strobel's books and radio commercials also distort the words of Carl Sagan, Steven Weinberg, Richard Dawkins, J. B. S. Haldane, Francis Crick, Stephen Jay Gould and Linus Pauling—all resolute atheists—giv-ing the vulgar misimpression that their words lend credibility to the theory of Intelligent Design.

THE *KALAM* ARGUMENT: LIPSTICK ON A PIG

The overriding goal for most of ID's spokesmen and writers is to be perceived as towering intellectuals by their fellow Republican churchmen. They know all too well that the professional scientific establishment dismisses their blind-faith dogma as pseudoscien-tific mysticism. So in an overly compensatory effort, advocates of Intelligent Design deliberately fill their sermons and books with complicated jargon and wordy gobbledygook in an attempt to look like intellectual supermen. For example, the age-old "First Cause" argument is no longer called the "First Cause" argument. Now, ID has repackaged this chestnut as the long-winded, speech-length *Kalam* argument. (Quite appropriately, the word *Kalam* is of Arabic origin meaning "speech.") The only difference between the *Kalam* argument and the First Cause argument is that the *Kalam* argument begs the question twice instead of only once.

The original First Cause argument was flawed in that it demanded a cause for *everything*, but then abruptly changed its rules midstream, flip-flopping that the rule didn't actually apply to God, Who *always* existed. As we discussed at length in Chapter 2, we can offer instead a much simpler supposition: that the mass-energy comprising our universe always existed. Such an assumption harmonizes beautifully with our physical laws of the conservation of mass-energy, which forbid Creation *ex nihilo* (i.e., out of nothing)—an essential tenet of ID philosophy.

We therefore have three possibilities:

(1) Mass-energy never existed and doesn't exist today. This possibility is inherently ridiculous because the universe obviously does exist. No one actually holds this view.

(2) Mass-energy did not exist at some point in the distant past; but it does exist today. This assumption would mean that the laws of physics were violated at least once through an *ex nihilo* Creation event.

(3) The mass-energy comprising our universe always existed. This assumption is far simpler than presupposing a highly complex series of Divine Creation miracles and a supernatural Being. The principle of Ockham's Razor—that the simplest explanation is usually the most accurate—prefers this supposition. Moreover, this supposition would not violate the mass-energy conservation laws since we are ruling out an *ex nihilo* Creation event. Mass-energy always existed. This proposition does not argue, however, that the universe as we *observe* it today always existed. We know our current universe had a beginning. But the eventual build-

> "It was, of course, a lie what you read about my religious convictions, a lie which is being systematically repeated. I do not believe in a personal God and I have never denied this but have expressed it clearly. If something is in me which can be called religious then it is the unbounded admiration for the structure of the world so far as our science can reveal it."
>
> —ALBERT EINSTEIN (1879–1955), in his biography *Albert Einstein: The Human Side*

ing blocks of our universe did always exist. The main objection to this hypothesis is psychological, rather than scientific, as we discussed in previous chapters.

In point of fact, there is actually a fourth possibility owing to vacuum fluctuation physics. Cosmologists have described the sudden appearance of matter out of what appears to be completely empty space. Matter may spontaneously appear in one of two ways: (1) from a preexisting energy field, or (2) from quite literally nothing. The reason why this latter appearance of matter— i.e., the zero-state theory—does not violate the mass-energy conservation law is that the matter produced in this way is composed equally of positive and negative energy: positive energy in the instance of material objects and negative energy in the generation of accompanying gravitational fields. When combined mathematically, both forms of energy precisely cancel out each other, resulting in a "zero state." It is quite possible that the universe as a whole may have a sum total of zero energy. Vacuum fluctuation physics is an esoteric field of study, but the important point to remember here is that, once again, the universe may be understood and explained through natural science, rather than supernatural mysticism.

It is also curious to note that, although String Theory is years—if not decades—from completion, ID apologists already claim to know the answers about the formation of the entire cosmos. It is therefore puzzling why they never submit their "research data" and "evidence" to any legitimate peer-reviewed scientific journal. Is it possible that ID has no true scientific research data or evidence to submit to the peer-reviewed journals? Could this absence of evidence explain why the percentage of scientists endorsing ID theory is trifling? A study published in *Nature* (July 23, 1998) revealed that, of the membership of the prestigious National Academy of Sciences, only 7 percent of its leading scientists believed in a personal God, much less in the "evidence" of the ID crusade. ID's greatest triumph therefore has been in convincing the general public that there is a controversy

> "At present there is not a single credible established religion in the world."
>
> —GEORGE BERNARD SHAW (1856–1950), British writer, in *Major Barbara*

raging among scientists over Intelligent Design. There is no *scientific* controversy whatever.

Intelligent Design proponents knew that their original First Cause argument was flawed so they contrived a "patch" in an attempt to salvage the necessity of Jehovah's existence. They changed their starting premise from "Everything needs a cause" to "Everything that begins to exist needs a cause." Since God didn't *begin* to exist (according to the Bible) and since the universe *did* begin to exist (according to ID's total lie about what cosmologists "agree"), ID leaders claim they have delivered scientific proof of God's existence.

There are three transparent blunders with this so-called *Kalam* argument. First, the argument that God exists and has always existed is a Biblical doctrine. So ID is "proving" God's eternal existence by constructing an argument that *assumes* God's eternal existence based on Scripture. And ID knows that the Bible is true because it's the Bible.

The second problem with the *Kalam* argument, as we discussed above, is the utterly dishonest claim that "cosmologists agree that the universe arose suddenly out of absolute nothingness." We can easily see here how one flawed premise quickly requires other flawed and dishonest arguments as supporting props.

The third fallacy involves the identity of the god whose existence is allegedly "proven" by the *Kalam* argument. Why couldn't the Intelligent Designer be Zeus, or Allah, or Apollo? There is nothing in the *Kalam* argument that even addresses this question. Yet, without rational explanation, ID worshippers know in their hearts that the intelligent Creator is Jesus' Father.

PLAYING WITH MARBLES

As we've seen, a mandatory doctrine of ID is that mass-energy could not always have existed. Supposedly, it magically popped into existence out of nothing and therefore requires a supernatural explanation. Ironically, few scientists would even contest the claim that a magically appearing universe required the assistance of a god (in one form or another). The real issue—obscured by ID subterfuge—is whether mass-energy always existed.

It is again imperative we understand that, contrary to popular misperception, Big Bang cosmology does not claim that mass-energy appeared *ex nihilo* at, or prior to, the Big Bang. Such a something-from-nothing appearance of energy or matter (as portrayed by the defenders of Intelligent Design) would violate the law of the conservation of mass-energy. Instead, Big Bang cosmology asserts only that, approximately 14 billion years ago, the mass-energy that now comprises the universe began its current period of expansion, due to an immense explosion.

So in a blatant self-contradiction, ID's "scientific proof" of God's existence requires a belief that our scientific laws were violated! While ridiculing secular thinkers for (allegedly) proposing a something-from-nothing appearance of the universe, it is actually the theologically enslaved ID proponents who hold this mystical something-from-nothing belief. Any belief in Divine Creation *ex nihilo* is an abandonment of the scientific principle of the conservation of mass-energy.

What "proof" does ID offer that mass-energy did not always exist? Since ID does not have—and could not possibly have—scientific proof that mass-energy did not always exist, ID instead retreats to philosophical musings and word games.

Philosopher William Lane Craig is revered in Fundamentalist pews for his defense of the *Kalam* argument. When asked by Lee Strobel in *The Case for a Creator* how we "know" that the building blocks of the universe aren't infinitely old, Craig used marbles to "explain":

> *"Imagine I had an infinite number of marbles in my possession, and that I wanted to give you some. In fact, suppose that I wanted to give you an infinite number of marbles. One way I could do that would be to give you*

the entire pile of marbles. In that case I would have zero marbles left for myself.

"However, another way to do it would be to give you all of the odd-numbered marbles. Then I would still have an infinity left over for myself, and you would have an infinity too. You'd have just as many as I would—and, in fact, each of us would have just as many as I originally had before we divided into odd and even! Or another approach would be for me to give you all of the marbles numbered four and higher. That way, you would have an infinity of marbles, but I would have only three marbles left.

"What these illustrations demonstrate is that the notion of an actual infinite number of things leads to contradictory results" (page 103).

Craig concludes,

"So the universe can't have an infinite number of events in its past; it must have had a beginning."

Craig is correct that if you mix finite and infinite numbers in a mathematical equation, you will indeed get contradictory and nonsensical results. But this fact is entirely *definitional*—i.e., it mathematically relates only to itself, rather than to the empirical universe. It's like saying "two plus two equals four; therefore, the cosmos sprang into being from nothing, proving a Creator's involvement." Craig's conclusion is a *non sequitur* (it doesn't follow). He is offering valid observations only about his self-created, self-contained universe of abstract numbers, rather than about the true, outside universe in which we actually live. As an admirably devoted Christian, Craig no doubt believes in the power of Biblical parables. But he has completely failed to demonstrate—or even attempted to demonstrate—the real-world applicability of his arithmetic parable through the scientific method. Unsurprisingly, therefore, Craig's arithmetic parable is wholly irrelevant to the law of the conservation of mass-energy. Consequently, it is unimportant whether Craig has lost three, half or all of his marbles. The mass-energy conservation law nonethe-less forbids Creation *ex nihilo*.

Craig similarly argues that the universe can't be infinitely old because an infinite length of time would have to precede the Big Bang—an infinite length of time which, by definition, could never have ended to permit the Big Bang to occur. In other words, in an infinitely old universe, we could never actually *arrive* at any specific moment in time.

Craig repeatedly misuses his mathematical infinities to "prove" a conclusion that is mathematically cohesive but empirically ridiculous. Let me demonstrate why: Suppose that you wish to walk a distance of one city block. Needless to say, before you can reach your final destination one block away, you must first traverse half of that distance (or half a block). Likewise, before you can reach your midpoint half a block away, you must first arrive at a point which is half of *that* distance (or a quarter of a block from your starting position). Before you can walk a quarter of a block, you must walk an eighth of a block, etc. All of these facts are incontrovertibly true and can certainly be extended to infinity (e.g., before you can walk 1/5000 of a block, you must walk 1/10000 of a block, *ad infinitum*). Applying Craig's theory about infinities to the real world, you could never arrive at your final destination one block away. Why not? Because you would first need to arrive at an infinite number of intermediate way-points—an infinity of waypoints that, by definition, is without end and therefore impassable. How could you possibly travel "beyond" an infinite number of anything?

Back to reality: It goes without saying that, despite the mathe-matical "impossibility" of your reaching an infinite number of waypoints, you can easily walk the length of a city block within two or three minutes at most. This example illustrates the clear distinction between ID's philosophical "proofs" of God's existence and the true world of experimental physics.

All cosmologies—whether secular or theological—are forced to contemplate an infinite regress, either in the form of mass-energy or in the form of a god. So the question again reverts to whether: (A) this infinite regress harmonizes with the mass-energy conservation laws (as I have been suggesting), or (B) whether a god violated the mass-energy conservation laws through an *ex nihilo* Creation event. Craig is back where he started, having made no forward progress whatever in his God-Did-It argument.

One may certainly believe by religious faith that God created the universe *ex nihilo*. But ID claims to possess scientific proof of Creation: "proof" in the form of self-contained definitions, flawed premises, *non sequiturs* and absolute misrepresentations of fact— misrepresentations which, even if true, would require that our laws of physics had been violated and that the Book of Genesis be dismissed as mere metaphor.

Furthermore, Craig's argument clearly begs the question yet again. For if his marble example actually proved that nothing could be infinitely old, then God could not be infinitely old either. Craig argues, however, that "God, the eternal, is timeless in his being." So, in other words, the rules don't apply to God because the rules don't apply to God—a barefaced illustration of the "special pleading" fallacy.

It is both meaningless and slippery to feign that "God is beyond time." What does this cliché actually mean in a scientific context? I don't know. Before His Creation of our universe, did God have no mental deliberations, no acts of love to bestow upon His heavenly host, no heavenly chores to discharge, no actions or thoughts of any kind? If God did engage in such thoughts or actions prior to His Creation of our universe, then, theoretically, these thoughts and actions could be enumerated or itemized, at least partially. Even though Craig would self-servingly define these pre-Creation activities as "before time" or "beyond time," couldn't these prior events be added to a tallied list of God's other praiseworthy attributes and actions? Wouldn't this list of God's pre-Creation activities—however incomplete it may be—show that an infinite regress of specific events is not only possible but *indispensable* if God is assumed to be infinitely old as Craig believes? In plain English, Craig claims that something *can* be infinitely old when it suits his purpose, but something *can't* be infinitely old when it doesn't suit his purpose.

Whether you define God's pre-Creation activities as "inside time" or "outside time" is purely a matter of preferential semantics rather than substance. What Craig really means is, "I don't want you to criticize any of my circular, question-begging, special-pleading arguments. I recognize that my no-infinite-regress marble game is particularly inconsistent and unconvincing. I am therefore going to define it as 'off-limits to criticism' by labeling God's pre-Creation activities, whatever they may have been, as 'beyond time.'" Craig's marble game is thus a cleverly veiled attempt to gag anyone who demands that his arguments for a Creator avoid the special-pleading fallacy.

The ID movement strives to prove the existence of a Creator by citing the complexity of the universe and the life therein. Yet ID's "explanation" posits the preexistence of even greater complexity: an Almighty Miracle Worker. ID "explains" complexity by presuming complexity, thereby merging its failed design argument with its failed First Cause argument.

As we discuss in Chapter 2, creationists fail to grasp what science even means by the term "explanation." A true scientific explanation must incorporate specific mechanistic descriptions of how an event occurred. If ID's preachers cannot explain how a Creator transformed nothing into something, then ID reverts to being a religion rather than a scientific explanation. Merely stating that "Creation was a Divine Miracle" does not fulfill the requisites of a scientific explanation. Once again, ID proponents are free to believe whatever they please about the origin of the cosmos, but their claim of having scientific "proof" of their religion is utterly empty.

Moreover, the very premise of the *Kalam* argument—i.e., "everything that begins to exist needs a cause"—has been flatly contradicted by the findings of modern quantum mechanics. The central *reason* why quantum mechanics is categorized as non-classical physics is its concept of non-causality at the atomic level, where physical states of "existence" and "nonexistence" are ultimately determined. The *Kalam* argument therefore fails on both the macro and micro levels.

William Lane Craig, like all creationists, is hypocritical when discussing the subject of causation. He demands absolute adherence to a strict determinist viewpoint—until the topic of human "free will" is introduced. Flip-flopping yet again, Craig is then forced by his religion and his Bible to claim that humans possess "free will," independent of external causes or exculpatory antecedents. Need I remark that Craig and his sympathizers cite laws of causation on a blatantly *ad hoc* basis?

William Lane Craig truly revealed ID's guiding principle when he said, "Should a conflict arise between the witness of the Holy Spirit to the fundamental truth of the Christian faith and beliefs based on argument and evidence, then it is the former which must take precedence over the latter, not vice versa" (*Reasonable Faith: Christian Truth and Apologetics, Revised Edition*, page 36).

Spiritual Rags to Riches

To me, what is among the most annoying habits of ID's writers is their peculiar tendency to plagiarize each other's life stories. Virtually every ID author doles out the identical biographical yarn that, before his awakening to the impeccable logic of Intelligent Design, he was a notorious atheist (e.g., immoral, crude, self-centered). I suspect that such a spiritual rags-to-riches tale goes over well at church revivals and tent meetings. But I have yet to locate a single bit of reliable, independent evidence to corroborate any such personal history of any well-known advocate of Intelligent Design. Their claims to having been morally depraved atheists appear more a theatrical stunt than a reflection of past reality. Such a smear and distortion of atheism, however, are perfectly consistent with past Fundamentalist propaganda. And—have no doubt—the Intelligent Design movement is a Fundamentalist revival disguised in a lab coat.

Another life experience common to many ID writers is that their "journey of discovery" from atheism to Jesus began only after a close family member became a born-again Christian. Several of ID's leading spokesmen—among them, Patrick Glynn and Lee Strobel—openly tell their audiences how a loved one's repentance from sin caused bitter arguments and serious marital problems until they themselves saw the light and repented from sin as well.

I am reminded here of the famous observation by Eric Hoffer that, when we are pressured by family circumstance to change our opinion about an important issue, our recantation is likely to be genuine, rather than insincere, so that we may honestly look ourselves in the mirror. We may preserve our self-respect if we turned to Jesus "because science pointed the way," but not when "our wives and in-laws nagged our balls off and whipped us into a Fundamentalist mentality." Hoffer's valuable insight also explains why ID's "evidence" of a Creator appears much more convincing to ID's own choir than it does to impartial observers.

Presumptuous Analogies

Generally speaking, Lee Strobel, William Dembski, Michael Behe, William Lane Craig, Hugh Ross and other ID authors are good writers and speakers, and use colorful analogies and examples in their books. The most common analogies they use to purportedly model the complex interactions of the universe include: (1) pocket watches, (2) computers and (3) mousetraps. We are told that each component in these various devices depends upon the presence and operation of other parts within the system. If you remove a single piece, then the entire system fails to function properly. Michael Behe has dubbed this interdependency the principle of "irreducible complexity." Citing these man-made devices, ID writers then extrapolate their analogies to the universe as a whole and to the complex lifeforms within the universe—thereby implying Intelligent Design of everything in the cosmos.

The fallacy of these arguments is that the analogies used by ID writers—e.g., pocket watches, computers, mousetraps—are, from the beginning, products of (human) intelligent design. Regardless of how we put together, disassemble or otherwise philosophically manipulate the pieces, ID analogies citing pocket watches, computers and mousetraps are invariably going to convey the strong impression of intelligent design because they *are* products of intelligent design. Yet again, ID incorporates into the very premises of its arguments what it claims to prove through its logic.

The late U.S. Senator Daniel Patrick Moynihan once noted that if your political adversary has trapped you into using his own terminology, then he has already won victory over you. Similarly, many rebuttals critical of ID fall into the fatal trap of adopting, for argument's sake, ID's own analogies. Many of these secular rebuttals to ID are brilliant works of science, and there is no doubt that the Harvard debating coach would award victory to the secularists. But to the general audience, any adopted analogy citing pocket watches, computers or mousetraps is going to leave a definite feeling in the air of Intelligent Design because these inventions are indeed products of intelligent design—our own. So if you're ever reading ID literature and you vaguely feel they are making a valid point about Intelligent Design, ask yourself whether the analogy in use is actually an example of human intelligent design. If it is, then dismiss the analogy as presuming its own conclusion.

God's Tsunami

On the morning of Sunday, December 26, 2004, as Christians worldwide celebrated the Christmas weekend, Earth's crust beneath the Indian Ocean began to shift violently. Within hours, a cataclysmic 9.0 earthquake caused an immense tidal wave to spread across the surrounding waters. As the tsunami reached shore on the Asian continent, hundreds of thousands of innocent men, women and children were swallowed by the sea and drowned. Untold others were maimed or left homeless and alone, their lives and families destroyed forever.

As ministers across America opened their Bibles that day for Sunday sermons, they repeated their assertion that Nature's perfect order reveals evidence of Intelligent Design. When asked by news media why God would cause or permit such horrible suffering by so many innocent people, Intelligent Design spokesmen responded only that "God has a purpose in all things." Appearing on the MSNBC program *Scarborough Country*, Anne Graham Lotz, daughter of evangelist Billy Graham, said very empathetically: "God didn't kill any extra people with this tsunami. Sooner or later, they all would have died anyway." Lotz then echoed the popular sentiment that "God has a purpose in all things."

To any rational observer, this catastrophic tsunami—and other earthquakes, hurricanes, tornadoes, floods, droughts, fires, famines and epidemics—are evidence not of a loving God, but of Nature's indifference to humanity. As we noted in Chapter 7, "the universe in which we live is located equidistant between absolute order and absolute chaos—a neutral position that we should *expect* from a universe impervious to our wishes."

Ignoring any real-world disaster or disorder which runs contrary to their theory of Intelligent Design, ID continues to claim that Nature's organization is evidence of a loving Creator. And it is here that ID daisy-chains one logical mistake to the tail of another. ID's argument is essentially this: Nature's behavior is too orderly to "just exist," so it must instead result from God—Who "just exists." Two errors are once again linked together as one, which ID then labels "a preponderance of evidence."

"Explaining" order by alleging preexisting order explains nothing, even when we incorrectly assume, for discussion's sake, that the limited degree of order we observe in the universe cannot possibly be explained by the laws of physics.

> "What I got in Sunday school . . . was simply a firm conviction that the Christian faith was full of palpable absurdities, and the Christian God preposterous . . . The act of worship, as carried on by Christians, seems to me to be debasing rather than ennobling. It involves groveling before a being who, if he really exists, deserves to be denounced instead of respected."
>
> —H. L. MENCKEN
> (1880–1956), editor and critic, in a letter to Will Durant

There is much evidence of intelligent design on Earth, but this intelligent design is that of human ingenuity. ID's defenders yap unceasingly about how perfectly fine-tuned our planet is for human survival. Yet these same ID spokesmen live in homes that are heated in the winter—to avoid freezing to death—and cooled in the summer—to avoid heat stroke and dehydration. If you arbitrarily placed an ID advocate at a random spot on Earth, he would probably die within moments, because 75 percent of Earth's surface is covered by water and is therefore inhospitable to human life. Force Lee Strobel to spend a night outdoors, naked, on the Siberian Plain, then ask him how perfectly fine-tuned his surroundings are to human survival.

From the moment we arise in the morning and brush our teeth (with man-made chemicals), until the time we switch off the man-made electric light and go to sleep in our man-made beds, our environment is filled with intelligently designed inventions that make life, as we're accustomed to it, possible and pleasurable. Human ingenuity has literally altered the natural landscape of our entire planet.

In the year 1900, a child born in the United States had a life expectancy of only 47 years. After a century of scientific progress, a child born in the year 2000 has a life expectancy of almost 80 years—an incredible achievement accomplished not through prayer, but through science. By contrast, the popular appeal of the Intelligent Design movement rests not on a scientific footing, but on the human psychological tendency known as *projection*. We fallaciously project our terrestrial perceptions of *human* intelligent design onto the vast, impersonal universe, thereby creating the illusion that the cosmos is governed by a magnified, human-like Intelligence.

Consciousness Equals Immortality?

Blending a creepy form of medieval mysticism with traditional religion, ID puts forth the fanciful argument that human consciousness can and does exist and operate independently of the human brain. Supposedly, our thoughts, emotions, perceptions and personalities have nothing to do with the processes of our brains, instead being mysterious evidence of our immortal "soul." Such a belief is called *dualism* in philosophical circles because it postulates the dual existence of both body and mind as separate and autonomous agents.

Although science-minded individuals have ridiculed dualism since the mid-1500s, we should recognize and appreciate that dualism is, even today, an indispensable element of all religious belief in immortality; for only when your personality is distinct and independent of your brain can *you* go flying out of your body to Heaven or Hell when your body dies.

The most immediate scientific objection to dualism is that, by any accepted laboratory standard or real-world experimentation, human consciousness is indeed a process of the human brain. Truly, we are stating the obvious here because this fact is easily provable. Brain injury can render a person unconscious for years or can change a person's entire personality, mental function and memory. Drugs, which act upon brain chemistry, affect the degree and nature of our consciousness. Even sleep results in our being unconscious for hours at a time. Is it really so unfathomable that we lose consciousness when our brains are totally destroyed at death?

Moreover, if consciousness is evidence that a soul—in addition to a mere brain—resides within every conscious body, then this "fact" is certainly good news for members of the animal king-

> "I have never seen what to me seemed an atom of proof that there is a future life."
>
> —MARK TWAIN (1835–1910), from Albert Bigelow Paine's *Mark Twain: A Biography*

dom since, clearly, animals too have consciousness of their environments and will therefore inherit eternal life as well. Animals see, hear, smell, taste and feel pain. In fact, certain animals boast eyesight, hearing and a sense of smell far superior to human capabilities. While their ability to intellectually ruminate is inferior to man's, animals undoubtedly possess some degree of consciousness by any standard definition of the word. If we are to believe therefore that animals do *not* survive death, then consciousness cannot legitimately be cited by ID as evidence of an immortal "soul." I find it difficult to grasp why ID, which wants so badly to be perceived as a scientific discipline, would even attempt to present medieval dualism as a supporting argument.

Lee Strobel's *The Case for a Creator* sinks to the scandalous level of a supermarket tabloid attempting to bolster the case for dualism. On page 257 of the hardcover edition, we are told about a hospitalized woman who died. According to J. P. Moreland, whom Strobel quotes with great admiration, this woman's "soul" flew out of her body and sailed through the hospital's roof. The disembodied "soul" then spotted a tennis shoe that had been abandoned on the roof—a particularly curious and trivial observation for a "soul" to make en route to Heaven. Apparently altering its travel plan in response to seeing the tennis shoe, the "soul" then flew back down through the hospital roof to dwell once again within the dormant woman, thus resurrecting her from the dead. News of this "miracle" was then told and re-told until it finally reached the ears of Lee Strobel, who offers this anecdote in his book as confirmation that we survive death.

What evidence do Moreland and Strobel present to us that this tennis-shoe resurrection story is true? Moreland is quoted by Strobel as saying, "We've got to be more than our bodies or else these stories would be ludicrous to us" (page 257).

If that is the standard by which we are to judge the credibility of this "evidence"—i.e., whether it sounds ludicrous to us—then I'll accept Moreland's own measuring rod. That Moreland and Strobel give any weight at all to such loony folklore is evidence only of their own gullibility.

Moreland then offers through Strobel the worst ID argument I have ever heard. You do not need my assistance in detecting its fallacies. Indeed, the only reason I bother to detail the following argument at all is that similar arguments are now beginning to surface in a variety of ID books—books that, let us remember, are now being offered as supplemental texts in your children's science classes.

Moreland tells us a tragic story about a young woman who suffered brain injury on her honeymoon. As a result of this accident, she lost all of her memories and much of her previous personality. She did not believe that she'd ever been married. She had to be shown videos of the wedding to be convinced that she even had a husband.

Instead of concluding from this story that the physical brain controls a person's consciousness, memory and personality, Moreland arrives at an especially bizarre interpretation of events:

"She was not a different person, though she was behaving differently. But she had totally different memories. She had lost her old memories and she didn't even have the same personality. What that proves is you can be the same person even if you lose old memories and gain new memories, or you lose some of your old personality traits and gain new personality traits" (page 260).

So Moreland argues that she was "the same person" after the accident, proving that "personhood" transcends the mere physical functioning of the brain. She was "the same person" apart from her physical self and would therefore survive as "the same person" even after her physical self stopped functioning altogether at death.

I wonder if Moreland has heard of the logical error known as *reification?* Reification means "to induce as truly existent an abstract idea or collection of observations." Moreland is illogically reifying the existence of a "soul" simply by labeling this brain-injured victim "the same person." While she certainly *was* the same person in some ways—e.g., she possessed the same DNA, she looked about the same, she had the same arms and legs—her personality, memories and consciousness were seriously affected by her brain injury. Her resulting disabilities obviously proved a direct link between physical brain structure and personality, memory and consciousness.

I'll let you decide which statement below is more scientifically accurate:

Statement #1: Even though the brain-injured woman had a different personality and memories after her accident, she was the same person. The fact that she was the same person shows that our personhood or soul exists independently from our bodies. Because our personhood exists independently from our bodies, our consciousness or soul will continue to exist even after our bodies have perished.

Statement #2: Following her brain injury, the accident victim was the same person in some ways but a very different person in other ways. While her legal rights as an individual and outward appearance remained the same, her brain injury resulted first in unconsciousness, then in a vastly different cognitive function, which included personality change and memory loss. Because her unconsciousness, personality change and memory loss began at exactly the same moment that her brain injury occurred, it is prudent to conclude that her brain probably controlled her consciousness, personality and memory. If our brains do control our consciousness, personality and memory, then it is highly unlikely, from a scientific perspective, that our consciousness, personality and memory survive brain death.

ID "explains" human consciousness by postulating preexisting Divine consciousness. ID therefore provides no actual explanation whatever for consciousness and merely engages again in question begging and endlessly circular argumentation. Science, however, explains the origin of consciousness by detailing the critical advantages consciousness brings to the struggle for survival. Obviously, a conscious animal can search for food, defend itself, and look for a mate far more efficiently than a vegetable.

> "My mind is incapable of conceiving such a thing as a soul. I may be in error, and man may have a soul; but I simply do not believe it."
>
> —THOMAS EDISON (1847–1931), in "Do We Live Again?"

Natural selection would therefore highly favor the development and refinement of consciousness in animal lifeforms. A belief in the *immortality* of consciousness, however, clearly falls under the heading of religion, rather than science.

Wild Misstatements of Fact

When I and others critique the shortcomings of the Intelligent Design movement, we tend to focus our criticisms on the logical errors so replete within ID literature. We point out that ID's conclusions do not follow logically from the factual premises of their own arguments. In other words, their arguments are *non sequiturs*. We tend to over-charitably concede, however, that the "facts" used as ID's initial premises are actually facts. Unfortunately, such charity is undeserved and misdirected. Through deliberate or inadvertent distortion, ID's leading spokesmen and authors thoroughly saturate their sermons and books with reckless exaggerations of fact. Let me cite a few typical examples:

• Hugh Ross is an ID lecturer and astronomer who released a DVD documentary, *Journey toward Creation*, attempting to imitate the look and feel of Carl Sagan's *Cosmos* but for born-again Fundamentalists. Arguing that God fine-tuned the universe for the benefit of earthly humans, Ross states: "In order for the universe to sustain even one life-support planet, each one of these ten billion trillion stars is a necessity. If the number of stars in the observable universe were any greater, or any fewer, life would be impossible."

All honest astronomers quickly concede that they, at present, have no exact count of how many stars exist in the universe. Over 99 percent of the stars in our universe are not visible to us from our position in the Milky Way galaxy. I'm wondering therefore how Hugh Ross knows that even *one* more star, or one *fewer* star, would spell catastrophe for life on Earth? NASA would certainly be interested in how Hugh Ross arrived at such a precise tally of stars and how he made his calculations. Is it possible that Hugh Ross is inventing or exaggerating "facts" to make his point for Intelligent Design?

In reality, the number of stars in our universe changes every day as new stars are born within gas-and-dust nebulae and old stars burn out, having exhausted their supply of hydrogen fuel. The only star truly essential to the continuation of life on Earth is our own sun. There is no such thing as a mandatory star-number.

• Ross on *The John Ankerberg Show*[1]: "If the Earth were one half of one percent closer to the sun, water on Earth would boil off. If the Earth were one half of one percent farther from the sun, all the water would freeze."

Factually, the distance of Earth from the sun routinely varies throughout the year—and from one year to the next—by far more than the "one half of one percent" that Ross claims would destroy life on our planet. There is no theoretical speculation involved here. Ross's statements are provably false, yet he is hailed as ID's foremost expert on astronomy.

• Ross on *The John Ankerberg Show*: "Only two percent of stars have planets around them."

How does Ross come to these definitive conclusions? Using the Hubble Space Telescope and ground-based observatories, we are only now beginning the search for planets surrounding distant stars. Perhaps NASA should save its time and resources by allowing Ross to divine the answers in advance.

• Ross on *The John Ankerberg Show*: "The position and the mass and the orbit of every solar system planet plays a critical role in life on Planet Earth."

Total nonsense! Most of the other planets could disappear tomorrow with no deleterious effect on Earth whatever. The sun plays a vital role, and the Moon one of lesser significance. But do you think the average person on Earth would even be aware— much less be annihilated—if Pluto or Mercury suddenly abandoned the solar system entirely? No. Moreover, even if, hypothetically, life did evolve on Earth because of the other planets, life would still be the result of—rather than the reason for—the planets' orbital positions.

• Ross on *The John Ankerberg Show*: "Only spiral galaxies can contain planets in stable orbits around their stars."

Once again, Ross is obviously making up these "facts" as he goes along to "prove" that Jesus came to the only planet in the entire universe with intelligent life. Personally, I do not know whether intelligent life exists elsewhere in the universe. I suspect that it does, but I cannot prove my belief to be a fact. Ross, however, refuses to admit that his belief (in Intelligent Design) cannot be proven and instead pulls "facts" out of his sleeve like a Las Vegas magician. Again, I am certain that NASA would be very interested in how Ross calibrated and cataloged the orbit of every planet in the entire universe to document his assertion.

In the only solar system that we know anything at all about, there is one planet that definitely supports life and another, Mars, that either supports life now below ground or could certainly have supported life in the past when rivers ran freely over its surface. Our own solar system is probably quite representative of countless others in the universe.

• A common statement made by ID apologists is that Jupiter routinely intercepts space debris that would otherwise strike and destroy Earth—the implication being that a Creator placed Jupiter in its orbit for the benefit of humanity.

Although Jupiter, like most planets and moons, does regularly intercept space debris, we must recognize that debris can and does strike Earth every day from any one of 360 degrees. Jupiter can intercept debris from, at most, 1 degree of arc (and probably far less than that). There is no reason to believe that the debris Jupiter intercepts is more dangerous to Earth than the debris falling to our planet from other directions in the solar system. Moreover, one could just as easily argue that Jupiter's gravitational field attracts debris toward Earth that otherwise would remain outside the solar system.

Amazingly, Lee Strobel in *The Case for a Creator* quotes astronomer and ID-advocate Guillermo Gonzalez as saying that Venus takes hits from the asteroid belt that otherwise would hit Earth (page 174).

I will give Gonzalez the benefit of the doubt and allow the possibility that Strobel misunderstood or misquoted him. But Earth orbits *between* Venus and the asteroid belt. Venus does not orbit—protectively or unprotectively—between the asteroid belt and Earth.

The errors and exaggerations cited above are but a tiny sampling of the almost innumerable misstatements of fact perpetrated by the champions of Intelligent Design. Clearly, they will say just about anything—true or false—to defend their Lord. The end justifies the means.

A detailed analysis of all the factual and logical errors in ID literature would require a multivolume, encyclopedia-length project. If I were to directly quote all the factual and logical blunders in Lee Strobel's books alone, such quotations would have to be so extensive that I would quickly cross the legal line from "fair use" to actual violations of federal copyright laws. Strobel, the supreme pontiff of ID, claims to be an objective journalist, humbly trying to collect all the relevant data. Yet, in his books, he admittedly interviews only those "experts" who he knows in advance are churchgoing, born-again Fundamentalists. It is therefore no coincidence that Strobel's publisher, Zondervan, is both the leading publisher of books on Intelligent Design and the world's leading publisher of Holy Bibles. Yet we are told that ID is not a religious belief but an objective scientific principle.

Forthcoming Nobel Prize?

Why should you take my word that ID argumentation fails the test of true science? Who am I? Chances are good that you never heard of me before reading this book. You may never hear of me again. I speak only for myself, rather than for the world's scientific establishment.

The world's scientific establishment, however, does have its own official means of recognizing and honoring science's greatest achievements. Nobel Prizes are awarded each year to those individuals whose groundbreaking discoveries have been verified and accepted by the true scientific community.

If we are to believe the words of ID's leaders and writers, then they have scientifically proven God's existence. Needless to say, this proof of God's presence would be the greatest scientific achievement of all time. What other scientific finding could possibly compare to proof of God's reality? J. J. Thomson's discovery of the electron, for which he won the 1906 Nobel Prize in physics, would pale in significance to the scientific discovery of God. Crick and Watson's Nobel-winning explanation of nucleic acids becomes small potatoes in comparison to the scientific detection of God. Even Einstein's equations of general relativity would be dwarfed in scope and impact by the scientific authentication of God's existence. So if the advocates of Intelligent Design have indeed succeeded in scientifically proving God to be a reality, then I fully expect their Nobel Prize to be forthcoming.

Will ID theory actually win a Nobel Prize? The thought is, at the same moment, both sad and amusing. Like snake handlers and charismatics who speak in tongues, the Intelligent Design movement is a congregation of religious fanatics localized primarily in conservative areas of the United States. The rest of the world, including the Nobel committee, pays no attention to their faith-based sermons.

As Sam Harris has stated so accurately, "There is sanity in numbers." If only *one* person truly believed in a magical Being, governing the universe from a magical city where our "souls" will fly after death, then this one person would be viewed correctly as indisputably insane. But because a majority believe this tale, the absurdity of the fantasy is undeservedly dissipated.

A Final Thought

"I'm a born-again atheist."

GORE VIDAL, writer

Let's suppose that you've read this entire book and you are still uncertain whether to embrace a secular or a theological view of the universe and mankind. If you reject a secular worldview and instead adopt Christianity, then I and other freethinking individuals will be mildly disappointed that we lost you as a compatriot, but we will respect your right to believe whatever you choose. Case closed.

If, however, you reject the teachings of ID and Christianity in general, then those who espouse those theological doctrines believe that you will be gruesomely tortured throughout all eternity for your decision. Your flesh will literally be set ablaze after you die, and you will be given a special, indestructible body Intelligently Designed to suffer unimaginable torment forever. Even your tongue will be set on fire according to Scripture (Luke 16:24). For your acceptance of secular science, you will be eternally barbecued by the devil. Although they are too embarrassed these days to publicly confess their certainty of eternal torture for all non-Christians, the Intelligent Design movement still believes that your fiery roasting is looming. If only on this basis, we should dismiss ID as both irrational and inhumane.

Chapter Notes

Foreword

1. Actually, they don't call it this: the Flying Spaghetti Monster is a spoof on creationist pseudoscience—more about this alternate deity and its "Pastafarian" followers can be found at www.venganza.org.
2. For more information about chemical clocks, see www.intothecool.com.

Chapter 4

1. Atmospheric gases near Earth's surface would actually burn up an arrow through friction if it were traveling 17,500 miles per hour close to the ground.
2. For accuracy, let me point out that, by official NASA nomenclature, the term "Space Shuttle" refers to the combination of orbiter (i.e., the space plane), external fuel tank and solid rocket boosters as these three elements are joined together on the launch pad and during ascent. The vehicle that circles high above the Earth with astronauts aboard is called the Space Shuttle *Orbiter*.
3. See Chapter 10—"Was America Really Founded upon Christian Principles?"—for a discussion of why the god of Deism, rather than the god of Christianity, was the "God" mentioned in the Declaration of Independence.
4. The origin of this "raw material" is discussed in Chapter 2—"Origin of the Universe: Natural or Supernatural?"
5. This calculation was published by John Gribbin in *Genesis: The Origins of Man and the Universe*. New York: Delacorte Press/Eleanor Friede, 1981.
6. In 1997, NASA's *Galileo* spacecraft discovered that Europa, one of Jupiter's four largest moons, is covered with an ocean of water, frozen on the top layers and, almost certainly, liquid beneath due to the warming effects of Europa's gravitational stresses. Because liquid water is essential to the formation of life, the Zone of Habitability may now extend all the way to Jupiter.
7. *Albert Einstein: The Human Side*, Princeton University Press, 1981.
8. The *New York Times*, April 19, 1955.
9. Pluto's orbit is very slightly askew to the solar orbital plane, indicating that Pluto is a captured Oort Cloud object rather than an original planet. The fact that Pluto is not a gas giant like Jupiter, Saturn, Uranus and Neptune also lends credibility to this theory.

Chapter 5

1. Readers unfamiliar with creationist literature may wonder whether these books really propose such zany explanations. I refer you to *The Genesis Flood* by Henry Morris and John G. Whitcomb, Jr. (Philadelphia: Presbyterian and Reformed Publishing Co., 1961). Other than the Bible, this book is probably the most sacred text of the creationist movement. *The Genesis Flood* is one of the books proposed by creationists for inclusion in your child's high school science curriculum.

Chapter 6

1. James Ussher (1581–1656), an archbishop of the Church of Ireland, is generally credited with publishing the first and most authoritative "proof" of the specific year of Creation. Although Ussher's precise date of Creation was not published until the 1650s, the Church had always believed that Earth was only a few thousand years old.
2. Page 156 of the soft-cover edition.
3. See *Science and Creationism*. New York: Oxford University Press, 1984.
4. Page 164 of *The Creation-Evolution Controversy*.
5. Eric Hoffer wrote in *The True Believer* that the opposite of the Fundamentalist Christian is not the avowed atheist. The opposite of both the Fundamentalist Christian and the avowed atheist is someone who is uninterested in questions of theology. I agree with Hoffer's observation.
6. Page 117 of *Lectures in Systematic Theology*.
7. After a song by the Platters.
8. For a detailed and chilling historical account of Christian witch burning, read Carl Sagan's superb book *The Demon-Haunted World: Science as a Candle in the Dark*.

Chapter 7

1. Despite innumerable biblical references to "the devil," contemporary Christians likewise view themselves as too elevated to use the term publicly. "Satan" has linguistically replaced "the devil," just as "Holy Spirit" has superseded "Holy Ghost." Do these semantic changes indicate that Fundamentalists are becoming slightly embarrassed by the content of their own Bible?
2. Our world is probably tilted slightly more toward order than disorder, both because man himself has artificially created order through shaping the landscape and because natural selection itself provides a built-in mechanism of preserving efficient lifeforms while eliminating the inefficient. In purely philosophical terms, however, Ayn Rand pointed out that our entire notion of "order" is derived from, and shaped by, what we

observe. To claim therefore that what we observe is "orderly" is a tauto-logical error.

Chapter 8

1. I define "antisocial sin" as any act condemned in the Bible as "sinful" that also infringes deliberately and needlessly upon the rights of others in society. Examples of "antisocial sin" are murder, rape, robbery, assault and battery, etc.
2. To support their contention that the majority of humanity will go to Hell, Church leaders also cite Matthew 22:13,14 and Luke 13:23,24, which follow respectively:

    "There shall be weeping and gnashing of teeth. For many are called, but few are chosen."

    "Then said one unto him, Lord, are there few that be saved? And he said unto them, Strive to enter in at the strait gate: for many, I say unto you, will seek to enter in, and shall not be able."
3. The term "free will," as employed by Christian theologians, is a blatantly unscientific concept, since an individual's genetic composition, upbringing and subsequent environment supposedly have no relevant or exculpatory influence on the formation of his religious character. In overt contradiction of their own doctrine of free will, however, theologians religiously employ the so-called Law of Cause-Effect to allegedly prove God's existence by deducing that everything (including the universe itself) must have a cause to account for its existence and behavior. Need I remark that theologians cite laws of causation on a strikingly *ad hoc* basis? I personally find it self-evident and incontrovertible that all human characteristics, decisions and behavior are rooted either in genetic predisposition, environmental influence or, in most instances, a combination of the two. The only reason that you're not a grasshopper is that your mother and father were not grasshoppers. If they had been grasshoppers, then your appearance, behavior, character and beliefs would differ radically from those you currently hold.

Chapter 9

1. Although not directly related to the internet, the entire Y2K frenzy was another classic illustration of groundless computer-related fear gone berserk.
2. Child pornography, in which children are forced to perform sexual acts with each other or with adults, is—and should be!—a crime. Since child pornography is by definition a crime, an increase or decrease in the volume of child pornography would directly raise or lower the crime rate to

that degree. So while every civilized person condemns child pornography, let us recognize that such illegal materials constitute only a minuscule fraction of 1 percent of the pornography in circulation. As an excuse for censoring the internet, anti-porn activists invariably bring up the hot-button issue of child pornography, which all sides unequivocally condemn already, and against which we already have tough and strictly enforced laws. The issue of child pornography is therefore a diversionary tactic used to distract attention from the real issue—the censorship of pornographic images of adults.

3. X-rated movie theaters and strip clubs are in fact usually located in high-crime areas, but only because conservative politicians enact restrictive zoning ordinances forcing sex-related businesses into these areas. Try opening a strip bar next door to a Baptist church or elementary school—you'll be forced elsewhere by a sanctimonious lynch mob.

Chapter 11

1. The *John Ankerberg Show*, seen on INSP, the Inspiration Network, bills itself as "the only nationally seen television program devoted exclusively to Christian apologetics."

Bibliography

The following books and articles either aided in the preparation of this volume or are suggested for further study.

Adler, Mortimer J. *How to Think about God*. New York: Macmillan Publishing Company, 1980.

Allen, Steve. *Meeting of Minds*. Los Angeles: Hubris House, 1978.

Aquinas, Thomas. *Basic Writings of Saint Thomas Aquinas*. New York: Random House, 1945.

Asimov, Isaac. *In the Beginning*. South Yarmouth, MA: J. Curley & Associates, 1982.

———. *Understanding Physics*. New York: Barnes & Noble Books, 1993.

Baggini, Julian. *Atheism: A Very Short Introduction*. New York: Oxford University Press, 2003.

Barker, Dan. *Losing Faith in Faith: From Preacher to Atheist*. Madison, WI: Freedom From Religion Foundation, 1992.

Behe, Michael J. *Darwin's Black Box: The Biochemical Challenge to Evolution*. New York: Free Press, 1998.

Bronowski, Jacob. *The Ascent of Man*. Boston: Little, Brown and Company, 1973.

Carnegie, Dale. *How to Develop Self-Confidence and Influence People by Public Speaking*. New York: Pocket Books, 1956.

———. *How to Win Friends and Influence People*. New York: Pocket Books, 1940.

Carrier, Richard. *Sense and Goodness Without God: A Defense of Metaphysical Naturalism*. Bloomington, IN: Authorhouse, 2005.

Carter, Jimmy. *Keeping Faith*. New York: Bantam Books, 1982.

Carter, Lee. *Lucifer's Handbook*. Van Nuys, CA: Academic Associates, 1977.

Craig, William Lane. *Reasonable Faith: Christian Truth and Apologetics*. Wheaton, IL: Crossway Books, 1994.

Dawkins, Richard. *The Blind Watchmaker*. New York: Norton, 1985.

———. *The God Delusion*. Boston: Houghton Mifflin, 2006.

Dembski, William A. *The Design Revolution: Answering the Toughest Questions about Intelligent Design*. Downers Grove, IL: InterVarsity Press, 2004.

Eller, David. *Natural Atheism*. Parsippany, NJ: American Atheist Press, 2004.

Ellis, Albert. *Is Objectivism a Religion?* New York: Lyle Stuart, 1968.

Ellis, Albert, and Robert A. Harper. *A Guide to Rational Living*. North Hollywood, CA: Wilshire Book Company, 1998.

Entzminger, Robert L. *Divine Word*. Pittsburgh, PA: Duquesne University Press, 1985.

Fearnside, W. Ward, and William B. Holther. *Fallacy: The Counterfeit of Argument*. Englewood Cliffs, NJ: Prentice-Hall, 1959.

Foote, G. W., and W. P. Ball. *The Bible Handbook for Atheists*. Austin, TX: American Atheist Press, 1977.

Frye, Roland Mushat. *Is God a Creationist?* New York: Charles Scribner's Sons, 1983.

Gaylor, Annie Laurie. *Women Without Superstition: No Gods—No Masters*. Madison, WI: Freedom From Religion Foundation, 1997.

Gilbert, Michael A., *How to Win an Argument*. New York: McGraw-Hill, 1979.

Godfrey, Laurie R. *Scientists Confront Creationism*. New York: W. W. Norton, 1983.

Gribbin, John R. *Genesis: The Origins of Man and the Universe*. New York: Delacorte Press/Eleanor Friede, 1981.

Harris, Sam. *The End of Faith: Religion, Terror, and the Future of Reason*. New York: W. W. Norton & Company, 2004.

Haught, James A. *Holy Horrors: An Illustrated History of Religious Murder and Madness*. Amherst, NY: Prometheus Books, 1999.

———. *Honest Doubt: Essays on Atheism in a Believing Society*. Amherst, NY: Prometheus Books, 2007.

———. *Science in a Nanosecond: Illustrated Answers to 100 Basic Science Questions*. Amherst, NY: Prometheus Books, 1991.

————. *2000 Years of Disbelief: Famous People with the Courage to Doubt*. Amherst, NY: Prometheus Books, 1996.

Hawking, Stephen W. *A Brief History of Time*. New York: Bantam Books, 1988.

Hazen, Robert M., and James Trefil. *Science Matters*. New York: Anchor Books, 1992.

Hoffer, Eric. *The True Believer*. New York: Harper & Row, 1951.

Jacoby, Susan. *Freethinkers: A History of American Secularism*. New York: Metropolitan Books, 2004.

Lewis, C. S. *Mere Christianity*. New York: HarperSanFrancisco, 2001.

Little, Paul E. *Know Why You Believe*. Downers Grove, IL: InterVarsity Press, 1968.

Martin, Michael, and Ricki Monnier. *The Impossibility of God*. Amherst, New York: Prometheus Books, 2003.

McDowell, Josh. *The New Evidence that Demands a Verdict*. Nashville, TN: Nelson Reference, 1999.

Mills, David A. *Overcoming Religion*. Secaucus, NJ: Citadel Press, 1981.

————. *Science Shams & Bible Bloopers*. Philadelphia: Xlibris, 2000.

Montagu, Ashley. *Science and Creationism*. New York: Oxford University Press, 1984.

Morris, Henry M., and Gary E. Parker. *What Is Creation Science?* San Francisco: Creation-Life, 1982.

Morris, Henry M., and John G. Whitcomb, Jr. *The Genesis Flood*. Philadelphia: Presbyterian and Reformed Publishing Company, 1961.

Narciso, Dianna. *Like Rolling Uphill: Realizing the Honesty of Atheism*. Tamarac, FL: Llumina Press, 2004.

Nourse, Alan E. *Universe, Earth and Atom: The Story of Physics*. New York: Harper & Row, 1969.

O'Hair, Madalyn Murray. *An Atheist Epic: Bill Murray, The Bible and the Baltimore Board of Education*. Austin, TX: American Atheist Press, 1970.

————. *What on Earth Is an Atheist?* Austin, TX: American Atheist Press, 1969.

Perakh, Mark. *Unintelligent Design.* Amherst, NY: Prometheus Books, 2003.

Price, Robert M., and Jeffery Jay Lowder. *The Empty Tomb: Jesus Beyond the Grave.* Amherst, NY: Prometheus Books, 2005.

Ross, Hugh. *The Creator and the Cosmos: How the Latest Scientific Discoveries of the Century Reveal God.* Colorado Springs, CO: Navpress Publishing Group, 2001.

————. *Journey toward Creation (DVD).* Pasadena, CA: Reasons to Believe, 2003.

————. *A Matter of Days: Resolving a Creation Controversy.* Colorado, Springs, CO: Navpress Publishing Group, 2004.

Russell, Bertrand. *Why I Am Not a Christian.* New York: Simon and Schuster, 1957.

Sagan, Carl. *Cosmos.* New York: Random House, 1980.

————. *The Demon-Haunted World.* New York: Random House, 1995.

————. *The Dragons of Eden.* New York: Ballantine Books, 1977.

Schroeder, Gerald L. *The Science of God.* New York: Free Press, 1997.

Smith, George H. *Atheism: The Case Against God.* Amherst, NY: Prometheus Books, 1980.

Strobel, Lee. *The Case for a Creator: A Journalist Investigates Scientific Evidence That Points Toward God.* Grand Rapids, MI: Zondervan, 2004.

Thiessen, Henry C. *Lectures in Systematic Theology.* Grand Rapids, MI: William B. Eerdmans, 1979.

Tucker, Wallace H., and Karen Tucker. *The Dark Matter.* New York: Morrow, 1988.

Wells, Jonathan. *Icons of Evolution: Science or Myth? Why Much of What We Teach about Evolution Is Wrong.* Washington, D.C.: Regnery Publishing, Inc., 2002.

Wysong, R. L. *The Creation-Evolution Controversy.* Midland, MI: Inquiry Press, 1976.

Young, Howard S. *A Rational Counseling Primer*. New York: Institute for Rational Living, 1974.

Quotation Resources

Brantlinger, Patrick. *Rule of Darkness: British Literature and Imperialism, 1830–1914*. Ithaca, NY: Cornell University Press, 1990.

Cardiff, Ira D. *What Great Men Think of Religion*. New York: Arno Press, 1972.

"Celebrity Atheist List" at www.celebatheists.com.

Del Rio Garcia, Eduardo. *Manual of a Perfect Atheist*. Austin, TX: American Atheist Press, 1994.

"Famous Non-Believers" at quinnell.us/religion/famous.

Green, Jonathon. *Cassell Dictionary of Cynical Quotations*. Sterling, 2000.

Haught, James A. *2000 Years of Disbelief: Famous People with the Courage to Doubt*. Amherst, NY: Prometheus Books, 1996.

Noyes, Rufus K. *Views of Religion*. Boston: LK Washburn, 1906.

"Religious Affiliation of History's 100 Most Influential People" at www.adherents.com/adh_influ.html.

Stenger, Victor J. *Has Science Found God? The Latest Results in the Search for Purpose in the Universe*. Amherst, NY: Prometheus Books, 2003.

Web Resources

American Atheists—www.atheists.org

Freedom From Religion Foundation—www.ffrf.org

Freethought Media—www.freethoughtmedia.com

Hellbound Alleee (Francois Tremblay and Alison Randall)—www.hellboundalleee.com

The Infidel Guy (Reginald Finley)—www.infidelguy.com

Kill the Afterlife (Aaron Kinney)—www.killtheafterlife.blogspot.com

Positive Atheism—www.positiveatheism.org

The Secular Web—www.infidels.org

■ Index

The quotations, sources, and subjects appearing in boxed sidebars are not indexed.

Index

ABOUT THE AUTHOR

© Zero G Corporation

David Mills has been an atheist for thirty years and has authored three successful books on the battle between science and religion. This book just might be his favorite. David has also written best-selling psychology and self-help literature for the Albert Ellis Institute in New York and for psychotherapy clients worldwide. During the 1980s, David worked as a journalist covering NASA's Space Shuttle program at the Kennedy Space Center.

Currently a homeschooling teacher, David's hobbies include computers, web-page design, singing, playing the guitar and piano, bowling multiple 300s, and assailing conventional wisdom at every opportunity. Born in 1959, David is single, lives in Huntington, West Virginia, and has one daughter, Sophia. For current contact information, go to: www.davidmills.net.

ABOUT THE AUTHOR OF THE FOREWORD

Dorion Sagan is a science writer who has authored and co-authored many books on evolution, most recently *Into the Cool*. He has also written for *Wired, Skeptical Inquirer,* the *New York Times, Natural History* and the *New York Times Book Review.* He is the son of astronomer Carl Sagan.